全国高等学校外语教师丛书·**科研方法系列**

U0750732

Data Elicitation
for Second and Foreign Language Research

第二语言研究中的数据收集方法

Susan M. Gass （美）
Alison Mackey （美）　著

外语教学与研究出版社
FOREIGN LANGUAGE TEACHING AND RESEARCH PRESS
北京 BEIJING

京权图字：01-2011-5094

Data Elicitation for Second and Foreign Language Research by Susan M. Gass and Alison Mackey / ISBN: 0-8058-6035-5

Copyright © 2007 by Lawrence Erlbaum Associates, Inc.

Authorized Licensed Edition from English language edition published by Routledge, part of Taylor & Francis Group LLC. All rights reserved.

本书原版由 Taylor & Francis 出版集团旗下的 Routledge 出版公司出版，并经其授权出版。版权所有，侵权必究。

Foreign Language Teaching and Research Press is authorized to publish and distribute exclusively the Licensed Edition. This edition is authorized for sale throughout the mainland of China. No part of the publication may be reproduced or distributed by any means, or stored in a database or retrieval system, without the prior written permission of the publisher.

本版本由外语教学与研究出版社在中国大陆地区独家出版、发行。未经书面许可，任何人不得以任何方式复制或发行本书的任何部分。

Copies of this book sold without a Taylor & Francis sticker on the cover are unauthorized and illegal.

本书封面贴有 Taylor & Francis 公司防伪标签，无标签者不得销售。

图书在版编目（CIP）数据

第二语言研究中的数据收集方法 ＝ Data Elicitation for Second and Foreign Language Research：英文／（美）盖苏珊（Gass, M.），（美）麦基（Mackey, A.）著. —— 北京：外语教学与研究出版社，2011.8（2020.7 重印）
（全国高等学校外语教师丛书. 科研方法系列）
ISBN 978-7-5135-1223-7

Ⅰ．①第… Ⅱ．①盖… ②麦… Ⅲ．①第二语言－数据收集－研究－英文 Ⅳ．①H003-39

中国版本图书馆 CIP 数据核字 (2011) 第 173060 号

出 版 人　徐建忠
项目负责　段长城
责任编辑　毕　争
责任校对　刘晓娟
封面设计　覃一彪　华　艺
版式设计　吴德胜
出版发行　外语教学与研究出版社
社　　址　北京市西三环北路 19 号（100089）
网　　址　http://www.fltrp.com
印　　刷　北京九州迅驰传媒文化有限公司
开　　本　650×980　1/16
印　　张　15.5
版　　次　2011 年 8 月第 1 版 2020 年 7 月第 11 次印刷
书　　号　ISBN 978-7-5135-1223-7
定　　价　57.90 元

购书咨询：(010) 88819926　电子邮箱：club@fltrp.com
外研书店：https://waiyants.tmall.com
凡印刷、装订质量问题，请联系我社印制部
联系电话：(010) 61207896　电子邮箱：zhijian@fltrp.com
凡侵权、盗版书籍线索，请联系我社法律事务部
举报电话：(010) 88817519　电子邮箱：banquan@fltrp.com
物料号：212230101

记载人类文明
沟通世界文化
www.fltrp.com

Contents

总　序

"全国高等学校外语教师丛书"是外语教学与研究出版社高等英语教育出版分社近期精心策划、隆重推出的系列丛书，包含理论指导、科研方法和教学研究三个子系列。本套丛书既包括学界专家精心挑选的国外引进著作，又有特邀国内学者执笔完成的"命题作文"。作为开放系列，该丛书还将根据外语教学与科研的发展不断增加新的专题，以便教师研修与提高。

笔者有幸参与了这套系列丛书的策划工作。在策划过程中，我们分析了高校英语教师面临的困难与挑战，考察了一线教师的需求，最终确立这套丛书选题的指导思想为：想外语教师所想，急外语教师所急，顺应广大教师的发展需求；确立这套丛书的写作特色为：突出科学性、可读性和操作性，做到举重若轻，条理清晰，例证丰富，深入浅出。

第一个子系列是"理论指导"。该系列力图为教师提供某学科或某领域的研究概貌，期盼读者能用较短的时间了解某领域的核心知识点与前沿研究课题。以《二语习得重点问题研究》一书为例。该书不求面面俱到，只求抓住二语习得研究领域中的热点、要点和富有争议的问题，动态展开叙述。每一章的写作以不同意见的争辩为出发点，对取向相左的理论、实证研究结果差异进行分析、梳理和评述，最后介绍或者展望国内外的最新发展趋势。全书阐述清晰，深入浅出，易读易懂。再比如《认知语言学与二语教学》一书，全书分为理论篇、教学篇与研究篇三个部分。理论篇阐述认知语言学视角下的语言观、教学观与学习观，以及与二语教学相关的认知语言学中的主要概念与理论；教学篇选用认知语言学领域比较成熟的理论，探讨应用到中国英语教学实践的可能性；

研究篇包括国内外将认知语言学理论应用到教学实践中的研究综述、研究方法介绍以及对未来研究的展望。

第二个子系列是"科研方法"。该系列介绍了多种研究方法，通常是一书介绍一种方法，例如问卷调查、个案研究、行动研究、有声思维、语料库研究、微变化研究和启动研究等。也有一书涉及多种方法，综合描述量化研究或者质化研究，例如：《应用语言学中的质性研究与分析》、《应用语言学中的量化研究与分析》和《第二语言研究中的数据收集方法》等。凡入选本系列丛书的著作人，无论是国外著者还是国内著者，均有高度的读者意识，乐于为一线教师开展教学科研服务，力求做到帮助读者"排忧解难"。例如，澳大利亚Anne Burns教授撰写的《英语教学中的行动研究方法》一书，从一线教师的视角，讨论行动研究的各个环节，每章均有"反思时刻"、"行动时刻"等新颖形式设计。同时，全书运用了丰富例证来解释理论概念，便于读者理解、思考和消化所读内容。凡是应邀撰写研究方法系列的中国作者均有博士学位，并对自己阐述的研究方法有着丰富的实践经验。他们有的运用了书中的研究方法完成了硕、博士论文，有的是采用书中的研究方法从事过重大科研项目。以秦晓晴教授撰写的《外语教学问卷调查法》一书为例，该书著者将系统性与实用性有机结合，根据实施问卷调查法的流程，系统地介绍了问卷调查研究中问题的提出、问卷项目设计、问卷试测、问卷实施、问卷整理及数据准备、问卷评价以及问卷数据汇总及统计分析方法选择等环节。书中对各个环节的描述都配有易于理解的研究实例。

第三个子系列是"教学研究"。该系列与前两个系列相比，有两点显著不同：第一，本系列侧重同步培养教师的教学能力与教学研究能力；第二，本系列所有著作的撰稿人主要为中国学者。有些著者虽然目前在海外工作和生活，但他们出国前曾在国内高校任教，期间也经常回国参与国内的教学与研究工作。本系列包括《英语教学中的学习策略培训：阅读与写作》、《听力教学与研究》、《写作教学与研究》、《阅读教学与研究》、《口语教学与研究》、《翻译教学与研究》等。以

《听力教学与研究》一书为例，著者王艳博士拥有十多年的听力教学经验，同时听力教学研究又是她完成博士论文的选题领域。《听力教学与研究》一书，浓缩了她多年听力教学与听力教学研究的宝贵经验。全书分为两部分：教学篇与研究篇。教学篇中涉及了听力教学的各个重要环节以及学生在听力学习中可能碰到的困难与应对的办法，所选用的案例均来自著者课堂教学的真实活动。研究篇中既有著者的听力教学研究案例，也有著者从国内外文献中筛选出的符合中国国情的听力教学研究案例，综合在一起加以分析阐述。

教育大计，教师为本。"全国高等学校外语教师丛书"内容全面，出版及时，必将成为高校教师提升自我教学能力、研究能力与合作能力的良师益友。笔者相信本套丛书的出版对高校外语教师个人专业能力的提高，对教师队伍整体素质的提高，必将起到积极的推动作用。

文秋芳

北京外国语大学中国外语教育研究中心

2011年7月3日

导　读

　　二语实证或实验研究通常包括下列要素：1）文献回顾，2）研究问题，3）理论框架，4）研究设计，5）数据收集，6）数据分析，7）研究发现与解释，8）研究结论。研究者研读和分析以往研究文献之后，参考以往研究的各个要素，基于以往研究中的问题或不足确定自己的研究方向和研究问题；根据研究问题构建自己的研究理论框架；根据研究问题和理论框架做研究设计，确定数据收集方法；根据确定的数据收集方法收集数据；然后分析数据，报告数据分析结果，概括研究发现，做出相应的解释和推论。尽管二语研究中的每一个环节都很重要，但毋庸置疑的是，研究发现和研究结论很大程度上取决于数据的收集。

　　如何收集数据通常是二语研究方法论著作的一个组成部分。这类论著有的用专门的章节讨论数据和数据收集方法；有的将数据和数据收集方法分散到各有关章节中进行介绍与讨论。《第二语言研究中的数据收集方法》一书是一本二语研究数据类型与数据收集方法的专著。因为这样的专著很少，所以可以说这是本书的第一个特色。

　　本书共八章。第一章为绪言，第二章至第八章分别从七个不同的视角，介绍二语研究常用的数据类型与数据收集方法。七个视角包括心理语言学视角、认知视角、语言学视角、互动视角、社会语言学与语用学视角、调查视角和课堂视角。从不同的视角论述二语研究数据类型与数据收集方法，是本书的第二个特色。第二章至第七章中的每一章首先指出相关研究领域的基本研究目的、研究方面或研究问题，然后大体按照自然数据、提示产出数据和提示应答数据的顺序，介绍各个领域常用的数据类型和数据收集方法，指出它们适用的特定研究现象或研究选题，最后附以真实的研究案例说明这些数据收集方法的实际运用。研究问题各种各样，数据类型和数据收集方法也多种多样。有些数据类型和数据收集方法可能适用于某些特定研究问题，而另一些可能更适用于另一些特定研究问题。将数据类型和数据收集方式与特定的研究领域或研究问题结合起来，附以真实的研究案例，是本书的另一个特色。第八章则从自然语境研究、实验语境研究和行动研究三个方面，介绍这三类研究常用的数据类型或数据收集方法。

本书有助于二语研究者们充分认识二语研究的不同研究视角、不同研究领域、不同研究问题以及相应的数据类型和数据收集方法，也有助于研究者们参照书中提供的研究视角、研究方面、数据类型、数据收集方式和研究案例开展自己的研究。

第一章　绪言

本书中的二语指：1）第二语言与外语环境中的学习；2）课堂与自然环境中的学习；3）第二、第三、第四语言及第N个语言的学习。二语研究大多是实证研究或实验研究，都涉及数据的收集与解释。二语研究中最难的任务之一就是确定数据收集方法。近年来，为了解答不断增多的各种各样的研究问题，二语研究领域数据收集方法如雨后春笋般涌现。然而，数据收集方法与研究问题之间的关系有时不是非常清楚。因此本书旨在建立与说明研究问题与数据类型和数据收集方式之间的关系。

本书按研究领域分章论述历年文献中出现的一些常用数据收集方法，并将这些数据收集方法与特定的研究领域联系在一起，使这些方法具有特定的研究语境。这些领域包括心理语言学、认知过程、认知能力与认知策略、语言学、互动、社会语言学与语用学、调查、课堂。每一章基本按照自然数据、提示产出数据和提示应答数据的顺序介绍各领域使用的数据收集方法。尽管不同的研究领域或研究问题可能需要使用某些特定的数据收集方法，但是许多方法是通用的，可以从一个研究领域很容易转用到另一个研究领域。创造性运用和组合运用不同研究领域的方法，对于多方印证数据和推进研究的发展，是正确和必要的。

在正式开始数据收集以前，一定要试测（1.1）。无论数据收集计划做得多么充分，数据收集工具设计得多么细心，都难免会有缺陷。试测的目的是，在正式开始数据收集前，通过小规模数据收集，考察数据收集计划与工具的可行性、可用性与完善性，并进行必要的调整与修改。

数据收集方法对研究至关重要（1.2），因为研究发现高度依赖研究使用的数据收集方法。许多研究领域有常用的数据收集方法，但并不意味着这些方法专属于这些研究领域或有对错之分。数据收集方法的选择与研究理论框架有关，更具体地说，与称之为构念的抽象概念有关，如水平、能力、动机等。数据收集要有构念效度，即数据收集方法要能够反映并测量出抽象概念代表的那些属性。保证构念效度的一种方法是对一个构念采用多种测量方式。数据收集方法的选择还在很大程度上取决于研究问题。特定的研究问题要求研究者选择特定的数据收集方法。根据特定的研究问题选用某些特定的数据收集方法时，要注意避免一些隐患（1.3），包括方法的不适用性和方法使用的不当性。

与数据收集有关的是复研与数据报告（1.4）。复研指一项研究的可复制性或可重复性，即某个人做的一项研究具有可以被他人重复再做的特性。《美国心理协会出版手册（第五版）》（2001）指出，"科学方法的精髓在于观察可以被他人重复或证实"。《二语习得研究》的编辑Albert Valdman（1990）指出，"使二语习得研究更可靠、更有效的方式就是重复研究"。重复研究可以介于真实复研与概念复研之间。真实复研是复制要重复的研究中的一切，概念复研是复制要重复的研究中的那些断言。如果一个研究的断言不适用于另一个环境或群体，那么这项研究的概括性或者效度就会令人质疑。为了使一项研究具有可复制性，就需要详细报告数据收集方式、数据收集工具和数据收集过程。

采用实验方法收集数据时，要考虑实验处理与数据收集之间的关系（1.5）。除了要考虑方法与研究问题的一致性之外，还要考虑：1）实验前后的数据收集方法是否有可比性；2）测量实验处理效果的数据收集方式是否适用于那种实验处理方式。

第二章　基于心理语言学的研究

基于心理语言学的二语研究主要关注学习者加工与使用语言的方式，具体包括：1）二语加工与一语加工比较；2）二语加工的结构、机制、表征与时间进程；3）二语信息的通达与综合；4）一语加工策略的迁移；5）学习者个体差异对二语加工的影响；6）二语加工技能与二语语法的同步性。基于心理语言学的二语研究对特定的研究方面或研究问题，常采用某些特定的数据类型或数据收集方法。

自然数据（2.1）中的犹豫或停顿、自我修正是基于心理学的二语研究经常关注的现象。犹豫或停顿的长度与位置、停顿之间的时间长度，常作为加工的表征，用于研究学习者二语系统出现的故障和出现故障的地方，从中推断学习者如何进行加工，加工了哪些方面。自我修正存在于各种话语之中，是学习者意识到自己话语中出现问题并试图纠正的表现。

提示产出（2.2）数据在基于心理学的二语研究中常用于计划效果的研究，如Ortega（1999）采用讲述故事的方式，收集了研究对象复述故事以及回顾访谈产生的提示产出语料，用于考察任务前计划对形式关注度的影响和对任务实施过程中语言输出的影响。

在基于心理语言学的二语研究中，提示应答（2.3）数据收集方法包括反应时、句子解读、诱导模仿、词汇联想、启动、词汇判断、跨形式启动、眼动、动窗、司柱普测试。

反应时（2.3.1）常用作语言加工的测量指标，考察人们如何处理某些语言成分。反应时常与语法判断或可接受性判断等其他数据收集方法一起使用。人们认为，判断不合语法句比判断合语法句用时多。受试对句子反应时越长，需要的加工"能量"越大。句子理解（2.3.2）常用于基于竞争模式的研究，考察人们利用哪些提示及如何利用这些提示理解句子中词与词之间的关系，考察这些提示与一语知识之间的关系。研究者向受试提供含有各种提示的句子，让他们判断谁是施动者，并记录他们的反应时。使用句子理解作为数据收集方法时需要考虑：1）句子呈现方式；2）句子数目；3）句子间停顿时间；4）任务说明；5）应答形式。诱导式模仿（2.3.3）常用于了解学习者语法系统的本质特征。诱导式模仿收集数据的方法是让受试听句子并重复听到的句子，同时将受试的重复录制下来。呈现给受试的句子通常含有特定的语法结构。受试对目标句准确重复的能力反映出其内在语法系统的特征。诱导式模仿也常用于加工研究，如输入加工研究。词汇联想（2.3.4）的目的是通过收集与分析学习者词汇联想的数据，了解学习者二语心理词典结构，二语语义网络形成的方式和特点，二语心理词典与一语心理词典的关系及异同。在词汇联想任务中，通常是给受试呈现一个词，让受试给出第一个出现在脑海里的词。应答类型可以是横聚合或纵聚合应答，也可以是语音或拼写应答。启动（2.3.5）实验先后给受试呈现启动项（prime）和目标项（target），受试需要以某种方式对目标项作出反应。当启动项对目标项有影响时，即视为产生启动（priming）。启动项呈现速度快，时间短，所以受试通常意识不到启动项的出现。句法启动指讲话者不断产出前面讲过或听到过的句子结构的倾向。句法启动实验可以有多种形式。一种形式是首先让受试听与重复一个语言项，并判断是否听过该语言项；然后让受试描述一张含有该语言项语境的图画，并判断以前是否见过该图画。第二种方式是给受试一些含有特定结构的句子片断，并让受试完成此片断；然后给受试更短的句子片断并能用启动项中的结构去完成。第三种形式是句子回想。

词汇判断（2.3.6）任务给受试呈现一些真词与假词，要求受试尽可能迅速、准确地判断出哪些是真词，哪些是假词。启动项与目标项之间可以在音、形、义上有关联，也可以没有关联。跨模态（词）启动（2.3.7）在二语研究中不多见。跨模态启动通常要求受试先听一个句子，然后对计算机屏幕上出现的一个词作出某种反应。这种方法常使用听力理解题来确保受试将注意力集中在听力理解部分。跨模态启动常用于考察先行词的重激活情况。采用跨模态启动方式时，要注意控制目标项的频率、长度等指标。跨模态词启动则要求受试在听句子的同时，眼睛盯着计算机屏幕上的一个定点。在某个时刻，一个测试词会取代定点，要求受试做词汇判断，并记录下反应时用于分析。眼动（2.3.8）方法正开始进入二语研究领域。眼动方法可以用于研究阅读过程。眼的跳动、停动与复动可以精确细微地反映阅读者的即时句子加工以及修正。眼动方法可以用于研究歧义源、解歧行为、语境对加工限制与词汇对加工限制之间的不同等方面。动窗（2.3.9）实验用于了解学习者对二语句子各种部分的加工情况。在动窗实验中，一个句子中的词在屏幕上一个接一个出现，但是每次在屏幕上只显示一个词。当下一个词出现的时候，前一个词自动消失。受试控制读的速度。当受试表示准备好接受新词时，下一个词才出现。当句子中的全部词都出现之后，受试按键表示句子是否合乎语法。动窗实验有不同的版本，其中一个是自控听力与阅读任务（2.3.9.1），另一个是选通变化（2.3.9.2）。司柱普测试（2.3.10）由词和背景色彩构成。词的背景色彩与词的意义可以相同，也可以不同。在司柱普测试中，要求受试尽可能快地说出一个刺激物的色彩，由此会导致抑制，因为受试要抑制住对词的语言加工。司柱普效应指人们对词义与背景色彩一致的反应比不一致的反应更容易和更迅速。

第三章　认知过程、能力与策略研究

认知过程、能力与策略研究的主要目的是了解二语学习者的内在过程和影响这些过程的因素，了解学习者使用的学习策略。人们可以用各种数据和数据收集方法调查学习者的认知过程、能力与学习策略。

研究者可以通过收集自然语境和媒介中的自然数据（3.1），了解语言学习的内部过程或策略。两种收集自然数据的方法是观察法与日记法。观察法（3.1.1）常用于课堂语境，有时也会用于人际交际的纯自然语境。研究者可以通过观察收集到大量感兴趣现象的数据。如果研究者长时间重复观察，可以对特定环境中的被观察者有更深入、多方面的认识。Macaro（2001）建议在课堂上从下列方面观察学生：1）唇动；2）填充语或某些话语标记语的使用；3）换语补偿策略的使用；4）请求同学帮助；5）试探说出某个词；6）用演绎法推理；7）关注每一个词；

8）对学习活动的计划；9）使用词典及使用频率。使用观察法时，观察者要尽力淡化观察者的存在效应，避免出现学生因意识到观察者的存在而刻意表现的情况。日记法（3.1.2）是收集自然数据来了解学习者内部过程的另一种方式。日记法的优点在于没有太多的限制，学习者可以按照自己的时间安排，记录自己语言学习的亲身感受、使用的策略、遇到的问题及解决办法等。本节根据以往的文献，提出了开展日记研究的指导方针，包括对记日记者的要求和对研究者的要求。

在认知过程、能力与策略研究中，提示产出（3.2）数据收集方法包括语言学习策略表、模拟回想、有声法、即时回想。语言学习策略一览表（3.2.1）由Oxford（1990）提出，是语言学习策略研究使用最多的工具之一。大多数语言学习策略量表包括5个等级，从"我总是或几乎总是如此"到"我从不或几乎从不如此"。模拟回想（3.2.2）是二语研究中的几种内省方法之一，用于考察学习者的思维过程或者策略。模拟回想通常使用某种提示物，如学习者的学习录像或二语作文，让学习者根据提示物内省他们在实施一项任务或参与一项活动时的思维。有声思维（3.2.3）也称作在线思维，通常是让学习者一边从事一项语言活动，一边口头报告思维。研究者将有声思维的录音转写成文字材料，称作有声思维记录。本节提出了采用有声思维方法的一些建议。即时回想（3.2.4）是让学习者在完成特定的活动之后立即进行回想。

提示应答（3.3）数据用于调查二语学习者在二语学习中可用的认知资源、认知能力等若干方面的问题。本节介绍两种提示应答数据的收集方式：能力测试与工作记忆测试。能力测试（3.3.1）本是为了预测学习者未来语言学习成效而设计的，后常应用于二语研究。本节重点推出的是The Modern Language Aptitude Test（MLAT），给出了MLAT的各个组成部分和一些测试题型及题例，并用Ehrman & Oxford（1995）的研究说明MLAT在二语研究中的应用。工作记忆测试（3.3.2）用于研究工作记忆与二语成效之间的关系。工作记忆不同于短时记忆和长时记忆，因为工作记忆不仅具有存储能力而且还有处理能力。工作记忆有不同的理论模型，因而有基于不同模型的工作记忆测试。基于加拿大模型的工作记忆研究发现，工作记忆上的个体差异与二语产出和加工有关。二语习得研究使用三种出自认知心理学的言语工作记忆测试：运算跨距、记数跨距和句子跨距。运算跨距任务给受试一道数学题，让其判断是否正确，随后给出一个单词。受试需要在接着做几道数学判断题后，回想该词。记数跨距任务分次给受试呈现图形，让受试数并记住图形的数目。在完成系列实验后，受试按照实验的顺序，回想每次出现的图形数。句子跨距任务在二语习得研究中使用最多。句子跨距任务给受试呈现2-6个句子。这些句子可以按升序呈现，也可以无序呈现。首先让受试判断句子的真实性、可接受性、句法或语义正确性。然后要求受试记忆某些东西，如一个词、一个字母等。基于英国模式的工作记忆研究发现，音位短时记忆与二语习得成效有关。音位短时记忆指在新词呈现后立即存储并准确回想的能力。

第四章　基于语言学的研究

基于语言学的二语研究主要关注语言表征，重点在语言形式分析，而不是语言加工分析。这个领域的二语研究者视二语习得为二语语法的习得和与二语学习与使用有关的加工策略的习得。

作者认为普遍语法理论是基于语言学的二语研究中占支配地位的语言理论。以普遍语法为理论框架的二语习得研究重点在描述与解释二语学习者的语言系统，尤其是二语学习者潜在的语言能力受普遍原则支配的程度。语言能力是一个抽象的构念，是学习者大脑中的潜意识存在，无法直接观察与测量。因此，人们通过产出、理解与直觉测量方式收集语言行为数据，从中推断语言能力。本章主要介绍基于语言学的二语研究使用的数据和数据收集方法。

自然数据（4.1）一般不适用于了解二语学习者有关什么是可能的，什么是不可能的语法知识。自然数据有时会用于基于普遍语法或形式语言系统的研究，如Lardiere（1998a）采用自然数据研究二语语法中动词移动的情况；Kumpf（1984）采用自然数据研究二语中介语的时态与语态使用情况。

提示产出（4.2）数据用于研究学习者某些特定的语法知识。提示产出数据收集方法有诱导模仿、图画描述、结构式诱导、故事讲述、句子组合。诱导模仿（4.2.1）常用于二语语法系统特性的研究。诱导模仿任务要求受试在听一些含有某种语法特征的句子之后，复述这些句子。研究者分析受试的复述语料，了解他们的二语语法知识。作者在本节中给出了一些使用诱导模仿方法的建议。图画描述（4.2.2）任务有助于研究者收集某个二语语法特征的足够样本。研究者可以使用一张或一系列能够诱导出某个语法特征的图画，让受试进行描述。结构式诱导（4.2.3）方法是图画描述的高级结构版，目的是考察学习者遇到基于规则的形态加工时表现的创造力。在结构式诱导任务中，研究者首先描述一张图画，从中提供目标动词，然后让受试用目标动词描述第二张图画，考察受试习得和使用该动词的情况。故事讲述（4.2.4）使用各种材料作为提示，可以有各种听众。故事讲述让学习者可以相对自由地选择各种语言结构表达他们的意思。研究者通过分析故事讲述语料，了解学习者的二语语言形式特征。句子组合（4.2.5）是一种收集复合句数据的方式，常用于关系从句的习得研究。句子组合任务通常给受试两个单句，让他们组合成一个句子。

提示应答（4.3）数据和数据收集方法是基于语言学的二语研究中常用的数据类型和方法。提示应答数据收集方法包括可接受性判断、量值评估、对错判断和句子比对。可接受性判断（4.3.1）是语言学研究中常用的一种方法，常用于让学习者陈述他们的二语中什么是可能的，什么是不可能的。多年来，围绕可接受性判断有众多的质疑和争议。因此，在使用这种方法时需要考虑众多的因素，如材料和程序的诸多方面。量值评估（4.3.2）是应用在诸多领域的一种很成熟的研究工具。当研究者不但希望了解受试对一些语言项的排序，而且还希望了解受试对各语言项的评价程度时，量值评估方法很有用。量值评估任务给受试一些语料，让受试对这些语料一一赋值。如果语料是一组句子的话，后面句子的赋值要参照前面句子赋值的标准。例如，受试给第一个句子的赋值是20的话，如果他认为第二个句子比第一个句子好一倍的话，那么他给第二个句子的赋值应该是40。对错判断（4.3.3）是考察人们如何理解句子所用的方法，广泛用于二语反身词的习得研究。句子比对（4.3.4）用于了解学习者有关合语法性与不合语法性的知识。句子比对通常在计算机上进行。首先在计算机屏幕上显示一个句子，让受试判断该句是否合语法。短暂停顿之后，出现第二个句子，让受试将第二个句子与仍保留在屏幕上的第一个句子比对，判断两个句子是否一致。从第二个句子出现起到受试按下判断键之间的时间被记录下来，用作研究数据。作者在本节中提出了使用句子比对所要注意的一些方面。

第五章　基于互动的研究

互动研究的关注点是互动如何促进习得，了解互动中各种成分的关系和各种目标语言项的学习，考察交际与习得的关系以及两者之间的调和机制。互动研究的前提假定是"交际压力激发语言学习"。互动假设认为，意义协商，特别是激发本族语者或高水平交谈者互动调整的协商，促进习得，因为它将输入、内在学习能力，选择性注意和产出性输出联系在一起（Long, 1996）。典型的互动研究过程包括：1）录制学习者的互动；2）标注互动；3）分析互动。

自然数据（5.1）有助于研究者加深了解在互动过程中人们使用语言的社会与语境特征。互动研究通常采用纵深研究模式收集与分析自然出现的互动，从定量描述角度揭示二语长时发展的各个方面，从定性解释角度探讨语言发展的社会认知与社会文化维度。Tarone & Liu（1995）采用纵深研究模式收集自然数据，描述了一个儿童从5岁到7岁的社会互动和二语发展。使用自然数据进行互动研究需要注意的是，在研究某一个特定语言结构的时候，收集的那部分数据中可能没有足够的案例可供使用。因此，研究者要么需要花费时间收集到足够例子的数据，要么需要采用其他辅助方式。另外需要注意避免录制对自然会话的影响。

提示产出（5.2）的任务形式包括图片描述、识别不同、完成故事、按图索路、达成共识、唤起意识。图片描述任务通常给一个学习者一张图片，让其向另一位看不到图片的学习者作描述。识别不同任务首先给受试两张或多张图片。这些图片除个别地方不同外，其他都相同。然后要求受试通过口头互动发现图片的不同之处。实施图片描述任务和识别不同任务可参照作者提供的指导方针。完成故事任务给不同的受试一个故事的不同部分，然后让他们把这些部分拼在一起成为一个完整的故事。按图索路让受试根据所给的地图和条件，找出最佳出行路线。达成共识任务让受试根据给定的情景或者条件，通过互动达成一致意见。唤起意识任务让学习者有意识根据特定的语言任务开展互动，以实现任务的目标。

提示应答（5.3）任务在互动研究中主要用于评价学习者对目标语的理解。这是因为提示应答任务通常要求受试按照对话者的指令操作物体。一个典型的提示应答任务是给受试一种厨房的图片和几张厨房用品的剪纸，让受试根据对话者的指令摆放这些厨房用品。

内省（5.4）是近些年来在互动研究中普遍使用的一种方法。内省数据通常有两种形式，一种是学习者在从事某项特定活动的同时说出自己的思维的方式，一种是像第三章介绍的模仿回想那样的回想方式。

第六章　基于社会语言学和语用学的研究

社会语言学与语用学都涉及研究语境中的语言，因此它们强调社会与语境因素如何影响二语习得与产出。基于社会语言学和语用学的二语研究的前提假定是，二语习得与产出在一定程度上受外部因素的影响，如指派的任务、对话者的社会地位、性别差异等。

自然数据（6.1）出现的自然语境很多。本节仅介绍使用口头数据与日记的研究。研究者们使用自然语境中的口头数据研究特定社会环境和语境中的二语习得与产出，包括语用行为的习得与产出。研究者们使用日记研究学习者的情感，了解学习者对不同学习语境和不同人群的态度以及考察学习者对语言学习的反思。开展日记研究可参照Bailey（1983）的日记研究五步骤。

提示产出（6.2）数据用于研究涉及社会语言学和语用学知识与使用方面的众多问题。收集数据的任务形式有叙述和角色扮演。诱导叙述的任务形式有访谈、无声电影、最少剧白电影短片。角色扮演一般有两种形式：开放式与封闭式。开放式是由两个或两个以上参与者根据特定情景互动的方式。封闭式与话语完成测验相同，但是采用的是口头形式，由参与者根据所给的情景，作出单向回应。

提示应答（6.3）的形式有话语完成测验、录像回放解读、配对身份。基于语用学的二语研究用得最多的方法大概就是话语完成测验。话语完成测验常用笔试形式。在话语完成测验中，受试根据给定的可以出现一定言语行为的情景，作出应答。话语完成测验的一种变体形式是给受试一些背景材料，并根据背景材料做得体性判断题。录像回放解读也是用于研究语用方面的课题，例如人们对语用不当的反应；也用于评价目的。配对身份方法也是社会语言学研究常用的方法。在配对身份实验中，说话者是能够流利说两种语言或两种方言的人，是具有两种语言身份的人。研究者为他们录音，然后让受试听录音，并回答一些与说话者有关的问题。

第七章　调查研究

调查方法常使用高度复杂的工具收集样本数据，通过对样本数据的分析得出概括性总体结论。二语调查研究使用的数据收集方法有问卷、访谈或这两种方法的组合。收集的数据可以作定性处理也可以作定量处理。问卷与访谈可以用于收集三类数据：事实类、行为类和态度类。事实类数据包括学习者的年龄、性别、社会经济地位、语言学习史等一些背景资料。行为类数据包括学习者的生活方式、习性、行动等资料。态度类数据包括学习者的态度、观念、观点、兴趣、价值等资料。

调查研究中的自然数据（7.1）可以采用观察、录音、录像的方式获得。人们通常用观察、访谈、问卷等方式收集数据，以用于三方印证。

调查研究中的提示产出数据可以采用问卷方式获得。问卷中的问项可以是开放式的（7.2），也可以是封闭式的（7.3）。开放式问项可以让回答者用自己的方式自由回答，自由表达自己的想法。开放式问项收集到的数据可以定性处理，也可以定量处理。封闭式问项的选择答案由研究者设定。相比开放式问项，通过封闭式问项获得的数据更容易量化处理和分析。选择何种问项取决于研究问题。如果只有大体研究方向而没有明确预设的研究问题，采用开放性问项可能更恰当。如果研究问题非常明确，采用封闭性问项可能更合适。如果必要的话，可以同时采用两种类型的问项。采用问卷的调查研究可以用于各种选题（7.4），包括语言态度、需求分析、二语学习策略、计算机熟悉度、语言焦虑、动机、交际愿望、修正反馈等等。问卷有优势也有需要注意的地方（7.5）。问卷有很多优势，如经济实用，操作便捷，渠道多样，可以大规模实施，容易重复与比较，既可以用于纵深研究，也可以用于横断研究。然而，问卷也有不少需要注意的方面。作者给出了问卷设计与使用需要注意的十个方面。

第八章　课堂研究

课堂研究指对二语课堂中各种教与学现象进行的系统考察、分析、描述、概括与解释。课堂研究可以由任课教师实施，也可以由外来研究者实施。课堂研究可以分成三类：自然课堂研究、实验课堂研究、行动研究。

自然课堂研究（8.1）是在原封未动的原始班级中进行的研究。研究者不介入教学过程，而是详细考察和了解课堂中的一切现象。在自然课堂研究中，人们常用观察法（8.1.1）收集数据，从中了解在特定课堂语境中的事件、互动和语言使用模式。观察手段包括使用观察表、场记和一些机械方式如录音、录像等。一些简单的观察表供人们给显见行为打勾或做标记。有些观察表不需太多推断。有些观察表则需要较多的推断，以确定某些行为的意义或者功能。有的观察表集中观察课堂话语中一些非常具体的方面，如修正性反馈等。使用机械方式收集数据有许多需要注意的方面，作者特别给出了这方面的指导建议。研究者在自然课堂进行观察，特别要注意观察礼节。作者也特别给出了课堂观察需要注意的礼节表。

实验课堂研究（8.2）不同于自然课堂研究，需要对原始班级随机分组，需要有控制组与实验组。在实验过程中，对实验组采用不同于控制组的教学方式或者实验处理方式，以考察处理方式的不同是否会带来二语学习或者使用上的差异。研究者需要尽最大努力控制各种不相关变量，以保证研究结果的唯一解释是实验处理方式而不是其他。

行动研究（8.3）有各种定义和名称，但是一个共同点就是，行动研究者通常是课堂任教者而不是外来研究者。任教者本人对自己课堂的各个方面开展研究，旨在改进自己的教学实践和教学质量。行动研究同其他研究一样，起始于困惑、疑问或者存在的问题。行动研究者或者教师研究者针对发现的课堂问题，可以从不同的视角，运用不同的方法收集与分析数据，详细考察涉及问题或者现象的特征、特点。教师研究者可以根据研究发现，提出处理方法，或者改变教学模式，然后加以实验，考察处理方法和教学模式改变的有效性。

马广惠

南京师范大学

2011年7月

Preface

In the process of writing our 2005 volume, *Second Language Research: Methodology and Design*, one chapter stood out: Chapter Three, entitled "Common Data Collection Measures." Although we included a great deal in that chapter, we also felt that there was much more that could be said. Sure enough, even though that chapter ended up being the longest in the book, upon reading it, many of our colleagues, co-authors, students, and editors expressed a desire to know more, asking us questions like "what about discussing the problems with this" and "I wish you'd included an example of that." Not only for them, but also for ourselves, we took up the challenge of demystifying the choice and creation of data elicitation techniques. The current book, devoted to data collection, is therefore an extension and expansion of this earlier chapter and, for those who want to delve further into the actual collection of data, can be used as a companion to our 2005 text.

One of the most difficult tasks when conducting second language research is identifying and deciding on ways to collect data. There are intricate relationships between research questions and data elicitation techniques, and with so many possibilities, it can be hard to keep all of the necessary considerations straight. Fortunately, a body of practical knowledge has been built up in this area, and we hope that this book takes a step toward synthesizing and systematizing it, thereby helping L2 researchers to be inventive without having to reinvent the wheel. In many graduate programs, students in disciplines such as applied linguistics, second language studies, TESOL, psycholinguistics, cognitive science, and educational linguistics are expected to collect data for projects, graduate seminar work, theses, and dissertations. Although many programs offer classes in research methods and design, there is clearly a need for a textbook that provides step-by-step examples and specific guidelines on how to collect second language data.

In this book we begin each chapter by discussing common research questions underlying data elicitation measures in that area, we then go on to identify relevant types of data according to a continuum that includes naturalistic language, prompted linguistic production, and non-linguistic experimental responses. Whenever possible, we provide the history and origins for some of the techniques, and we also provide detailed descriptions in terms of "how to's," summaries of published studies that have made use of the techniques described, and discussions not only of advantages, but also of common misconceptions, caveats, and/or limitations related to various techniques. Interested readers can then seek out the studies we have summarized, both for further details and to better understand the usefulness and relevance of the technique to their own research. We hope that our book will stimulate researchers to use data elicitation measures with an understanding of their strengths and limitations and, when appropriate, to modify and combine techniques to match their own research needs.

There are many individuals to whom thanks are due. First, we are grateful to our editor, Cathleen Petree of Lawrence Erlbaum Associates, for her (as usual) unwavering support for this project and for obtaining extremely useful external reviews of both the proposal and the final product. Both Susan Gass and Alison Mackey had research assistants, and we are indebted to them for their help in many ways. At Michigan State University, Robin Roots showed her usual keen ability to pinpoint problems and suggest alternative wording. Both Robin and Junkyu Lee found and summarized many relevant articles. At Georgetown University, Rebecca Sachs, in particular, contributed enormously to this effort, and served as an extremely talented editor. Jaemyung Goo, Mika Hama, Rebekha Abbuhl, and Bo-Ram Suh also assisted in important ways. All of our assistants provided library work and advice, criticisms, and occasionally even praise. Their careful work and contributions greatly improved the final version of this text. We are also grateful to Jane Ozanich and Jenefer Philp, who graciously contributed some of the drawings (those on p. 118 are the work of Jane Ozanich, those on p. 121 are by Jenefer Philp, and those on pp. 117 and 130 are by Jamie Lepore Wright). We appreciate their willingness to share their artistic talents with us. Finally, we sincerely thank the aforementioned colleagues and students who encouraged us to write this book. We have learned a great deal ourselves in the process and hope that it helps to answer some of the questions they had.

CHAPTER 1

Introduction

How Do Second Language Researchers Decide on Data Elicitation Measures?

When we read research reports in journals or books, we can easily be lulled into a false sense of security. The straightforwardness and simplicity of the reporting, while often necessary for publication, can obscure the trials, tribulations, difficulties, and, in some cases, significant problems that were part of the research process. The passage from generating an idea for a research question to publishing a report is rarely tidy or obvious; it is a long and arduous undertaking. Furthermore, since we cannot control every eventuality, compromises in data collection and analysis are often necessary. These sorts of details usually are not disclosed in the reports that we read. To give just one example, because of the attrition of participants, it is quite common for researchers to have to eliminate variables or factors that are potentially of interest. A lack of participants or data in a study can force researchers to narrow their focus or to separate a large study into smaller studies, dealing with separate variables each time. For clarity and parsimony in reporting, however, these developments may be glossed over in the final report. Although there are many potential problems along the road for researchers to be aware of when conducting studies, this book deals in detail with perhaps the most significant one of all: the collection of the data.

Second language research relies heavily on empirical and often experimental studies that involve the interpretation of data. The term *second language* is used in this book as a cover term to include, *inter alia*: (1) learning in both second and foreign language environments, (2) learning in both classroom and naturalistic settings, and (3) learning a second language as well as learning a third, fourth, language, and so on. The terms *acquisition* and *learning* are used interchangeably, meaning only that non-primary language acquisition is the focus.

One of the most difficult tasks when conducting research in such a broad field is identifying and deciding on methods of data collection. In recent years, to answer an increasing variety of research questions, the field has witnessed a burgeoning of techniques to elicit data. At times, however, the relationship between the techniques of elicitation and the questions being asked has been obscured. In this book, our goal is to demystify the process of data collection. We present suggestions for collecting data in relation to a wide range of research areas and, in so doing, provide a detailed picture of the many different techniques available for eliciting data on the knowledge and use of language, intuitions about language, and/or attitudes toward language. Data collection in second language research is clearly a multi-dimensional topic. This book reflects that fact by exploring some of the common measures that have appeared in the literature over the years and across a range of domains of SLA research.

In Mackey and Gass (2005), we pointed out that data elicitation techniques are limited only by one's imagination. For expository purposes in the current text, we have divided the book into chapters according to research area, contextualizing elicitation techniques by linking each to a specific area of second language research. We opted to begin with the brain in areas of cognition, move to memory, mind and language and then move to interaction and sociolinguistic context and end with the classroom. Each chapter deals separately with data collection for studies based on psycholinguistics (processing), cognitive processes, capacities and strategies, linguistics, interactions, sociolinguistics and pragmatics, surveys, and classrooms. Within each chapter we have organized the data collection methods according to a continuum ranging from naturalistic data, prompted production data to prompted response data—a classification scheme based on Chaudron's (2003) exposition of data collection methods. Whereas some research questions appear to call for eliciting and measuring language learners' spontaneous speech (naturalistic data), for others it may seem more appropriate to use formal tools to collect written or spoken language production (prompted production data) or to elicit specific responses to prompts (prompted response data).

At the same time, an important consideration when using any elicitation instrument is to understand its advantages and limitations, as well as to realize that many techniques are versatile enough to shift easily between research areas and elicit data to address a wide range of questions. Thus, in contextualizing each technique within a specific area of research, it is not our intent to suggest that these techniques are limited to those research areas (and vice versa), but simply to illustrate common practice. Indeed, creative uses and combinations of techniques from a range of areas are often appropriate and necessary both to triangulate data and to move research forward. As will be discussed in more detail below, no measure is foolproof, and each must be tried before actually using it for collecting data. In this book, where appropriate, we also provide some historical context, discussing the origins of the data collection techniques presented. Finally, for illustrative purposes, we present descriptions of published second language studies in boxed insets, as well as samples of data collected using the different techniques.

1.1 PILOT TESTING

Before delving further into the details of data elicitation techniques, a caveat: Regardless of how carefully researchers have designed their studies, they should never simply assume that their data collection methods will work. A crucial issue that must be kept in mind in the data-gathering process is the importance of pilot testing. A pilot study is generally considered to be a small-scale trial of the proposed procedures, materials, methods, and (sometimes) coding sheets and analytic choices of a research project. The point of carrying out a pilot study is to finalize these essential components, to uncover any problems, and to address them before the main study is carried out. A pilot study is therefore an important means of assessing the feasibility and usefulness of the data sampling and collection methods and revising them before they are used with the research participants. While it might seem that careful prior planning would allow researchers to skip this step, it is in fact critical to allocate additional time to conduct pilot tests, as they can reveal subtle flaws in the design or implementation of the study—flaws that may not be readily apparent in the plan itself, but that could otherwise prove costly and time-consuming, perhaps even leading to the loss of valuable and irreplaceable data.

Since pilot studies sometimes result in data that might be useable for the main study, it is important to note the constraints imposed by human subjects committees or institutional review boards (also referred to as ethics review boards, discussed extensively in Mackey & Gass, 2005), which must approve research conducted in most university or institutional settings. Some researchers choose to seek permission from their institutional review boards

3

to carry out their experiments in such a way that if they do not encounter problems with their pilot-testing, they can use those data for their main study as long as exactly the same procedures are used. However, not all institutions will give blanket permission for this, and many will not consider requests for the retroactive use of data. It is therefore worthwhile to investigate these issues while also keeping in mind that it is a rare pilot study that does not result in some sort of revision of materials or methods.

1.2 THE SIGNIFICANCE OF DATA COLLECTION MEASURES

One goal of second language research is to uncover information about learner behavior or learner knowledge independent of the context of data collection. However, research findings are highly dependent on the data collection measures used. As such, although many research domains have common measures associated with them, and while the choice of a measure may be related to the theoretical framework within which the research is conducted, there should be no single prescribed elicitation method for a given domain, nor is there necessarily a "right" or "wrong" elicitation method for a given context. At the same time, saying that numerous elicitation measures can be used in the various areas of second language research does not imply that one method is as good as another; rather, the choice of one method over another is highly dependent on the research question being asked.

Also important to consider in data collection is the concept of construct validity, which refers to the degree to which the phenomenon of interest is adequately captured. It is often difficult to capture a particular construct, such as proficiency, aptitude, or motivation, with one measure. In cases such as these, construct validity can be enhanced when multiple estimates of a construct are used. For example, if we consider the construct "amount of input" and its relationship to some part of acquisition, construct validity might be enhanced if a variety of factors, such as length of residence, amount of language instruction, and the language used in the participants' formal education, are considered.

We mentioned above that research questions can dictate, to a certain extent, a researcher's choice of data collection method. Let us consider what this means by looking at some hypothetical examples. In each of these examples, we refer to specific elicitation techniques, each of which is dealt with in this book and appears in the subject index.

Researching a Grammatical Structure

After years of teaching Japanese, you recognize that English-speaking learners of Japanese have great difficulty with passives. You perform an extensive literature review and find out that there are theoretical reasons for this, so you decide to investigate the issue further. The task in front of you is to gather data from learners of Japanese to determine exactly which faulty generalizations they may be making. In other words, which language forms are used by learners at various stages of Japanese proficiency? Once you have determined the type(s) of data you need to elicit (i.e., samples of Japanese passives), your next task is to determine how to elicit the appropriate data.

Your first thought, before pilot testing, is to have learners describe pictures that depict various actions (e.g., a man being hit by a ball, a dog being kissed by a boy). Unfortunately, the learners, who are experts at avoidance, produce very few examples of the structure in question. You then modify the task and tell the learners to start with the object of the action. You even point to the man and the dog in the pictures. This does not work very well, either, and the learners do not do what you have asked. You are thus left with the question: Did they not produce the requisite passive because (1) they do not have the linguistic knowledge to do so, (2) the active sentence is easier to formulate, or (3) they did not understand how to carry out the task? Only the first interpretation will help you in dealing with your research questions but there are too many possibilities for you to be able to interpret the data legitimately. It is therefore necessary to question the value of this elicitation method.

You then realize that you have to "force" the issue and make the learners behave in a way that allows you to be confident that you are obtaining information that reflects their actual knowledge about passives. There are a few ways that this is commonly done in second language research. One way is to use what are known as acceptability/grammaticality judgments, in which a list of grammatical and ungrammatical sentences is presented to learners who are then asked to indicate whether they consider them acceptable Japanese sentences or not. This is followed by a request to the learners to correct those sentences they have judged to be incorrect. Forcing correction allows researchers to ensure not only that their target of investigation (e.g., passives) is included in the sample of sentences, but also that learners are indeed focusing on passives. Another way to gather information about passives is through "elicited imitation." In this method, sentences are read to learners (usually in the form of audio recordings to ensure that everyone hears the same sentences at an identical rate and with identical intonation), and the learners are asked to repeat them. As with acceptability judgments, researchers can control all aspects of the sample sentences. A third possibility for eliciting information about passives is known as "truth-value judgments," which might be particularly useful in the case of Japanese passives because some of the differences in language forms involve subtle meaning differences. With truth-value judgments, learners are given short contextualized passages with relevant sentences embedded in them. Following each passage is a question designed to ascertain whether or not the learners can correctly interpret the meaning of the passage.

Thus, the investigation of a particular grammatical structure offers a number of possibilities for data elicitation measures, the choice of which will depend on the questions being asked (e.g., acceptability judgments or elicited imitations if researchers wish to gather information about grammatical knowledge, or truth-value judgments if the focus is on subtle meaning differences). In any event, specific research questions can be used to narrow the choice of data collection measures.

Interaction Research

Suppose your research interest is to find out whether recasts or negotiation will lead to faster development of relative clauses in a second language.[1] You find groups of English learners of Italian who are at four different stages of development in their knowledge of relative clauses. For each group, half of them will serve in your "recast" group and the other half in your "negotiation" group. You first give a pre-test to ensure comparability of groups. Everyone then completes a picture-description task in which feedback is provided by a native speaker of Italian, either in the form of recasts or negotiation. At the end of the session, you give the learners a post test on relative clauses and then a delayed post test three weeks later. You find that there are no differences between the groups. When you go back to analyze the actual transcripts of the sessions, however, you realize that your findings are probably due to a lack of examples of relative clauses in the data.

This example illustrates how important it is in task-based research first to ascertain whether or not tasks will, in fact, elicit the targeted grammatical structures and provide opportunities for interactional feedback. Since relative

---

[1]Recasts occur when an incorrect non-native speaker (NNS) utterance is repeated in a more target-like way while maintaining the original meaning.

Example: NNS: I have three bird my picture.
         NS: You have three birds in your picture?

Negotiation occurs when learners and their interlocutors try to understand the meaning or form of an utterance.

Example: NNS: I see bud my picture.
         NS: You see what in your picture?
         NNS: I see bud my picture.
         NS: Bud?
         NNS: Yes
         NS: Do you mean bird?
         NNS: Ah, bird, yes.

clauses are frequently used to differentiate one object or person from others (e.g., *the boy who is wearing a red hat is my brother*—in other words, not the boy who is wearing the green hat), researchers targeting relative clauses must make sure that their tasks are consistent with the normal function of relative clauses and involve learners identifying an object or person from among others. In sum, researchers need to ensure (through piloting) that each elicitation measure yields the kind of data that will be useful in addressing their research questions.

Researching Pragmatics

Assume that you want to conduct research on the pragmatic problems that a particular group of students might have (e.g., English speakers learning Chinese). You have further limited your area of research to interactions between English learners of Mandarin and their Mandarin-speaking professors. You obtain permission to observe interactions between these two groups of people in order to determine what sorts of pragmatic errors may occur, but after five days of observations, you have little in the way of consistent results. Why might that be the case? One reason might be that you have not sufficiently narrowed down your research question. For example, you might be considering too many pragmatic functions (e.g., complaining, apologizing, requesting, inviting) rather than constraining the data. A second reason is that waiting for language events such as these to occur often depends on luck. You might end up with some interesting examples that could be fodder for insightful qualitative analyses, but if you are looking for sufficient examples to be able to make quantitative generalizations, you may need to force the issue through written discourse completion tests or well-designed role plays. In their simplest form, discourse completion tests present learners with specific contexts in which responses are required. Role plays involve acting out situations and are also useful for establishing particular contexts. An elicitation method could involve a learner and a researcher sitting at a table when the researcher pretends to accidentally knock over a glass of water. What the learner actually says to accept the apology could then be recorded.

As can be seen through the examples above, research questions can help to guide researchers in selecting appropriate elicitation measures. In conducting research, researchers must understand how data elicitation methods relate not only to their general areas of research, but also to their more specific research questions.

1.3 ELICITATION PITFALLS

As we begin a research project, the first question that confronts us is the identification of a research area; the second task is to narrow the area down into
manageable research questions. Once that happens, there are myriad ways for
collecting appropriate data to answer our questions. In section 1.2, we discussed how research questions can guide researchers into selecting one particular technique over another and we presented situations in which certain
techniques might be ineffective. In addition to the problem of choosing techniques that turn out to be inappropriate, there are also inappropriate ways of
using techniques that might otherwise be suitable. In what follows, we present
some examples of such inappropriate uses. Unfortunately, when we use an
elicitation technique inappropriately, we are left with the regrettable situation
of not knowing what interpretation to give to our data.

Example 1: Acquisition of relative clauses

Purpose: To determine whether second language learners can recognize
acceptable versus unacceptable relative clauses in a second
language after three years of language study.

Instrument: Acceptability judgment task. Learners are presented with 20
sentences in the second language and are asked to judge whether
those sentences are acceptable or not. Example sentences follow:
1. That's the girl that loves Johnny.
2. That's the family which has five dogs.
3. That's the house that was just painted.

Problem 1: Let's assume that some of the learners indicate that all three
of these sentences are incorrect. We might conclude that they
do not have appropriate knowledge of English relative clauses
since all three are acceptable English sentences. However, given
the particular technique that we used, we actually have no idea
why the sentences were marked wrong. At least two possibilities
come to mind: (1) The learners have no knowledge of English
relative clauses, or (2) they believe that it is inappropriate to
use contractions in writing.

Problem 2:   Let's assume a different response pattern: The learners mark 1 wrong and 2 and 3 correct. Again, at least two possible interpretations are possible: (1) The learners have no knowledge of English relative clauses, or (2) they believe that that cannot be used as a relative marker with animate referents.

Conclusion: Without asking learners to correct what they believe to be the specific errors responsible for their choices, we cannot have confidence in our interpretations of the data.

Example 2: Working memory and proficiency

Purpose: To determine (1) whether the effect of corrective feedback on the learning of relative clauses in a second language is the same for learners with low working memory capacity versus for learners with high working memory capacity, and (2) whether this is related to proficiency. The target language is English, and the native languages of the learners are Japanese, Korean, Arabic, and Hindi.

Instruments: a. Reading span test. Because it is not logistically possible to give the reading span test in the native languages of the learners, the test is given in English.

              b. Spot the difference task. Learners are given two similar drawings with 10 differences. Their task is to describe the pictures to one another in pairs in order to find the 10 differences. The sessions are audiotaped.

Problem: The results of a language based working memory task in a second language may be confounded with proficiency if the learners in the study are at different developmental levels.

Conclusion: When doing research using working memory tests, research-ers need to be able to tease apart working memory capacity and second language proficiency, for example, by giving a language neutral working memory test (e.g., spatial span or digit span) or by giving working memory tests in the learners' native language.

Example 3:   Acquisition of complex sentences

Purpose: To determine whether Japanese or Spanish learners of English
                have better knowledge of complex sentences (e.g., Before the
                man robbed the bank, he studied the bank's layout).

Instrument: The learners listen to example sentences and repeat them (see
                Chaps. 2 and 4 on elicited imitation).

Background: The two groups are matched according to their results on a
                placement test used in their intensive English program.

Problem: The results show that the Spanish learners perform better
                than the Japanese learners. However, a closer inspection of
                the learners' placement scores shows that the placement test
                only included a grammar and vocabulary test. Given that the
                elicitation technique involved a listening measure, one cannot
                be sure whether the learners' abilities on a skill crucial to the
                technique itself were indeed matched.

Conclusion: It is imperative that groups of learners be truly matched on
                the measures relevant to a particular technique.

Example 4:   Verb tense

Purpose 1:   To elicit present, past, and future tense by asking English
                learners to respond to particular questions.

Instrument 1:   The researcher asks the following:
                Tell me what you did yesterday.
                Tell me about a typical day for you.
                Tell me how you like to spend your free time.
                Tell me about the town you live in.
                Tell me your plans for the summer vacation.

Problem 1:   Learners may use verb forms other than the intended ones.

Purpose 2:   To elicit past tense forms in Spanish by native speakers of
                English.

Instrument 2:   Participants view a picture for one minute, then turn the
                picture over and read instructions designed to prompt a past
                tense narration of the events.

Problem 2:	Below is a response in Spanish from one of the participants, again along with an English translation.
	Response in Spanish: Bueno, mientras el señor Gonzalez está leyendo se ve [eh] que *en el otro lado de la pared va caminando su esposa, pues se supone que es su esposa con un regalo muy grande, una caja muy grande que obviamente es un regalo ...* [*the story continues*]
	[Good, while Mr. Gonzalez is reading, you see [eh] that on the other side of the wall his wife is walking, well you assume that it is his wife with a very big gift, a very big box that is obviously a gift ...]
Conclusion:	All prompts must be piloted to ensure that they will actually elicit the data appropriate to answer the research question. In this example, the researcher wanted to elicit past tense, but there were no exemplars of the past.

Before devoting a considerable amount of time and effort to a research project, researchers want to be sure that the results will be attributable to the correct causes. As shown by the problematic examples in this and the previous section, methods of data collection are crucial in this respect.

1.4 REPLICATION AND DATA REPORTING

With any discussion of data elicitation comes the issues of replication and data reporting, two concepts that are inextricably linked. It is well understood that replication is important to the development and maintenance of any field of study. If the results of a study are valid, they should be able to be replicated. As the *Publication Manual of the American Psychological Association, Fifth Edition* (a manual that is used by most of the second language research field) points out, "The essence of the scientific method involves observations that can be repeated and verified by others" (American Psychological Association, 2001, p. 348). Likewise, Albert Valdman, the editor of the journal *Studies in Second Language Acquisition,* has asserted that "the way to more valid and reliable SLA research is through replication" (1993, p. 505). Generally speaking, there are two primary reasons for replication: verification and generalizability. As we will point out below, these issues are often fused in second language studies.

Replication studies do not often find their way into the published pages of literature on second language research. One reason behind the dearth of replication studies, as Valdman (1993) acknowledges, is that, "to be sure, in replication one loses the aura of glamour and the exhilaration of innovation" (p. 505). This sentiment is echoed by van der Veer, van Ijzendoorn, and Valsiner (1994), who state, "As these replication studies do not yield novelty, but rather check the reliability of the original results, they are less valued in a community where (limited) originality is highly valued" (p. 6). This speaks to the political and career reasons for which an individual might decide not to pursue replication studies.

There are also disciplinary reasons behind the difficulties involved in replication. A second language researcher can replicate the instruments, tasks, and general setting of a study; however, when dealing with linguistic behavior, individual characteristics such as prior linguistic background and knowledge come into play, and these are often extremely difficult to replicate for a variety of reasons. Polio and Gass (1997) discuss a continuum of replication studies (see also Hendrick, 1990 and van der Veer et al., 1994), ranging from virtual to conceptual. Virtual replications, in which everything is copied, are clearly almost impossible. No group of participants is going to be identical to another group. However, conceptual replications are feasible and can provide important supporting or disconfirming information. In these studies, researchers need to be conceptually true to the original, carefully considering the theoretical claims of the original research. If the claims cannot be extended to a different setting and to a different group of participants, then the generalizability (and, by implication, the validity) of the original study can be called into question. It is in this sense that it is difficult to interpret the results of a replication study. While true replication is possible in some sciences, the fact that it is not usually possible in second language studies leaves researchers with two questions when results diverge: Are the results different because they are not generalizable, or are they different because there is an issue of verification of the original results?

Related to replication is the issue of data reporting. When writing up results, regardless of the audience, it is generally agreed that researchers should provide sufficient detail to allow others to replicate their studies. Thus, all of the procedures, tasks, and instruments must be thoroughly described. For example, if the participants were asked to read a passage, then that passage should ideally be included. If there were comprehension questions following that passage, those questions should be included as well. However, there are usually space limitations in journals that make it impossible to include all of the pertinent information. In such instances, researchers wishing to replicate others' studies are usually advised to contact the authors for further details. For instance, it may not be necessary for an author to specify the type of tape recorder or transcriber used in a study, but it may be appropriate to provide copies of the instruments to people who ask for them, or to explain the type of analytic machine used when doing spectrographic analyses of speech because the degree of analyticity is dependent on the equipment used.

1.5 RELATIONSHIPS BETWEEN TREATMENTS AND DATA COLLECTION

When conducting experimental research, it is important not only to consider whether the data elicitation techniques are used appropriately in relation to particular research questions, but also to keep in mind two other issues that we raise in this section: (1) whether the data elicitation measures employed before and after a treatment are comparable with each other (i.e., the relationship between pre- and post-tests) and (2) whether the modes of data collection that are selected to measure the effects of a treatment are suitable for that type of treatment.

It should be obvious that in a study considering the effects of a treatment, the pre- and post-tests need to be comparable. Determining the reliability and comparability of testing instruments is not always an easy task, and since it goes beyond the scope of this book, we refer the reader to standard statistics books for further discussion. Nonetheless, it is easy to imagine the problems that arise if a pre-test is easier, more difficult, or simply different from the post-test. For one thing, there is little guarantee in these situations that observed "improvements" are due to the effects of the treatment. A simple solution might be to give the same test twice. However, given that learners might remember the items from the first test, researchers would not be able to have confidence in the interpretation of these scores, either.

The second issue, regarding whether the tests employed reflect the treatment, can usefully be discussed in the context of interaction-based research, where the conflict is likely to arise. Interaction-based research generally involves collecting data from learners in a task-based setting, establishing a baseline of second language use, and then determining whether learning has occurred due to a treatment. In this type of research, specific tasks are used to elicit data from learners who are involved in interactions with other learners, with native speakers of a language, or with their instructors. One approach is to argue that the pre- and post-test data collection measures should involve the same type of task that is used in the treatment, thereby ensuring familiarity with the task and helping to eliminate the influence of one particular task on the results. Another is to assert that different measures of learning are necessary to avoid practice effects and to enhance generalizability. Both arguments have value, but the decision as to how to measure learning is ultimately a trade-off that researchers must consider in relation to their own studies. The first possibility may be able to show a more local effect, the limitation being that researchers cannot conclude whether the newly-demonstrated knowledge truly represents a change in the learners' knowledge base to be drawn on in other areas of performance. In contrast, measuring learning by means of an unrelated task (e.g., an acceptability task—or a task involving reaction times) suggests greater generalizability of results, with the advantage of providing data that indicate a change reflecting knowledge usable in a wider variety of contexts.

1.6 CONCLUSION

As mentioned earlier, this book is organized according to research domains that are currently prominent in second language research. We conclude this chapter by stressing again that there is significant crossover from method to different domains of SLA research. For example, data collected via stimulated recall protocols can be used in many different domains of SLA research, ranging from research on interaction and noticing to research on sociolinguistics and pragmatics. Similarly, while we present acceptability judgments in chapter 4 on language-focused research, they can be a general source of information on learning following a variety of experimental treatments and are thus associated with many different approaches and domains.

This chapter was intended to provide information on some of the basics involved in selecting and using data elicitation measures. The measures that we have chosen to describe here do not represent an exhaustive list; in fact, a complete list would be difficult given the increasing number of recent innovations and combinations of methods. We turn next to a discussion of the data collection methods often associated with research based on psycholinguistics.

CHAPTER 2

Psycholinguistics-Based Research

What sorts of questions underlie data elicitation measures in L2 research based on psycholinguistic approaches?

In this chapter, we focus on measures that seek to determine what learners are doing while they are using language. The emphasis in processing-based research is on the actual mechanisms involved in using language. In general, psycholinguistic research addresses questions related to how learners process and use an L2. Much of it is experimental in nature and uses online techniques[1] to answer questions related to internal cognitive processes.

As Felser (2005, pp. 95-96) notes, studies of L2 processing seek to answer, *inter alia*, the following questions:

1. What are the architectures, mechanisms and representations that underlie L2 processing, and how do they differ from those that underlie first language (L1) processing?
2. To what extent are learners able to access and integrate different information sources when processing the L2 input?
3. What is the time course of L2 processing, and how does it differ from that of L1 processing?
4. Do learners transfer processing strategies from their native language to the L2?
5. How do individual differences in L1 background, age of acquisition,

---

[1]We use this term somewhat loosely. In a technical sense, an online experiment has its probe and response internal to the stimulus, as opposed to a response following a probe, as would be the case in a task that requires participants to react in some way to a preceding stimulus. That is, online techniques involve responses to ongoing stimuli. This chapter includes standard online techniques (e.g., moving window tasks), as well as those that involve timed responses to stimuli (e.g., sentence interpretation tasks measuring reaction times).

L2 proficiency or working memory capacity influence L2 processing?
6. Do L2 processing skills develop in conjunction with, or separately from, the L2 grammar?

Thus, second language psycholinguistic research seeks to identify and understand learners' mental processes in real time during their use (production or comprehension) of a second language.

2.1 NATURALISTIC DATA

As mentioned above, psycholinguistic research is often experimental in nature, and it is not common to use naturalistic data to answer questions regarding learners' processing of language. Nonetheless, there are some questions that can be addressed through naturalistic data and even some areas where naturalistic data are most appropriate. To give just two examples, researchers can examine learners' hesitations and/or pauses as indications of processing time in authentic speech situations and can consider self-repairs to be potential indications of some level of awareness of problems. Obviously, this assumes that speech performance can provide information about the cognitive processes that underlie that performance.

Hesitations and pauses are often researched within the general context of fluency. Researchers seek to identify temporal variables that they might relate to psycholinguistic aspects of production and that they can then use to compare the speech of native and non-native speakers. One such research area concerns the length and placement of pauses, which often come at sentence or clause boundaries among more fluent speakers, but which can give the impression of dysfluent speech when they occur at non-boundary points. Another aspect of research involving pauses is the consideration of the length of time between pauses; that is, how much non-paused speech can an individual maintain? The main assumption is that, when a speaker encounters some difficulty (which could take the form of searches for vocabulary, syntax, or other linguistic information), the system breaks down and the individual cannot maintain the speech flow.

Related to this discussion of hesitations and pauses are the concepts of automatic and controlled processing (see McLaughlin, 1990), which have been prevalent in the psycholinguistic literature. In language performance, speakers must bring together a number of skills from perceptual, cognitive, and social domains. While L2 use may require a good deal of conscious control at first, these skills may eventually become automatized and put to use with greater ease. That is, when there has been a consistent and regular link between a certain kind of input and an output pattern, an associative connection may be activated and the process may become automatic. Pauses and/or hesitations are suggestive of a breakdown in a learner's system and may also provide some indication to the researcher of the locus of the breakdown.

An example of how hesitations can be used to reveal processing information comes from Pawley and Syder (2000). The examples come from native speaker data but illustrate how naturalistic data might also be used to gain information about second language learners' processing. The authors argue that, at least in complex sentences, speakers first construct grammatical frames before encoding lexical content. They use the following two examples from naturalistic data to support their psycholinguistic claim.

(1): Pauses
1 Well, re / -recently here ah-um there was a race relations act brought out-
2 in which, um yyou cannot do anything whatsoever,
3 which tends to discriminate—against *either race*

Most noteworthy here are the pauses before and after "in which" (line 2), which the authors argue suggest reflection on the part of the speaker. Pawley and Syder explain that the speaker first had to think about his choice of a modifying clause. Following this reflection, the speaker selected a structure relativizing the prepositional phrase "in which" out of the modifying clause. Finally, the speaker "encoded the full lexical content of the modifying clause" (p. 191). In fact, both of the embedded clauses in this example (the second occurring in line 3) are bounded by pauses.

In example (2), we also see the speaker apparently searching for a phrase.

(2): Hesitations and pauses
1 Now—since there's such a/ah—what?-*chain* of relationships,—
2 um—the/the/they go from family to family,
3 so—the kids may live in a different family.—
4 And if a Maori calls up ah I—in a town,
5 anywhere he goes
6 he'll be welcomed.
7 Because th-they are/ a very friendly people.—
8 So that/ um no matter where you're from,
9 y/go in/ ah ah um
10 a Maori walks into another Maori house
11 and he'll be welcomed.—
12 He'll have a place to stay for the night,—
13 they' give 'im food,
14 and he'll stay as long as he likes.

There are a number of interesting psycholinguistic inferences that can be made from this passage. First, the beginning of the extract contains a dependent clause with the word "what" suggesting that the speaker is searching for the right phrase. The pause after "so" in line 3 further suggests that the wording of the *so*-clause has not yet been encoded. Below is the authors' interpretation of the remainder of the extract.

> J continues with a fairly complex grammatical sentence (clauses 4-7) which is broken into two intonational sentences. The first, conditional clause is put together hesitantly while J evidently gropes for a locative phrase. The complex main clause that follows ("anywhere he goes he'll be welcomed") is built around a formulaic expression and is produced as continuous speech. Another brief pause precedes a reason clause (7); the latter appears to be formulated into two stages, with one hesitation before "because" and another in the clause core, between verb and noun phrase.
>
> Several interesting developments now occur. J begins another complex reason clause (lines 8-9) but is not satisfied with his first formulation and abandons it. He reformulates, then stays in the coordinating style for five consecutive clauses (10-14). It is noteworthy that during this series of simple clauses, there is not a single intraclausal pause. J's fluency in clauses 10-14 contrasts with his hesitancy during the earlier, more complex constructions (p. 192).

Examples (1) and (2) show how psycholinguistic inferences can be made from naturalistic data, in particular, through examining hesitations and pauses as they occur in natural speech and through investigating when they occur in certain types of language (e.g., complex constructions) compared to others (e.g., simple constructions).

Another phenomenon that can be investigated through naturalistic data is self-repair. Self-repairs are common in all types of speech, both that of native speakers and that of non-native speakers. They can be interpreted as indicating that speakers recognize problems with what they have said (e.g., grammatical, lexical, or content-related problems) and are making an effort to correct their utterances. The study presented in Box 2.1 considers issues of timing in self-repair, using a mixture of naturalistic data and prompting. The goal was to elicit relatively naturalistic language data through role plays and to measure the timing of various aspects of the self-corrections that naturally occurred. In addition, the study employed prompting to gain insight into language learners' psycholinguistic processes. The results are interpreted with respect to two psycholinguistic theories of speech production: interactive activation spreading (Dell, 1986; Stemberger, 1985) and perceptual loop theory (Levelt, 1983, 1989, 1993).

Box 2.1: A Study Using Role Plays and Interviews to Examine Self-Repairs in Second Language Speech

Kormos, J. (2000). The timing of self-repairs in second language speech production. *Studies in Second Language Acquisition, 22,* 145-167.

This study investigates underlying psycholinguistic processes in second language speech production as evidenced by the timing of different types of self-corrections. It also explores how proficiency level might influence the speed with which learners can detect and correct errors.

The study involved 30 native speakers of Hungarian learning English at three levels of proficiency. In order to elicit the data to answer these research questions, each participant was asked to perform a one-on-one information-gap role-play task with the researcher, which was recorded, followed by a retrospective interview conducted in Hungarian. During the interviews, the participants listened to the recordings of their own speech and were asked to state the problems they had experienced as they were trying to formulate their messages and what they had done to solve the problems.

Self-repairs were classified into one of four types depending on the assessments made by the participants: different information, appropriacy, error, and rephrasing. In addition, Kormos analyzed the digital recordings to determine various measurements for each correction, in milliseconds: (1) the error-to-cut-off time (i.e., "the time between the onset of the error and the point at which the flow of speech was interrupted" [p. 151]), (2) the cut-off-to-repair time (i.e., "the interval between the cut-off point and the onset of repair" [p. 151]), and (3) the amount of time taken for the correction itself. The total time of self-repair was calculated by adding up these three measurements.

The analysis of the timing data revealed that lexical errors and pragmatically inappropriate lexical choices have very similar detection times, a finding that may indicate that, while parsing an utterance, a lexical item's pragmatic features are monitored along with its argument structure and phonological and semantic form. The author considers this indirect support for the assumption that lexical entries contain pragmatic information in addition to grammatical, phonological, and semantic specifications. Kormos also found that the amount of time used for the lexical, grammatical, and phonological encoding of repairs is affected by L2 proficiency level "which is caused by the difference in the degree of automaticity of these mechanism at various stages of L2 development" (p. 145). In addition, evidence in this study that linguistic errors are detected significantly earlier than problems of inappropriateness and different information is taken

(Box 2.1 Continued)

Box 2.1 Continued

> to support both the activation spreading and perceptual loop theories, which assume that speech monitoring and comprehension involve the same mechanisms.

It is interesting to note that, while Kormos would have been able to conduct an analysis of self-repair timing using only naturalistic data, she would have been limited in the inferences she was able to make. Eliciting retrospective information from the learners themselves regarding the nature of their self-repairs provided more insight. This illustrates one way in which psycholinguistic research can be enhanced by using more proactive data elicitation techniques in addition to simply examining learners' spontaneous language production. It should be clear from this example that, while naturalistic data (or the relatively naturalistic data obtained through role plays) can be used to explore psycholinguistic processes, supplemental methods can facilitate deeper investigations that produce more direct evidence.

2.2 PROMPTED PRODUCTION

In the preceding section, we dealt with naturalistic data and the inferences that can be drawn from them. There is another type of data that we turn to in this section—that of prompted production. A question that arises in second lan-guage research is the effect of planning. When learners are given the opportunity to plan, what will they say during a second language task? Planned discourse lies somewhere between the naturalistic data discussed in the previous section and the psycholinguistic experiments of the following sections. Box 2.2 presents an example of this sort of research.

Box 2.2: A Study Using Planning to Provide Psycholinguistic Information

Ortega, L. (1999). Planning and focus on form in L2 oral performance. *Studies in Second Language Acquisition, 21,* 109-148.

This study examines the effects of pre-task planning on the focus on form that learners engage in during planning time and on their linguistic outcomes during the actual performance of the task. There were two main research questions in the study, which asked (1) what learners do while planning, how they allocate attentional resources, and whether they take advantage of opportunities to focus on form, and (2) whether pre-task planning increases the "syntactic complexity, lexical range, accuracy, and fluency of planned output" (p. 121).

Sixty-four English-speaking learners of Spanish formed 32 dyads in which one person was assigned the role of listener and the other the role of speaker. (Only the performance of the speakers was analyzed.) There were four experimental groups, with four dyads in each group and two experimental conditions for each dyad (with and without 10 minutes of planning time). After the participants completed a familiarization task, they performed two story-retelling tasks. Thus, each dyad performed a planned and unplanned task with a different story for each, and the stories and planning conditions were counterbalanced across the groups. For each story, the speakers were given a visual stimulus (an 8-picture strip) and heard a tape-recorded oral version in the L1 prior to each of the retellings. This was intended to reduce individual variation in the story lines and to reduce the cognitive load of the task. Below are the instructions for the familiarization task, which was done without planning.

Speaker Instructions

This activity will take around 10 minutes. You will listen to a story in English, and you will also be able to follow the story in pictures. Your task is to tell the story in Spanish afterwards to your partner. Your partner only has a set of jumbled pictures, and (s)he has to find out which pictures belong to the story and in which order the things in her/his pictures happened. (S)he needs to get the complete story from you, but cannot ask you questions or interrupt you. Therefore, try your best when you tell the story, so (s)he can solve the riddle.

Step 1:

You will be shown a story in pictures, and you will also listen to the story in English on the tape, so that you have a clear and complete understanding of it.

Step 2:

You have to tell the story to your partner, so that she finds out which of the pictures that (s)he has belong to the story, and what is the order in which things happened. Please, try to use only Spanish in your story, and to be clear and specific, so that your partner can find out about her/his pictures.

These instructions were reviewed orally prior to each subsequent story-retelling task. In the planned condition, the speakers listened to a taped version of the story while looking at the picture strip. This was followed by 10 minutes of planning time, which they were told they could use however they saw fit. They were allowed to take notes but were told not to write complete sentences and knew that they would not be able to refer to their notes during the retelling. In the unplanned condition,

(Box 2.2 Continued)

Box 2.2 Continued

the story was told immediately following the aural/visual prompts. In order to build communicative need into the tasks, the listeners were asked to complete written tasks based on their partners' retellings in both conditions.

Following each story-retelling task (familiarization, planned, and unplanned) was a retrospective interview, the goal of which was mainly to determine what the speakers had been doing during their 10 minutes of planning time. Regarding the planned task, the researcher asked: How did you spend your time? What did you do during the preparation time? What would you say your focus was when you prepared the story? Did you write a lot?

The results suggest that learners are able to focus attention on formal aspects of language during the planning stage and that pre-task planning increases their focus on form. Planning removes some of the cognitive load as well as communicative pressure, which frees up attentional resources for the task itself, allowing for utterances with more varied and complex syntax. Additionally, there are greater possibilities for learners to make form-function connections and recognize their gaps in knowledge. Ortega argues that pre-task planning involves "instances of competence-expanding episodes that promote hypothesis-testing, restructuring, and development" (p. 138).

2.3 PROMPTED RESPONSES

In this section, we discuss prompted responses, which do not involve spontaneous, communicative language production, but rather present participants with stimuli which they must then respond to in some way. One measure used in such studies is reaction time, which is a way of determining how quickly a participant responds to presented stimuli. Others to be discussed below include sentence interpretation, elicited imitation, word association, priming, lexical decision, eye movement, moving window, and Stroop tasks.

2.3.1 Reaction Time

Reaction times have been argued to shed light on how people process certain parts of language and are frequently used as a measure that (indirectly) reflects processing. In reaction time experiments, times are generally measured in milliseconds.[2] It is assumed that the more time it takes to respond to a sentence,

---

[2]In addition to self-made programs, there are commercially available programs for measuring reaction times, as well as for doing psycholinguistic research in general. The following are three such programs:

the more processing "energy" is required. For example, if someone is asked about the acceptability of sentences in English, it would be predicted that a 7-word sentence such as *I saw a big beautiful cat today* would take less time to respond to than a 7-word sentence such as *Who did Ann say likes her friend?* because the second sentence represents a more complex syntactic structure (and, hence, a greater processing load) than the first.

Reaction time measures are often used as a supplement to other kinds of elicitation techniques, for example, grammaticality or acceptability judgments used as a means of determining linguistic knowledge (Chap. 4). Underlying the use of reaction times in conjunction with these measures is the assumption that it takes longer to judge an ungrammatical sentence because a learner has to

---

a. *E-Prime* (Version 1.1) [Computer software]. Pittsburgh, PA: Psychology Software Tools, Inc. E-Prime is a user-friendly graphical experiment generator used primarily in psychology research. It includes applications for designing, generating, and running experiments, as well as collecting, editing, and analyzing data. (See http://www.step.psy.cmu.edu/scripts/index. html and a useful article using E-Prime at http://www.lrdc.pitt.edu/Schunn/research/papers/ macwhinneyetal2001.pdf retrieved April 14, 2006.)

Data can also be exported to external statistical tools such as Statistical Package for the Social Sciences (SPSS). The graphical environment allows users to select and specify experimental functions visually, and the paradigm wizard provides basic experimental models that users can modify to fit their goals. The package includes E-Studio (the graphical interface), E-Basic (a customizable scripting language into which the graphical representations are compiled), E-Run (an application affording stimulus presentation and data collection precise to the millisecond), E-Merge (an application allowing the combination of single session data files into multisession data files, and keeping a data file history), E-DataAid (a data management feature allowing users to filter, edit, and export their data), and E-Recovery (a backup mechanism in case data is unexpectedly lost or corrupted).

b. *PsyScope*. (Retrieved December 3, 2005, from http://www.psyscope.psy.cmu. edu). Similar to E-Prime, PsyScope (designed for Macintosh computers) is a program for the design and control of experiments, primarily used in psychology research. As of 2003, PsyScope development has ceased; however, the software is compatible with Mac systems from OS7 to OS9, including the Classic environment in OSX, as well as with all Apple hardware produced in the last 6 years. PsyScope 1.2.5 is available free of charge (although unsupported). The developers kindly request that the following citation be referenced in any manuscripts that report results based on the use of PsyScope: J. D. Cohen, MacWhinney, Flatt, and Provost (1993).

c. *Nesu* (Retrieved December 3, 2005, from http://www.mpi.nl/tools/nesu.html). This program is designed by the Max Planck Institute and can also be used to run online psycholinguistic experiments presenting auditory and visual stimuli. Although complex experiments may require additional programming, there is a graphical interface that makes it easy to design simple experiments, and support is available via e-mail from the technical staff at the Max Planck Institute. A recent version (Nesu2000) runs on Windows; additional hardware requirements include a NesuBox (which can plug into a computer's printer port), a sound adapter such as Soundblaster Live, a display adapter such as Matrox 550, and a push button box.

attempt to match the sentence with some structural description in the learner's grammar. In the case of an ungrammatical sentence, there is no structural description, hence the delay. In Box 2.3, we see an example of a study that used reaction times in addition to the more typical grammaticality judgments.

Box 2.3: A Study Using Reaction Times as a Supplement to Grammaticality Judgments

White, L., & Juffs, A. (1998). Constraints on Wh-movement in two different contexts of non-native language acquisition: Competence and processing. In S. Flynn, G. Martohardjono, & W. O'Neill (Eds.), *The generative study of second language acquisition* **(pp. 111-130). Mahwah, NJ: Lawrence Erlbaum Associates.**

This study considered the acquisition of English by two groups of Chinese speakers: one that had studied in an English-speaking environment (Canada) and the other whose only exposure to English was through schooling in China. The grammatical focus was *wh*-questions, and two tasks were used to elicit data: a timed grammaticality judgment task administered via computer and an untimed written question formation task. The timed task provided the researchers with information on the learners' processing.

Each of the 60 *wh*-questions used for the timed task (30 grammatical questions and 30 ungrammatical) appeared on the computer screen one at a time. The participants read each question, pressing a green key if they thought it was an acceptable English sentence and a red key if they thought that it was not acceptable. The instructions encouraged them to respond as quickly as possible to each sentence, and any responses that were more than 2.5 standard deviations slower than the mean were excluded (for a discussion of these sorts of exclusions, see Mackey & Gass, 2005). Only accurate responses were included in the analysis.

Response times revealed differences according to question type and provided additional information beyond what might have been gleaned from accuracy data alone. For example, the Canada group took longer to judge sentences with extracted subjects than with extracted objects, and both the Canada group and a NS control group took longer to judge sentences when subjects were extracted from nonfinite clauses than when objects were. These results allowed the researchers to conclude that certain types of sentences do indeed cause processing difficulties. The results from the China group differed in that they took longer to respond to sentences with extracted objects than extracted subjects and the response to extraction from nonfinite objects was longer than extraction from nonfinite subjects. It is likely that exposure is a contributing factor.

Reference

Mackey, A., & Gass, S. (2005). *Second Language Research: Methodology and design.* Mahwah, NJ: Lawrence Erlbaum Associates.

Another example of research using reaction times as a supplement can be found in sentence interpretation tasks. We address this in section 2.3.2 below.

2.3.2 Sentence Interpretation

Sentence interpretation is frequently used in research based on the Competition Model (Bates & MacWhinney, 1982; MacWhinney, 1987). The Competition Model has spawned a great deal of research that focuses on how learners process information. The major concern is what information people use in coming to an understanding of the relationships of words in a sentence. For example, when we hear or read a sentence such as *Sally kissed John*, how do we come to an interpretation of who kissed whom? In English, we rely on word order (i.e., the first noun is typically the agent), as well as meaning, the animacy status of lexical items (if the sentence were *The pencil kissed John*, for example, we might be confused), and morphological agreement. Not all languages use these same criteria (called *cues*), and not all languages assign the same degree of importance or strength to each criterion. In other languages, for instance, case markings are a dominant cue, and word order is less important. The advantage of sentence interpretation tasks is that researchers can learn which cues learners use in comprehending L2 sentences and how those cues might be related to L1 knowledge.

In second language research based on the Competition Model, experiments often involve presenting sentences containing various cues. For example, learners whose native language uses cues and cue strengths that differ from those of the target language are presented with sentences designed to contain conflicting cues and are then asked to determine what the subjects or agents of those sentences are. In addition to eliciting responses as to who is the "doer" of the action, researchers examine reaction times as a way of reflecting the online processing of cue competition. An underlying assumption is that fast responses will occur in cases of little cue competition. As MacWhinney and Pléh (1997) point out, however, the situation is far more complex in that "strong cues tend to saturate the on-line processing system" (p. 71). This means that reaction times are not greatly affected when there is a particularly strong cue. Additionally, frequent structures may have stronger effects on on-line role assignment than on offline interpretations. Box 2.4 presents a study of native speaker cues within the context of the Competition Model.

Box 2.4: A Study Using Sentence Interpretation and Reaction Times to Investigate Cue Types

Mimica, I., Sullivan, M., & Smith, S. (1994). An online study of sentence interpretation in native Croatian speakers. *Applied Psycholinguistics, 15,* 237-261.

This study investigated Croatian speakers' uses of various types of cues for assigning relationships among words during sentence comprehension. The 14 native speakers of Croatian who participated were asked to determine the agents (who was the *doer* of the action) of various ambiguous sentences. Four types of cues were included in the study: two morphological cues (case inflection and gender agreement), one semantic cue (animacy), and one syntactic cue (word order). Cue strength, cue convergence, and cue competition were systematically varied, and some of the target structures resulted in ungrammatical sentences where the gender and case information competed.

In order to elicit data in this study, the participants heard sentences while viewing pictures representing two nouns on a computer screen. The participants were asked to determine which noun was the "doer" of the action and to push the button corresponding to that picture. They were told that there was no "right" answer and that they could respond as soon as they had an interpretation, even if the sentence was not finished. The computer program recorded both their responses and their reaction times.

Based on these sentence interpretations, the researchers concluded that case was the strongest cue for these participants, while the semantic cue (animacy) had the smallest effect. When morphological information was ambiguous, participants relied on word order. As expected, cue competition was found to result in longer reaction times; however, cue strength and cue convergence did not lead to faster reaction times, suggesting that those variables did not facilitate sentence theta-role assignment. These results are partially consistent with the Competition Model. Importantly, in Croatian, the processing of grammatical cues seems to be separate from the processing of animacy contrasts, suggesting a more modular system than that proposed by the Competition Model.

As with many elicitation methods, there is a great deal of variation in the procedures used for sentence interpretation tasks. Some issues to consider are listed below. All of them are important to keep in mind when designing a study in which sentence interpretation is used as an elicitation technique.

Factors to consider in designing sentence interpretation tasks

- Are the sentences read or tape-recorded? When sentences are read, it is often difficult to neutralize natural intonational biases. This can lead to a lack of consistency and is particularly important when using unusual sentences such as *The pencil the cat saw.*
- How many sentences are included? In order to control fatigue and avoid compromising the reliability of the study, it is usually necessary to limit the number of sentences used. While a study by Sasaki (1997) used 144 sentences, most researchers have used between 27 and 54.
- What is the pause time between sentences? There appears to be no widely accepted standard.
- What are the instructions? A typical set of instructions is presented in Harrington (1987, p. 360):

You are going to hear a tape with a series of very simple sentences. After each sentence is read you will have to interpret it: you should say which one of the two nouns in the sentence is *the subject of the sentence*, that is, *the one who does the action.*

In the Harrington study, half of the participants were given the "syntactic bias" instructions first (*the subject of the sentence*), while the other half were given the "semantic bias" instructions first (*the one who does the action*).

- In what format are the responses given: oral or written?

2.3.3 Elicited Imitation

Elicited imitation is often used to determine the nature of learners' grammatical systems (see Chap. 4). The basic assumption underlying elicited imitation is that if a given sentence is part of a person's grammar, it will be relatively easy to repeat; if it is not part of the person's grammar, it will be difficult. Thus, a sentence such as "Elicited imitation is used in many experiments to determine grammaticality" is not difficult (for native speakers of English, at least) to repeat accurately and fluently. On the other hand, for a sentence such as "Elicited imitation will have had to have been used to determine grammaticality," repetition would be more difficult despite the fact that the two sentences contain a similar number of words. Elicited imitation goes beyond rote memory and repetition; rather, sentences are assumed to be "filtered" through one's grammatical system.

In elicited imitation tasks, sentences are presented to participants audi-torily (i.e., either via audiotape or orally by the researcher), and the participants are then asked to repeat them. The sentences are typically designed to manipulate certain grammatical structures, and the participants' ability to repeat them accurately is seen as a reflection of their internal grammatical systems. A crucial factor in designing suitable test sentences is to keep their lengths at an appropriate level, generally a level that exceeds a learner's ability to memorize and repeat. Thus, sentences that might be appropriate for early-level learners might be inappropriate for more advanced-level learners.

Elicited imitation is also commonly used within the context of processing research. For example, for researchers investigating input processing, a central question involves the determination of how input becomes intake. Attention to form is considered to be a mitigating factor. Assuming that attention to form is driven, at least in part, by salience, other appropriate questions involve asking what determines what is salient and what information learners are able to use as they process L2 input. The study presented in Box 2.5 illustrates how elicited imitation can be used to study input processing.

Box 2.5: A Study Using Elicited Imitation to Study Input Processing

Barcroft, J., & VanPatten, B. (1997). Acoustic salience of grammatical forms: The effect of location, stress, and boundedness on Spanish L2 input processing. In A. Pérez-Leroux & W. Glass (Eds.), *Contemporary perspectives on the acquisition of Spanish, Volume 2: Production, processing, and comprehension* (pp. 109-122). Sommerville, MA: Cascadilla Press.

This study, situated within the framework of input processing, assumes that a prerequisite to attention to form is acoustic perceptibility. It investigates learners' ability to repeat linguistic structures with various characteristics in order to determine which of the following factors affect their perception of grammatical forms: (1) the form's location in an utterance, (2) the presence of stress, and (3) whether the form is bound or unbound.

Participants were 18 native speakers of English with limited exposure to Spanish (i.e., no more than two years of Spanish in high school, no college-level Spanish courses, and no more than one week of vacation in a Spanish-speaking country). Fifteen stimulus sentences (including nine target sentences), which were designed to be similar with respect to their numbers of words and syllables, were tape-recorded and presented once each to individual participants, who were asked to repeat as much as they could within a ten-second period. A second tape recorder recorded their responses. Each response was given a score of 1 if correct and 0 if incorrect. Scores were then summed across all participants

---

for each of the factors listed above (location, stress, and boundedness). The learners' performance on these elicited imitations led the authors to conclude that stressed items are more salient than unstressed items and that utterance-initial items are more salient than medial or final items. Boundedness, however, was not found to play a role for these beginning learners.

2.3.4 Word Association

Word association tasks have often been used in psychoanalysis as a way of gaining access to a patient's mind. In second language research, a similar assumption can be made, the idea being that learning something about the word associations that learners make may provide a window into how their lexicon is organized. In other words, second language researchers are interested in understanding the semantic networks that learners have and how those networks come to be.

In a typical word association task, respondents are presented with a word and asked to provide the first word that comes to mind. There are a number of linguistic bases for these associations. One type of response, in which the response completes a phrase, suggests a syntagmatic relationship, akin to collocational knowledge. Thus, a word such as *comb* would evoke a response such as *hair*. Another type of response is a paradigmatic response, in which the response is part of the same word class as the stimulus. This category of responses includes synonyms and antonyms; thus, *hot* might elicit *cold*. Other responses, relying on word form, are known as clangs and are phonological or orthographic in nature. A response in this category might be seen in the case of the stimulus *nap* eliciting the response *nab*. The important point to remember about word association tasks is that they are able to provide information about the organization of the L2 lexicon as well as its relationship to the L1 lexicon.

Box 2.6: Two Studies Using Word Association to Investigate Semantic Networks

Meara, P. (1978). Learners' word associations in French. *Interlanguage Studies Bulletin, 3,* 192-211.

   This study was carried out in the U.K. with 76 English-speaking students (all girls) in their final year of studying French in preparation for a 0-level exam.

(Box 2.6 Continued)

Box 2.6 Continued

The learners were given a list of 100 French words and were asked to write down, for each one, the first French word it called to mind. There was a wide range of responses, many of which were similar to those of French native speakers, but of particular interest was the fact that, in general, the participants appeared to rely more on form than on meaning in making their responses. Meara took this finding to suggest a non-semantic organizing principle to these learners' second language lexicons.

*****

Wilks, C., & Meara, P. (2002). Untangling word webs: Graph theory and the notion of density in second language word association networks. *Second Language Research, 18,* 303-324.

This research, which involved a computer simulation followed by a human experiment, aimed to develop an elicitation tool to quantify differences in L1 and L2 lexical network density. In the computer-simulated portion, the numbers of associations in randomly chosen sets of words were calculated in order to provide initial information about general lexicon properties and to enable the detection of quantifiable differences between L1 and L2 lexical association networks.

The predictions were then tested in the human experiment, in which 60 participants completed a 40-item questionnaire using the same sets as the computer simulation. Half of the participants were native speakers of English who had completed one year of university-level French study, while the other half were native speakers of French. Each item on the questionnaire was made up of a set of 5 words randomly selected from the *Français Fondamental* word list (a list comprised of the approximately 1000 most frequent words in French, excluding grammatical items): for example, *blouse, cheminée, co-ter, feu, tort* (in approximate English translation, smock/blouse, fireplace, to cost, fire, fault/wrong). The participants were instructed to read each set of words, to circle any two words in a set that they considered to be associated (circling the two with the strongest link if more than two were associated), and to circle no words if they perceived no associations. They were allowed 20 minutes for the exercise.

In general, the native speakers of French were found to circle more pairs of words than their non-native counterparts, as predicted by the simple model of the mental lexicon. However, Wilks and Meara also observed that the mean number of circled associations was far higher for both native speakers and L2 learners than their computer simulations had predicted. Their results using this data elicitation technique led them to argue that the density of connections between words is higher than most researchers might assume it to be, even for L2 speakers.

2.3.5 Priming

In priming experiments, two stimuli are presented successively, with the first one being the *prime* and the second the *target*. The participant must respond to the target in some way, and priming is said to occur when there is an influence of the prime on the target. A variant is masked priming, whereby the prime is presented immediately prior to the target with little intervening time and no intervening items. In masked priming experiments, participants are not aware of the prime, given the rapidity of the presentation. In fact, the prime is often presented for a short enough period of time that respondents are not even aware of its presence (Kinoshita & Lupker, 2003). Syntactic priming refers to a speaker's tendency to repeatedly produce the syntactic structure of a previously spoken or heard structure (Bock, 1990, 1995; Bock & Griffin, 2000). Thus, when speakers have a choice between two structures, they are more likely to opt for the one that they have previously encountered, even when the newly produced utterance contains different lexical items.

According to McDonough (2006), priming tasks can be conducted in a number of ways. One means is through a two-part experiment in which a sentence repetition segment is followed by a picture description task. In the first part, participants hear and repeat an item and then have to decide if they have heard it before. In the second part, they describe a picture that provides a context for the structure in question and then make a decision about whether or not they have seen the picture before. The recognition part of these tasks aims to deflect the participants' attention from the real task of describing.

A second technique involves presenting participants with written or oral sentence fragments that they are then asked to complete. Some of the fragments are primes and have been manipulated in such a way that the participants will produce a particular structure as they complete the sentences. This is followed by presenting them with shorter fragments that can be completed using one of two structures. The claim is that syntactic priming is evidenced when the shorter fragments are completed using the same structure that was used when completing the prime fragments more often than when those fragments followed something different.

A third technique in syntactic priming research is sentence recall, which involves three parts: First, a computer screen quickly presents a sentence one word at a time. Second, there is a distractor task, and finally, participants repeat the original sentence aloud. At issue is the structure of the repeated sentence: Does it have the same structure as the one that was read, or does it have the structure of a previous sentence?

Recent studies have investigated priming within the context of second language research (see Gries & Wulff, 2005). Box 2.7 below describes a study examining priming within a dyadic context.

Box 2.7: A Study Using Syntactic Priming in Dyadic Interaction to Investigate the Acquisition of Dative Constructions

McDonough, K. (2006). Interaction and syntactic priming: English L2 speakers' production of dative constructions. *Studies in Second Language Acquisition, 28,* **179-207.**

This study investigated syntactic priming during conversational interaction. Two questions guide the research: Does syntactic priming occur in interaction between two non-native speakers? And do second language learners increase their use of a target structure following primes of that structure? The target structures were prepositional and double-object datives (Experiment 1) and double-object datives (Experiment 2).

Because McDonough was concerned with priming in an interactive setting, she used what is known as *confederate scripting* (Branigan, Pickering, & cleland, 2000), in which a task is carried out between a participant and an individual who is a partner of the researcher (i.e., who is working with a specific conversational goal in mind). The idea behind confederate scripting is that interlocutors will be more likely to use a form that has just been used because it reduces the processing load involved in language production. The task involves the interlocutors describing a set of pictures to one another, using verbs written under the pictures, so that each interlocutor can identify the pictures being described. The confederate is given a script, and the order of picture description is such that the confederate's prime precedes the participant's target.

In Experiment 1, 50 learners of English as a second language participated. They were divided into two groups; one group heard the prime first and then described the picture (comprehension group), and the second group heard and repeated the prime first and then described the picture (production group). Evidence of syntactic priming was found for prepositional datives, but not for double-object datives, and there was no effect for the different priming conditions.

Experiment 2 further investigated the lack of syntactic priming for double-object datives, attempting to determine whether exposure to only double-object datives (a more advanced structure than prepositional datives) would suffice to bring about a priming effect. The design of this experiment was the same as Experiment 1, with 54 ESL learners participating. Again, no evidence of syntactic priming was found for double-object datives.

Reference

Branigan, H., Pickering, M., & Cleland, A. (2000). Syntactic co-ordination in dialogue. *Cognition, 75,* B13-B25.

2.3.6 Lexical Decision

In lexical decision tasks, participants are presented with real words and non-sense words and are asked to determine as quickly and accurately as possible whether the groupings of letters shown make up legitimate words. The target words often follow primes that vary in their relationship to the targets. For example, control primes are unrelated to target words, while semantic primes have related meanings. Previous research using lexical decision tasks has shown that native speakers are faster to respond to target words when they are preceded by semantically-related primes and slower to respond to target words when they are preceded by orthographically- or phonetically-related primes. The study in Box 2.8 illustrates how a lexical decision task has been used to investigate age-of-acquisition effects on learners' L2 lexicons.

Box 2.8: A Study Using a Lexical Decision Task

Silverberg, S., & Samuel, A. G. (2004). The effect of age of second language acquisition on the representation and processing of second language words. *Journal of Memory and Language, 51,* 381-398.

This study examines the organization of bilinguals' and L2 learners' lexicons through the use of a lexical decision task. The participants, all native speakers of Spanish, varied according to proficiency and age of acquisition of English as a second language. They were divided into three groups: high-proficiency early L2 learners (n = 24), high-proficiency late L2 learners (n = 24), and low-proficiency late L2 learners (n = 24).

The L2 priming words chosen for this study had a variety of relationships to the L1 target words; some were semantically related, some were orthographically related, and some were unrelated. For others, it was the L1 translation of the L2 prime that was orthographically related to the L1 target. The authors reasoned that semantic priming effects would indicate that the participants' L1 and L2 lexicons shared a conceptual level of representation, while orthographic priming would indicate sharing at a lower level.

Lexical decision tasks require a careful balance in the frequency of the target words as well as a well-thought-out determination of the appropriate interval to use between word onsets. This study varied stimulus onset asynchrony (SOA) among blocks (350, 500, and 650 ms) and also counterbalanced the stimuli such that the four types of primes were used in equal numbers for each participant, but the participants were presented with each target word only once, using different primes for different participants. Participants saw a list of two to five items in lowercase letters, followed by a target item in capital letters, and were instructed to decide whether each target item was a word or not and to push a button ("yes" or "no") indicating their answer.

(Box 2.8 Continued)

Box 2.8 Continued

> This method of data elicitation allowed Silverberg and Samuel to determine that high-proficiency early L2 learners do show semantic facilitation, suggesting that they have developed a shared conceptual level for the L1 and L2. The high-proficiency later L2 learners were found to demonstrate orthographic inhibition, which the researchers interpret as indicating a shared lexical level. The low-proficiency later learners, however, showed no cross-lexical priming effects, suggesting that their L1 and L2 lexicons are separate.

2.3.7 Cross-Modal (Lexical) Priming

Cross-modal priming has not received wide recognition in second language research, but it is worthy of mention given its possibilities for use in future studies. The technique generally involves two tasks: Participants listen to a sentence and then respond in some way to a word that appears on a computer screen. Comprehension questions are often included as well in order to ensure that the participants are focusing attention on the listening part of the task and comprehending the oral input.

Cross-modal priming tasks (see Marinis, 2003) are often used to determine reactivation of antecedents. In a typical experiment, participants hear sentences such as the following: "The soldier is pushing *the unruly student* violently into the street. *Who* [1] is the soldier [2] pushing (*t*) [3] violently [4] into the street?" Words appear on a computer screen at one of four possible points (see above) and participants are asked to decide whether the word is a word or a nonword. These *words* are a) semantically related to the antecedent, b) unrelated to the antecedent or c) nonwords. In the sentences presented above, taken from their experiment, the antecedent of "*who*" would be "*the unruly student*," represented in the second sentence by a trace (*t*). While the participants are being given an auditory presentation of this second sentence, the semantically related word "school" appears (visually) simultaneously with the position of the trace. (Alternatively, an unrelated word such as "blouse" or a nonword such as "fipple" might appear, or a word might appear simultaneously with a different part of the auditory stimulus.) The learners' first task is a lexical decision (see section 2.3.6), and their accuracy and reaction time data are recorded (see section 2.3.2). The idea is that if antecedents are, in fact, reactivated at gap positions, then any semantically-related words presented there will enjoy short reaction times, while decisions on unrelated words and non-words will require more time. However, there should be no such differences at syntactically irrelevant parts of the sentence. In designing the data elicitation instrument for this technique, it is important to ensure that visual targets are matched on the parameters of frequency and length (number of syllables and letters).

A related task is a cross-modal lexical priming task. In this type of task, participants listen to a sentence while watching a fixation point on the computer screen. At a certain point (usually immediately following an ambiguous word), a test word replaces the fixation point and the learners must make a lexical decision about it. Their reaction times are then measured and analyzed. In the following example, presented in Box 2.9, the researchers decided to use naming rather than lexical decision because naming does not involve metalinguistic knowledge and is not susceptible to post-lexical processing strategies.

Box 2.9: A Study Using Cross-Modal Lexical Priming

Li, P., & Yip, M. (1998). Context effects and the processing of spoken homophones. *Reading and Writing: An Interdisciplinary Journal, 10,* 223-243.

This study was part of a two-experiment report, the first of which is described in Box 2.14 on the gating paradigm (a variation on the moving-window technique). Here we consider the second of these experiments, investigating Chinese-English homophone processing. Twenty Chinese-English bilinguals (Cantonese as the home language, English as the academic language) listened to Chinese sentences with English homophones embedded in them. The embedded words (8 nouns and 8 verbs) were pronounced with Cantonese phonetics. The auditorily presented sentences were either neutral or biased toward the meanings of the homophones. The learners' task was to name words that were presented visually: English target words (the same as the homophones), Chinese target words which were similar in phonological structure, and unrelated targets with no phonological similarities to the Chinese and English targets. Li and Yip found that the participants were faster at naming the English targets than the Chinese targets and take this to suggest a facilitative visual effect for the English targets despite the fact that the stimulus sentences were in Chinese.

2.3.8 Eye Movement

Eye-movement studies are beginning to find their place in second language research. With appropriate eye-tracking equipment, one can gain a wealth of data regarding the processes involved in reading, for example. As Frenck-Mestre (2005) notes, "recording [the] jumps, stops and re-takes provides a to-the-letter, millisecond-precise report of the readers' immediate syntactic processing as well as revisions thereof" (p. 175). There are a number of research areas that can be investigated with eye-movement tracking. For example, researchers can determine sources of ambiguity (i.e., when and where processing difficulties begin) and what individuals do to resolve them. Eye tracking can also be used to determine differences between contextual and lexical constraints on processing (Altarriba, Kroll, Scholl, & Rayner, 1996). The study presented below in Box 2.10 deals with bilingual language activation through eye-movement studies.

Box 2.10: A Study Using Eye-Movement Tracking

Marian, V., & Spivey, M. (2003). Competing activation in bilingual language processing: Within- and between-language competition. *Bilingualism: Language and Cognition, 6,* 97-115.

Marian and Spivey investigate the nature of bilingual language processing in terms of whether bilinguals activate their two languages selectively or in parallel fashion. To this end, spoken language processing in Russian-English bilinguals was examined in two eye-tracking experiments, a specific goal of which was to control for language mode, known to be a key factor in bilingual lexicon activation.

Fourteen participants were recruited for each experiment. The recording of their eye movements was made using a headband-mounted ISCAN eye-tracker which contained two cameras. The scene camera, which was "yoked with the view of the tracked eye," captured an image of the participant's field of view, while the eye camera provided "an infrared image of the left eye and tracked the center of the pupil and the corneal reflection" (p. 101). These outputs were superimposed and recorded onto a Hi8 VCR. Instead of computer presentation, this study utilized naturalistic displays, using real objects, miniature replicas, or toy replicas. All objects were located on a 61 cm by 61 cm white board set, which was divided into nine equal squares. Eye movements were coded as fixations on these objects.

In Experiment 1, on L2 processing, ten sets of stimuli were selected, with care taken to include only concrete nouns of comparable frequency and familiarity across languages. [a] The exemplars were selected to be clear, comparable in size, and able to be placed on a table and moved around. Each set was made up of three objects: a target object (e.g., plug), a within-language competitor object whose

---

[a]Zeno, Ivens, Millard, & Duvvuri (1995) for the English word frequencies and Lenngren (1993) for the Russian word frequencies

name in English overlapped with the English name of the target object (e.g., plum), and a between-language competitor object whose name in Russian overlapped with the English name of the target object (e.g., *plat'e* [dress]). Experiment 2, on L1 processing, also used an equal number of stimuli in each set: a target object (e.g., *sharik* [balloon]), a within-language Russian competitor (e.g., *shapka* [hat]), and a between-language English competitor (e.g., shark). In each experiment, there was an approximately equal amount of phonological overlap for the between-language and within-language competitor words.

Four conditions were created in both experiments, with the participants experiencing 10 trials each of within-language competition, between-language competition, simultaneous competition, and a control in which there was no language competition. The instructions were recorded by monolinguals in both cases: an English native speaker in Experiment 1 and a Russian native speaker in Experiment 2. They instructed the participants to (1) look at the central cross, (2) pick up a target object, (3) pick up a filler object, and (4) pick up another object in the display in each of the 40 trials. Pseudo-randomized order was used in order to block the consecutive occurrence of a target or competitor. The trials were then coded as containing zero or greater-than-zero fixation on the between-language competitor object, the within-language competitor object, and the associated filler (control) object within the same squares. Comparisons were made between the proportion of eye movements in the control condition to the competitor objects in the other conditions.

Participants showed consistent within-language competition during both L2 (Experiment 1) and L1 (Experiment 2) processing. However, Experiment 2 did not show a significant difference in the proportion of eye movements to between-language competitors when compared with eye movements to the non-overlapping control fillers. The results support previous findings of parallel activation of lexical items, but suggest that the magnitude of between-language competition effects may vary across first and second languages and may be mediated by a number of factors, such as stimuli, language background, and language mode.

References

Lenngren, L. (Ed.). (1993). *Chastotnyi slovari sovremennogo russkogo yazyka* [Frequency dictionary of modern Russian language]. Uppsala: Acta Universitatis Upsaliensis.

Zeno, S., Ivens, S., Millard, R., & Duvvuri, R. (1995). *The educator's word frequency guide.* Brewster, NY: Touchstone Applied Science Associates.

2.3.9 Moving Window

In a moving-window experiment, words or phrases are presented on a screen one at a time, with each successive word appearing after participants indicate that they are ready. In other words, it is the participant who controls the reading speed. Once a new word or phrase appears on the screen, the previous word disappears, and after an entire sentence has appeared, the participant presses a button to indicate whether the sentence is grammatical or ungrammatical. An example of a study using this technique is presented in Box 2.11.

Box 2.11: A Study Using a Moving-Window Technique

Juffs, A., & Harrington, M. (1995). Parsing effects in second language sentence processing: Subject and object asymmetries in *wh*-extraction. *Studies in Second Language Acquisition, 17, 483-516.*

In this paper, Juffs and Harrington address the issue of the accessibility of Universal Grammar (UG) through an online study of subject/object asymmetries in long-distance *wh*-movement. The authors argue (1) that NNSs have grammatical knowledge comparable to that of NSs, insofar as that knowledge is part of UG, and (2) that the behavioral difference associated with subject/object *wh*-extraction is an issue of parsing and not a matter of competence. There were two research questions:

(1) Do advanced adult Chinese learners of English perform as well as native speakers on judgment tasks involving ungrammatical and grammatical long-distance *wh*-extraction?

(2) Is there evidence for parser-based difficulties on the judgment tasks?

Juffs and Harrington used a moving-window technique to investigate differences between long-distance object extraction (*Who did Jane say her friend likes?*) and subject extraction (*Who did Ann say likes her friend?*). Their main concern was to investigate the source of any differences, focusing on both processing time and linguistic knowledge (acceptability judgments were also used in their experiment).

They constructed 54 sentences for acceptability judgments, including five types of grammatical *wh*-movement and four types of ungrammatical *wh*-extraction violating Subjacency, and measured both accuracy and reading time. Twenty-six Chinese speakers who were studying English in the US and 25 English native speakers participated in the study. They were asked to make grammaticality judgments (by pressing either "possible" or "not possible") in both a moving-window condition and a full-sentence condition.

Juffs and Harrington found that the learners' performance on object extraction from finite clauses was comparable to that of the native speakers, as was their accuracy level on ungrammatical sentences. On the other hand, the learners were less accurate than native speakers in performing subject extractions. The researchers conclude from this that difficulties in performance with subject-extracted movement do not illustrate an absence of grammatical competence, but rather are characterizable as parsing difficulties.

Moving-window techniques can provide information about the amount of time used to process various parts of a sentence. In other words, because it is the participant who indicates readiness to move on to each subsequent word, researchers can determine which parts of a sentence require additional processing time. When using acceptability judgments as part of a moving-window study, one must be careful to make sure that participants understand what it means to make a judgment of acceptability. Essential components include an explanation of what "intuition" means, together with the fact that there are no right or wrong answers. An example from Juffs and Harrington (1995, p. 515) is presented below. This is an acceptability judgment task, but with a focus on processing time.

Instructions

Speakers of a language seem to develop a "feel" for what is a possible sentence, even when they have never been taught any particular rules. For example, in English, you might feel that sentences (a) and (c) sound like possible sentences, whereas (b) and (d) do not.

a. Mary is likely to win the race.
b. Mary is probable to win the race.
c. It seems that John is late.
d. John seems that he is late.

In this experiment, you will read sentences word by word on a computer screen. Concentrate on how you feel about these sentences. Native speakers of English often have different intuitions about such sentences, and there are no right or wrong answers. Tell us for each one whether you think it sounds possible or impossible in English.

Read each sentence carefully before you answer. Think of the sentences as spoken English and judge them accordingly. Work as quickly and accurately as you can.

There are a number of variations on the moving-window technique. In the two sections that follow, we deal with two: (1) self-paced listening and reading tasks (SPLT/SPRT) and (2) the gating paradigm.

2.3.9.1 Self-Paced Listening and Reading Tasks (SPLT/SPRT). Many SPLT and SPRT studies target grammaticality, ambiguity, or syntactic complexity. As discussed above, in these studies, it is the participant who controls the speed with which the stimuli are presented, the assumption being that longer listening and reading times reflect greater processing difficulty. The quickness with which respondents comprehend sentences as they unfold online provides researchers with information about the points where sentences are difficult to process, where something unexpected appears, or even where some sort of reanalysis takes place, as in the case of garden-path sentences.

Box 2.12: A Study Using a Self-Paced Listening Task (SPLT)

De Jong, N. (2005). Can second language grammar be learned through listening? *Studies in Second Language Acquisition, 27,* 205-234.

This study addresses two research questions: (1) Can comprehension of a target structure lead to implicit or explicit knowledge of that structure that is available for both comprehension and production? and (2) Do tasks requiring the production of that structure delay learning?

Fifty-nine L1 speakers of Dutch participated in this study of a "miniature language system" based on Spanish. The target structure was overtly agreeing and invariable adjectives. Participants were randomly assigned to one of three groups. The first group received receptive training with the target structure, and the second received both receptive and productive training. The third group acted as a control group and participated in training tasks that did not contain the target structure. Instead, the target rule was explained to the control group immediately before the post-tests. Training took place in four 90-minute sessions over a two-week period and included vocabulary training, sentence training, and target structure training (where applicable). All training tasks were presented aurally, and all participant responses were oral.

To examine learning, De Jong employed a number of measures, including vocabulary tests, a match-mismatch test, a speeded grammaticality judgment test, production tests, questionnaires, and a self-paced listening task (SPLT). As an online measure of comprehension, the SPLT was considered to indicate the speed of input processing, with longer times interpreted as signaling greater processing difficulty. Each target sentence was split into five sections, and participants were instructed to push a button to proceed from section to section, going through the

---

sentences as quickly and accurately as possible. To make sure that they comprehended each sentence, they were also asked to push a button indicating whether or not the sentence matched a picture. One word was critical for determining this, and it was expected that slower listening times for the last element would indicate slower processing of the target structure.

Finding that the control group performed better than the experimental groups on many of the learning tests, De Jong concludes that the short training period may have biased his study in favor of explicit learning. Neither experimental group performed at chance, however, indicating that some learning was taking place. De Jong speculates that both implicit and explicit learning were likely occurring.

Box 2.13: A Study Using a Self-Paced Reading Task (SPRT)

Papadopoulou, D., & Clahsen, H. (2003). Parsing strategies in L1 and L2 sentence processing: A study of relative clause attachment in Greek. *Studies in Second Language Acquisition, 25,* 501-528.

This study examines alternative models of language comprehension, considering data from L1 and L2 Greek parsing strategies in resolving the attachment of ambiguous relative clauses. The models make conflicting predictions regarding relative clause attachment in Greek. Some models predict low attachment, because Greek allows relative clauses to be headed by complementizers and is therefore not constrained by a requirement that relative pronouns be attached to salient discourse entities—namely, higher Determiner Phrase (DPs). Other models predict a preference for high attachment, given that Greek has relatively free word order and the structurally-based parsing strategy of predicate proximity would tend to attach an ambiguous modifier to a constituent close to the predicate of the sentence.

Native speakers of Greek and 47 advanced L2 learners of Greek with various L1 backgrounds (Spanish, German, and Russian) completed an acceptability judgment task in which they rated sentences on a scale from 1 to 5 according to their acceptability. The sentences were temporarily ambiguous in that later information disambiguated the relative clause attachment, and the assumption was that sentences in which the disambiguations matched the initial parsing preference should be rated higher. A subset of 16 learners also participated in a computer-based self-paced reading task (SPRT). In this task, there were 24 critical sentences and 72 fillers, which the participants were told to read as quickly as possible. The sentences were presented segment-by-segment following the pressing of a button, and the intervals between button presses were measured. To ensure that the participants paid attention to the content, they were also required to answer a content question (yes/no) after each sentence.

(Box 2.13 Continued)

Box 2.13 Continued

> Based on data from the acceptability judgments and the SPRT, the researchers conclude that attachment preferences are influenced by the phrase that is modified (genitive vs. prepositional phrase), and that those preferences are stronger for Greek native speakers. They also argue that L1/L2 differences may reflect different parsing strategies; that is, the L1 parser seems to integrate ambiguous information into a structural representation online, while the L2 parser seems to rely more on lexical cues and wait for disambiguating information before continuing the parse.

2.3.9.2 Gating Paradigm.

The gating paradigm allows researchers to determine the amount of phonetic/acoustic information that is necessary in order to identify a word. It is conducted as follows: A participant hears fragments of a word (which increase in duration) one at a time until the whole word is heard. At each point that a new fragment is introduced, the participant is asked to identify the word being said, thereby giving researchers information regarding the point at which a word becomes recognizable.

Box 2.14: A Study Using the Gating Paradigm to Study the Processing of Homophones

Li, P., & Yip, M. (1998). Context effects and the processing of spoken homophones. *Reading and Writing: An Interdisciplinary Journal,* **10,** 223-243.

This study is concerned with the effects of context and tone on the processing of homophones. It involved two experiments: one using the gating paradigm, to be discussed here, and one using a cross-modal lexical priming task, discussed above in Box 2.9.

Twenty native speakers of Cantonese participated in the gating paradigm experiment, which was modified to fit the purposes of the study. In effect, rather than asking the participants to identify the words being presented, the researchers asked them to "identify the homophones that either match or do not match the sentence context" (p. 226). The 60 homophones used in this study differed in terms of the lexical tones associated with each syllable. Each was preceded by a sentence context containing a bias toward one or the other of the homophone's meanings. The sentences were read by a native speaker of Cantonese and then digitized and presented to listeners in a gating format, controlled using PsyScope (see footnote 2b). In the first gate, participants heard the preceding context up to the beginning of the target homophone. The next gate contained the first gate along with 40 milliseconds of the homophone. This continued until the last gate, which included the entire homophone. For each presentation, listeners identified the last word of the sentence (all homophones were at the end of the sentence). Participants wrote their answers in Chinese characters and then pressed the space bar to trigger the next item.

The results showed that context is a major factor in the processing of Chinese homophones. Less than half of the acoustic information is required when the context biases listeners toward a specific meaning. With regard to Chinese at least, tonal information comes in late in homophone identification and often plays a secondary role to context.

2.3.10 Stroop Test

The Stroop test (Stroop, 1935) involves naming the color that a word is printed in when that color may be the same as the meaning of the word itself (e.g., the word *red* written in red) or when there is a mismatch between word and color (e.g., the word *red* written in blue). It requires responding as quickly as possible to a stimulus by stating the color of the stimulus, which often involves inhibition, because respondents may have to hold back their linguistic processing of the printed word. The Stroop effect, or the fact that responses to matches are produced more easily and quickly than mismatches, is generally explained in one of two ways: (1) with respect to speed of processing-that is, interference occurs because naming colors is a slower task than reading words, making it so that word-reading needs to be inhibited, and (2) with respect to selective attention-that is, difficulty occurs because color-naming requires more attention than word-reading. In second language research, a picture-word interference version of the Stroop task has suggested that bilinguals demonstrate inhibition for semantic distractors and facilitation for lexical form distractors during picture naming in an L2 (Hermans, Bongaerts, De Bot, & Schreuder, 1998). Box 2.15 provides an example of a study using a Stroop task.

Box 2.15: A Study Using a Stroop Task

Miller, N. A., & Kroll, J. F. (2002). Stroop effects in bilingual translation. *Memory & Cognition, 30,* 614-628.

Miller and Kroll raise the question of whether bilinguals show semantic inhibition and form facilitation in naming words during a translation-based Stroop task. A key manipulation involves whether the distractors following the words to be translated are presented in the output or the input language.

(Box 2.15 Continued)

Box 2.15 Continued

In Experiment 1, Miller and Kroll recruited 15 English-Spanish and 20 Spanish-English bilinguals in order to replicate a study by La Heij, de Bruyn, Elens, Hartsuiker, and Halaha (1990), in which Dutch-English bilinguals were found to exhibit Stroop-type effects in a translation task when performing translations from their L2 (English) to their L1 (Dutch). The participants in Miller and Kroll's study were presented with 96 stimuli via computer, with half of the targets in English and half in Spanish. Distractor words were presented in the output language (i.e., in the L1 when participants translated from L2 to L1 and in the L2 when they translated from L1 to L2). They were either related or unrelated to the meaning or form of the spoken translation, such that if the translation was to be from *cuchara* to *spoon*, for example, a semantically-related distractor would be *fork* and a form-related distractor would be *spool*. The participants had to press a key in order to display the word to be translated in the middle of the computer screen. This was followed by the appearance of a distractor in the same location, and the participants were asked to say the correct translation of the target aloud. In Experiment 2, the participants were 17 English-Spanish and 19 Spanish-English bilinguals who had not participated in Experiment 1. The procedures were the same, except that the distractor words were presented in the input language and were related to the meaning or form of the target word to be translated.

The results of Experiment 1, consistent with previous research on picture naming, showed that semantically related distractors were associated with Stroop-type interference, while form-related distractors produced facilitation. However, in Experiment 2, the distractor words had little impact on translation performance, leading the authors to argue that "language cues related to the nature of the input in translation may serve to reduce competition among lexical competitors" (p. 614).

References

La Heij, W., de Bruyn, E., Elens, E., Hartsuiker, R., & Helaha, D. (1990). **Orthographic facilitation and categorical interference in a word translation variant of the Stroop task.** *Canadian Journal of Psychology, 44,* 76-83.

2.4 CONCLUSION

Psycholinguistic research is often able to provide insight not only into issues of online processing, but also into issues of grammar and the intersection between grammar and processing. This chapter has reviewed and illustrated some of the most common techniques for eliciting psycholinguistic information from L2 learners. Most of these methods have been adopted directly from the psychology literature. What is important to remember is that, with virtually all of the examples of data elicitation measures that we have presented in this chapter, numerous variations and changes can be made, and often are, depending on specific questions or circumstances of the research. For example, in studies where disambiguation is the object of inquiry, we might envisage using a moving-window technique, but rather than having learners answer questions about grammaticality, a question such as "Does this make sense?" could be used to guide the responses. In other words, participants would continue to press a button to move a sentence across the screen word by word as long as the sentence continued to make sense.

The data collection techniques presented in this chapter do not, of course, represent an exhaustive list, but simply point the way to a range of techniques. Many of them require access to a psycholinguistic lab, or at least to psycholinguistic equipment. For more information in this area, Marinis (2003) provides some suggestions as to the amount and kind of space, hardware, and software that is helpful or necessary for conducting psycholinguistic research.

CHAPTER 3

Cognitive Processes, Capacities, and Strategies-Based Research

Research on cognition and strategies is often aimed at investigating second language learners' internal processes together with the variables that influence these processes and determining the selection of strategies that learners employ. Learning strategies are particular actions, steps, or techniques employed by learners, often consciously, to assist their L2 learning. There are a number of ways of gaining access to information about learners' internal processes. It is important to keep in mind that even though these may provide a window through which insights may be gained, what learners say they do is not always the same as what they actually do. The following are some ways of gaining information about learners' strategies:

- Observing learners while they are engaged in language learning tasks.
- Carefully structured observations, sometimes using equipment such as eye-tracking sensors, may provide additional information about cognitive processes.
- Tracking learners' behaviors on a variety of measures (e.g., via computer using a keyboard tracking program).
- Querying learners directly (e.g., in an interview) or indirectly (e.g., through a questionnaire) about their use of strategies or processes in general, or for specific information about what they do when attempting a particular task.
- Obtaining retrospective information from learners about how they learn (e.g., through analyzing learners' journals, in which they have been asked to write comments about how they think they learn).
- Asking learners to provide online commentary about how they are

carrying out a language task (i.e., to speak their thoughts aloud while they are engaged in a task, such as verbalizing while they complete a crossword puzzle in an L2).

The following sections elaborate on some of the resources that researchers can use to elicit information on learners' cognitive processes, capacities, and learning strategies, including observations and diaries (naturalistic data); introspective methods, such as think-alouds and stimulated and immediate recalls (prompted production data); and measures that give us information about cognitive capacities, such as aptitude tests and working memory tests (prompted response data).

3.1 NATURALISTIC DATA

One of the ways in which SLA researchers can gain greater access to learners' internal processes and strategies is through collecting data in naturalistic settings and media, such as observations and diaries. We will now consider how these techniques can be used as data collection methods.

3.1.1 Observations

Observations in second language research are frequently carried out within classroom contexts; less often, due to logistical problems, they may sometimes be conducted in purely naturalistic contexts of interpersonal communication. Some types of observation are associated with experimental contexts as well, of course, but here we are concerned with observations that are as naturalistic as possible. In general terms, observations allow researchers to collect large amounts of data on behaviors of interest. When researchers repeat observations over time, the data can provide deeper and more multilayered understandings of participants in particular settings. Macaro (2001) provides several useful suggestions for ways we may consider conducting observational research on strategies used within the classroom. He suggests observing:

- when students are moving their lips, which might be an indication that they are preparing themselves to speak by practicing under their breath,
- to what extent and which students appear to be buying time by using such markers as "uh" or "well" or other discourse markers designed to show that they wish to keep their turn,
- to what extent students are employing the compensation strategy of circumlocution (finding alternative ways of saying something they don't know how to say),

- which students are asking a classmate for help when they don't understand,
- which students are sounding out words before saying them,
- which students are reasoning by deduction ("it must mean this because of this"),
- which students are focusing on every word rather than the gist, perhaps by observing them as they move their finger from word to word,
- which students plunge straight into [an] activity and which students spend time planning their work, and
- which students use a dictionary and how often. (p. 66)

Whereas such observations can provide substantial information about what is happening in a classroom, there are also methodological issues of which researchers need to be aware. One of the most obvious concerns for observations is the "observer's paradox" (Labov, 1972), which refers to the fact that, although the goal of most observational research is to collect data as unobtrusively as possible, the mere presence of an observer can influence the linguistic behavior of those observed. There is also some possibility of the Hawthorne effect, which occurs when learners perform better due to positive feelings at being included in a study. Simply put, if learners realize that they are under observation, then their performance might change because of the fact of the observation. In order to minimize these limitations, researchers need to find ways to mitigate the effects of their presence. For example, if the goal of a study involves observing the use of a second language among immigrants at their place of work, researchers may try to visit the job site repeatedly, gradually making the participants more accustomed to their presence so that they can blend into the background of the workplace. Participant observation is another approach that researchers may take to avoid these problematic issues. Participant observation occurs when a learner is a participant in the group they are studying. For example, an SLA researcher may choose to learn a second language, and at the same time, study themselves and their classmates.

3.1.2 Diaries

Second language diaries, also referred to as L2 journals or learner autobiographies, are another means of obtaining information about learners' internal processes. In diary studies, learners are able to record their impressions or perceptions about language learning, unconstrained by predetermined areas of interest. Diaries can yield insights into the learning process that may be inaccessible from the researcher's perspective alone. Even in studies that provide a structure for the diary writers to follow (e.g., certain topics to address and guidelines for the content), researchers are still able to access the phenomena under investigation from a viewpoint other than their own. In addition, because diary entries can be completed according to the participants' own schedules, this approach to data collection allows for flexibility. The example presented in Box 3.1 is a diary study investigating learner-internal processes in SLA.

Box 3.1: A Study Using a Diary to Explore Learner-Internal Processes and Language Learning Experiences

Schmidt, R., & Frota, S. N. (1986). Developing basic conversational ability in a second language: A case study of an adult learner of Portuguese. In R. Day (Ed.), *Talking to learn: Conversation in second language acquisition* (pp. 237-326). Rowley, MA: Newbury House.

In Schmidt and Frota's (1986) study, Schmidt used a diary to record his experiences learning Portuguese in Brazil. He described his experiences in Portuguese language classes, as well as his daily interactions while living in Brazil, including not only the specific L2 forms that he was taught in class, but also those he observed during conversations and found himself using. Additionally, he met with his coresearcher, a native speaker of Portuguese, for periodic communicative second language testing. Through an examination of his diary entries and the results of testing, Schmidt and Frota were able to discover an interesting pattern: Schmidt consistently reported noticing forms in the input shortly before acquiring them. His diary revealed many interesting patterns:

"V and I were waiting for the bus when A spotted us and came over and talked for a few minutes. After he left, V complained that A speaks very simplified Portuguese to me and speaks much too slowly. I protested that I have really needed slower than normal speech. However, it's true that I now understand almost everything A says to me ... I need more challenge than this, new blood. Perhaps I should propose the vampire principle for SLA" (p. 246)

As Schmidt and Frota noted (p. 279) "R learned and used what he was taught if he subsequently heard it and if he *noticed* it" (p. 279, emphasis in the original) and, finally, as Schmidt was leaving, his language began to take off

"I'm suddenly hearing things I never heard before, including things mentioned in class. Way back in the beginning, when we learned question words, we were told there are alternate short and long forms. ... I have never heard the long forms, ever, and concluded that they were just another classroom fiction. But today, just before we left Cabo Frio, M said something to me that I didn't catch right away. It sounded like French que' est que c'est only much abbreviated ..." (p. 280).

Guidelines for Conducting Diary Studies
(Based on Bailey, 1990, and Bailey & Ochsner, 1983)

Diarists should ...

- Describe characterizations of their own personalities, making note of qualities and attitudes that might affect the language learning process.
- Set up favorable conditions for writing so that it does not become a dreaded chore.
- Make sure to choose a place for writing that is free of interruptions.
- Schedule a time each day (e.g., immediately after class) to write in the diary.
- Try to be systematic, thorough, and honest.
- Ask whether there is evidence for particular claims; support ideas with actual examples of interactions and language use to make sure that insights are substantiated.
- Try not to worry about writing style, grammar, or organization. It is more important to record memories while they are still fresh so that the data will be as accurate and complete as possible.
- Try not to edit thoughts while writing. Diaries can always be censored later, if necessary.
- Focus on particular areas of interest. It will not be possible to write about everything.
- Reread the diary entries later and try to find patterns in the data.

Researchers should ...

- Provide a structure for diarists to follow (e.g., guidelines for the content, such as particular topics to address). A lack of structure can make analysis more difficult.
- Keep the diarists' personal feelings in mind; some people are more comfortable than others with self-examination.
- Consider the data analysis phase. Some diarists may feel more comfortable recording their thoughts in oral form, and this may produce more data than written diaries tend to. However, this may also require hours of transcription on the part of the researcher for the purposes of data analysis. Weigh the trade-off between "overwhelming quantity and the possible depth of quality added by electronic recordings" (Bailey, 1990, p. 220).
- Make use of software programs available to facilitate the task of data analysis (e.g., NVivo, discussed later) or Talkbank (http://www.talkbank.org—retrieved April 14, 2006).
- Triangulate the data with external information, such as test scores, written compositions, and observations.

Although diary research is undoubtedly able to produce valuable information when undertaken conscientiously, one of the main concerns in this area is the fact that keeping a diary requires commitment on the part of the participants to provide frequent and detailed accounts of their thoughts about learning. This can be a significant burden. In addition, due to the lack of structure in many diary entries, data analysis can become a complex affair, making it difficult for researchers to find and validate patterns in the data. There are, however, software programs available to facilitate the task. As just one example, NVivo (http://www.qsrinternational.com—retrieved 4/14/06) is designed to assist researchers in textual analysis; it allows researchers to create links and compare patterns, which in turn helps them to detect emerging themes. We now move on from this sort of spontaneous and free data to consider more constrained data—that is, data obtained through prompted production.

3.2 PROMPTED PRODUCTION

Introspective methods, which tap participants' reflections on their own mental processes and behaviors, originated in the fields of philosophy and psychology (see Gass & Mackey, 2000, for more information about the origins and use of introspective methods in second language research). The use of introspection assumes that what takes place in consciousness can be observed at some level, in much the same way that one can observe events in the external world.

Verbal reporting is a special type of introspection. It consists of gathering protocols, or reports, by asking individuals to say what is going through their minds as they are solving a problem, for example. A. Cohen (1998) outlines three primary types of verbal reporting used in second language research:

1. Self-report. With self-report data, researchers can gain information about a learner's general approaches to a given task. For example, a statement such as "I am a systematic learner when it comes to learning a second language" might be found on a typical second language learning questionnaire, and learners may be asked to use a scale to indicate how true or false this is of them (e.g., see Box 3.2 for a discussion of the Strategy Inventory for Language Learning).

2. Self-observation. In self-observation, learners report on what they have done, either within a short period of the event or retrospectively. An example would be a learner saying something like the following: "I read over the passage quickly, pausing for words and phrases that I did not understand" (p. 34). Such self-observations refer to specific linguistic events and are not as generalized as self-report data.

3. Self-revelation, also known as "think-aloud." Here, participants provide ongoing reports of their thought processes while performing some task; for example, a learner may think-aloud while correcting an essay written a week earlier.

Introspective reports are often classified according to time frame, mode (oral or written), task type (e.g., think-aloud or retrospective), and amount of stimulus for the task. The following sections illustrate these distinctions through discussing a commonly used questionnaire on language learning strategies and the methods of stimulated recall, think-aloud, and immediate recall; example studies are also described.

3.2.1 The Strategy Inventory for Language Learning (SILL)

The Strategy Inventory for Language Learning (SILL), developed by Oxford (1990), is one of the most commonly used instruments for assessing language learning strategy use. Most of the SILL's items involve 5-point scales ranging from "always or almost always true of me" to "never or almost never true of me." Learners are asked to respond to items such as the following: "I use a combination of sounds and images to remember new words" (to assess memory strategies) and "I work with other language learners to practice, review, or share information" (to assess social strategies).

Strategies for Language Learning (SILL)

Direct Strategies	Indirect Strategies
1. Memory Strategies	1. Metacognitive Strategies
• Creating mental linkages (e.g., grouping, associating, elaborating)	• Centering your learning (overviewing and linking with already known material, paying attention, delaying speech production to focus on listening)
• Applying images and sounds (e.g., using imagery, semantic mapping)	
• Reviewing thoroughly (structured reviewing)	• Arranging and planning (finding out about language, organizing, setting goals and objectives, identifying the purpose of a language task, planning for a language task, seeking practice opportunities)
• Employing action (e.g., using physical response or sensation)	
	• Evaluating (self-monitoring, self-evaluating)

Direct Strategies	Indirect Strategies
2. Cognitive Strategies	2. Affective Strategies
• Practicing (repeating, formally practicing with sounds and writing systems, recognizing and using formulas and patterns, recombining and practicing naturalistically)	• Lowering your anxiety (using progressive relaxation, deep breathing or meditation, music, laughter)
• Receiving and sending messages (getting the idea quickly, using resources for receiving and sending messages)	• Encouraging yourself (making positive statements, taking risks wisely, rewarding yourself)
• Analyzing and reasoning (reasoning deductively, analyzing expressions, analyzing contrastively across languages, translating, transferring)	• Taking your emotional temperature (listening to your body, using a checklist, writing a language learning diary, discussing your feelings with someone you know)
• Creating structure for input and output (taking notes, summarizing, highlighting)	3. Social Strategies
3. Compensation Strategies	• Asking questions (asking for clarification or verification, asking for correction)
• Guessing intelligently (using linguistic clues, using other clues)	• Cooperating with others (cooperating with peers, cooperating with proficient users of the language)
• Overcoming limitations in speaking and writing (switching to the mother tongue, getting help, using mime or gesture, avoiding communication partially or totally, selecting the topic, adjusting or approximating the message, coining words, using a circumlocution or synonym)	• Empathizing with others (developing cultural understanding, becoming aware of others' thoughts and feelings)

Source: Adapted from Language Learning Strategies: What Every Teacher Should Know (pp.38, 58, 136, 152), by R. Oxford, 1990, New York: Newbury House.

Interestingly, pointing to definitional problems, Dörnyei (2005) has questioned work on learner strategies, maintaining that, because strategies are commonly seen as processes, actions, and thoughts that are consciously selected by learners, they are therefore different from other cognitive processes in learning. In his view, it is important to note that "the construct of learning strategies has been found to be less helpful for researchers when conducting in-depth analyses of the antecedents and ingredients of strategic learning" (p.195). Dörnyei suggests, therefore, that research can be directed at more dynamic and process-oriented learner factors such as "self-regulated learning," a term that has been introduced from the educational psychology literature, as opposed to strategies, which he refers to as "surface manifestations" (p. 195).

3.2.2 Stimulated Recall

Concomitant with an ongoing shift toward examining cognitive factors in second language research, there has been a recent proliferation of studies using stimulated recalls. Stimulated recall is one of several introspective measures available to second language researchers. To explore learners' thought processes or strategies, researchers can prompt them to recall and report thoughts that they had while performing a task or participating in an event. Gass and Mackey (2000) provide an extensive description of stimulated recall, together with examples of its use. Importantly, stimulated recalls are conducted using a stimulus; for example, learners may be shown a videotape so that they can watch themselves carrying out the original task while introspecting about their thought processes at the time, or they may be given one of their written products in the L2 so that they can comment on their linguistic revisions, motivations, and thought processes along the way. Box 3.2 describes two studies in which stimulated recall has been used.

Box 3.2: Two Studies Using Stimulated Recall to Determine Perceptions of Feedback

Mackey, A., Gass, S., & McDonough, K. (2000). How do learners perceive interactional feedback? *Studies in Second Language Acquisition, 22,* 471-497.

The authors used stimulated recall in a study designed to examine learners' perceptions about interactional feedback. Ten ESL learners and seven learners of Italian as a foreign language participated in the study. Each participant carried out a picture-differences task with a native (English) or a near-native (Italian) interlocutor, and interactional feedback on morphosyntax, phonology, lexis, and semantics was provided when necessary. Each task-based activity was videotaped and played for each learner immediately after it was completed. In this stimulated recall session, learners were allowed to pause the tape whenever they wished to describe their thoughts at the time of the interaction. The researcher also paused the tape after episodes in which interactional feedback had been provided and asked learners to recall their thoughts at the time when the interaction was going on. The stimulated recall sessions, which were audiotaped, were conducted in English for both groups (i.e., the L1 for the Italian learners and the L2 for the English learners). Stimulated recall allowed the researchers to find that, whereas the learners tended to have relatively accurate perceptions about lexical feedback, they often did not perceive morphosyntactic feedback accurately.

*****

(Box 3.2 Continued)

55

Box 3.2 Continued

Swain, M., & Lapkin, S. (2002). Talking it through: Two French immersion learners' responses to reformulation. *International Journal of Educational Research, 37,* **285-304.**

In a study designed to investigate the role of reformulation as a form of written feedback on French immersion learners' written production, Swain and Lapkin utilized stimulated recall in an effort to gain access to some details of the learners' cognitive activities, such as their noticing of changes. Two learners were shown a 5-minute videotaped lesson on French pronominal verbs and carried out a jigsaw task collaboratively, first orally and then in writing. Their written version of the story was reformulated by a native speaker. The learners were given an opportunity to compare their original text with the reformulated version for 10 minutes, marking changes with a highlighter and sometimes commenting on the differences they noticed. They were then shown a videotape of their noticing activity (when they compared the two texts). The tape was stopped whenever the learners had noticed differences between the two texts, and the learners were asked to make comments on the differences they had observed at the time. The stimulated recall session was implemented in English, the learners' L1. A posttest was carried out after the stimulated recall session, followed by an interview with each learner. Swain and Lapkin's approach led them to the conclusion that learners' reactions to reformulation and their collaborative dialogues, in which they can resolve many of their language problems together, can be an important part of the language learning process.

Like many other methodologies, stimulated recall must be used with care and requires meticulously structured research designs to avoid pitfalls. Potential limitations include issues of memory and retrieval, timing, and instructions. The following are some recommendations based on our earlier textbook on stimulated recall (Gass & Mackey, 2000, pp. 54-55).

Recommendations for Stimulated Recall Research

- Data should be collected as soon as possible after the event that is the focus of the recall. This is to increase the likelihood that the data structures being accessed are from recent memory. Retrieval of an event that happened at a time distant from the time of retrieval may result in recall interference, and as the event becomes more distant and less sharply focused in memory, there is a greater chance that participants will say what they think the researcher wants them to say.

- The stimulus should be as strong as possible to activate memory structures. For example, in a stimulated recall of oral interaction, participants can watch a video if the recall is performed immediately after the event. If it is more delayed, then participants can read a transcript of the relevant episodes in addition to watching the video.
- The participants should be minimally trained; that is, they should be able to carry out the procedure, but should not be cued in to any particular aspect of the event. Piloting will be helpful here. Often, simple instructions and a direct model will be sufficient in a stimulated recall procedure. Sometimes, the collection instrument itself will be enough (e.g., in the case of a questionnaire or a question-and-answer interview). Again, one must be careful not to be so specific that participants only follow the model.
- The amount of structure involved in the recall procedure is strongly related to the research question. Generally, if participants are not led or focused, then their recalls will be less susceptible to researcher interference. If they participate in the selection and control of stimulus episodes and are allowed to initiate recalls themselves, then there will again be less likelihood of researcher interference in the data. However, as already discussed, completely unstructured situations may not always result in useful data.

Adapted from *Stimulated Recall Methodology and Second Language Research* (pp. 54-55), by S. Gass & A. Mackey, 2000, Mahwah, NJ: Lawrence Erlbaum Associates.

3.2.3 Think-Aloud Protocols

In think-aloud protocols, also known as online protocols, learners are usually asked what is going through their minds as they are concurrently solving a problem. Through this procedure, researchers can gather information about the ways in which people approach problem-solving activities. In second language research, examples of think-aloud tasks can be seen in a series of studies by Leow (1998), which investigated issues of attention in second language learning through the use of L2 crossword puzzles. The data elicited through this method can be quite rich, as can be seen in the excerpt. The following are the instructions he gave to the university-level learners of Spanish in his study (p. 137), along with an example of one of the learners' think-alouds. The italicized print indicates words in Spanish; the boldface print indicates words that the speaker was generating online but had not yet written down.

Instructions and Example of a Think-Aloud Protocol from Leow (1998)

Instructions for Think-Alouds

Here is a crossword puzzle similar to the ones you have done in class. ... Use the clues provided and see if you can successfully complete this crossword. As you do the crossword, <u>try to speak aloud into the microphone your thoughts WHILE you perform the task for each word, NOT AFTER</u>. Include the numbers of the clues also while you are thinking aloud. Please try to speak in a clear voice.

Portions of transcript of a learner's verbal protocol

Vertical now ... 2 down, OK I have an *o* here butI don't know why because in 1 across I have *se morio* but I guess it has to be ***murio*** because 2 down has to be *un* [changes *o* to *u*] ... OK I have to but it must be *tu* so it means that 7 across for the past tense of *dormirse* must be ***durmio*** instead of *dormio* [changes *o* to *u*]... OK third person plural form of the verb *pedir* they asked for, 5 down ... *pedieron* [pause] OK I am wondering whether because I have ***pidieron*** [spells out] and I am thinking it should be *pe-* but that would make it *dormeo* with an *e* instead of *i*, ... I guess I will see how the other ones go and take a look at that one again ... OK, the opposite of *no* is *sí* which means that for 1 across I have *mentieron* but it should be ***mintieron*** for the third person plural past tense of *mentir, mintieron* [changes *e* to *i*] <u>which makes me now realize that **pidieron** with an *i* is probably right since the *e* in mentir changes to an *i* so the *e* in *pedir* is also going to change to an *i* as well</u> ... OK 12 down, the opposite of *no* is *sí* which means that where I have *corregio* it becomes ***corrigio*** *corrigio* so the third person singular of past tense *corregir* is ***corrigio*** [changes *e* to *i*] ... <u>looks like all the *e*'s are becoming *i*'s in the *stems*</u> ...

From "Toward Operationalizing the Process of Attention in SLA: Evidence for Tomlin and Villa's (1994) Fine-Grained Analysis of Attention," by R. Leow, 1998, *Applied Psycholinguistics, 19,* 146.

Box 3.3 describes an example of an experimental study using think-aloud protocols in order to examine the relationships among intake, awareness, and types of exposure. It also includes the think-aloud instructions, which are slightly more elaborate than those used by Leow (1998).

Box 3.3: A Study Using Think-Aloud Protocols to Investigate Awareness

Rosa, E., & O'Neill, M. D. (1999). Explicitness, intake, and the issue of awareness: Another piece to the puzzle. *Studies in Second Language Acquisition, 21,* 511-556.

In a study designed to investigate how intake may be related to reported levels of awareness and types of exposure to input, Rosa and O'Neill had participants produce think-aloud protocols while completing an L2 problem-solving task. The types of exposure, ranging from relatively implicit to explicit, differed according to whether or not the learners received formal instruction on the targeted forms and whether or not they were told to search for rules.

The 67 participants (native speakers of English in their fourth semester of university Spanish study) were asked to carry out a multiple-choice jigsaw puzzle task, through which they were presented with the target structure, Spanish contrary-to-fact conditionals in the past. The task contained 10 puzzles, and the participants were not allowed to go back to a previous puzzle once they had moved on to the next puzzle. They were instructed to think-aloud concurrently in the following manner:

> In this experiment we are interested in what you think about when you complete this task. In order to find out, we are going to ask you to THINK ALOUD as you put together the puzzles, from the time you start the task until you finish the task. We would like you to talk CONSTANTLY. We don't want you to try to plan out what you say or try to explain to us what you're saying. Just act as if you are alone in the room speaking to yourself. What's most important is that you keep talking, and talk clearly and loudly enough into your microphone. We will not be able to help you in any way. You can think aloud either in Spanish or in English. Do you understand what we want you to do? You will have 15 minutes to complete the puzzles. (p. 525)

The results of this study showed that both degree of explicitness and level of reported awareness were related to intake. The formally instructed participants made more improvement than those in an implicit training condition. They also tended to report awareness at the level of understanding (i.e., verbalizing rules and often testing hypotheses about the forms) more than would have been expected had awareness been unrelated to training condition. Similar results were found for the rule-search condition in terms of levels of reported awareness. Furthermore, it was found that the learners who reported awareness at the level of understanding improved more than those who reported awareness at the lower level of noticing (i.e., explicitly mentioning verb forms, but not formulating rules) and those who did not verbally report being aware of the targeted structures.

(Box 3.3 Continued)

Box 3.3 Continued

> Interestingly, no significant differences were found between the groups of learners who made reports of noticing and those who did not. The authors suggest that this may be due to the eclectic nature of the latter group, about half of whom made substantial improvements and half of whom made little or no gain. They propose that some of these learners may have been aware of the targeted structures without verbalizing their awareness completely. For example, one participant made comments such as, "I wanna check that the grammar matches it too" (p. 541). However, not knowing specifically what she was referring to, the researchers coded the think-alouds conservatively in order to avoid imposing their own inferences on the data. Although the think-alouds gave them insights into the nature of the learners' input processing, they admit that they likely did not have access to all of the noticing that actually occurred.

The examples from Leow (1998) and Rosa and O'Neill (1999) deal with individuals' thoughts about grammar problems. Box 3.4 describes a study by Morrison (1996), demonstrating a different use of think-alouds. This time, the focus is on talk between two learners.

Box 3.4: A Study Using Think-Aloud Protocols in Pairs to Investigate Lexical Awareness

Morrison, L. (1996). Talking about words: A study of French as a second language learners' lexical inferencing procedures. *Canadian Modern Language Review, 53,* 41-75.

> Morrison's study was concerned with the inferencing strategies used by L2 French learners when encountering unknown vocabulary words in an authentic reading passage. Learner A and Learner B read the text individually and were then asked to think-aloud together about the meanings of the underlined words. The following excerpt is taken from their discussion of the word *piétons,* 'pedestrians.'
>
> A2   OK, '*piétons.*'
> B3   I think that's *pedestrian.*
> A4   OK ...
> B5   I had no idea when I was writing ...
> A6   Me either, but I have to admit, unfortunately *pedestrian* didn't—that's good. I didn't think of that—it's so obvious. But for some reason I thought it had to do with something like ... just because it said modern urban city, so I thought of just like, sort of like *businessman.*
> B7   Mmm. (oh)

A8   I thought there was some sort of French word for like modern *city dweller.*

B9   Right.

A10 I didn't think of *pedestrian.* But that's right. I think it's *pedestrian.*

B11 I think even, because you see 'pied' and you think foot.

A12 I didn't think of that. But, definitely.

B13 And so, I think it has something to with that. But, again, in there, I had absolutely no idea. I think it's even, when you read the rest of this, this ...

A14 thing, that's when you understand. That's why now it makes sense.

B15 Exactly

A16 But I should have figured it out.

B17 You ... different perspectives, you know think, because, you know they talk about being on the road on the street, and the way, you know, they carry themselves on the street and stuff, and right away you think, you know, *pedestrians.* Right?

A18 Yeah.

B19 Like, that's who you'd find on the street.

A20 Uh-huh. Yeah

B21 So

A22 Yeah, I think you're right

B23 I think it has something to do with that. So '*piétons*' (writing) *pedestrian*

A24 And I think also, you're right, the 'pied' and then even just 'picd' *pedestrian*, for the ...

B25 Yeah, like 'pied,' 'pied,' that's what—

A26 Yeah, OK

B27 ... so *pedestrian* ...

A28 And I guess also because you don't have *pedestrians* in the country, countryside. Like you wouldn't call it a pedestrian...as in roads, as in...

B29 Yeah, when you think *pedestrians*, you think...

A30 ... modern cities

B31 the city, city life ...

This example presents two learners in the process of reporting their earlier thoughts, together with the new inferencing strategies they use to refine their understanding. These include using their L2 French knowledge (B11, A24), as well as various contextual clues from further on in the passage (A6, B13, B17) and their real-world knowledge (B19, A28). The example shows the development of their comprehension of this word through collaboration and the integration of these strategies.

As with stimulated recalls, think-aloud protocols must be carried out with care. The following basic recommendations are adapted from Macaro (2001).

Recommendations for Think-Aloud Protocols

- Give participants a specific task to perform (reading and writing tasks work best).
- Make sure that they understand what they have to do and that they are comfortable with the task. In general, they should be told that you want to know what they are thinking when they are performing the task.
- Find a similar task and demonstrate how a think-aloud works, or have the participants practice the procedure themselves with a different task. The latter is often preferable because, if the researcher models the task, learners might be inclined to use the particular strategy that the researcher has used.
- Record the session.
- Participants may need to be encouraged when there is insufficient think-aloud data. Avoid using phrases like "Are you sure?" and evaluative comments like "That's good." Instead, use only phrases like: "What makes you say that?"; "What made you do that?" (e.g., if they are looking up a word in a dictionary); "What are you thinking at this moment?"; "Please keep talking."
- After the session, listen to the recording of the think-aloud and code the data according to a predeveloped coding system.

Adapted from *Learning Strategies in Foreign and Second Language Classrooms* (pp. 62-63), by E. Macaro, London: Continuum.

3.2.4 Immediate Recalls

A technique used to elicit data immediately after the completion of the specific event to be recalled is known as immediate recall. It can be distinguished from stimulated recall in that a stimulated recall may or may not occur immediately following the event. Because of its temporal proximity, immediate recall does not always contain an additional stimulus (e.g., videotape, audiotape, written product). Immediate recall can be distinguished from online recall techniques such as think-alouds in that it does not occur simultaneously with the event. For example, in an experiment involving interaction data, an immediate recall might take place after one conversational turn (where the turn is 10 to 15 seconds in length, for example) during a larger conversational session. A stimulated recall would take place after the entire conversation, using a tape of the conversation as a stimulus. Online recall is difficult to implement in interaction research, but immediate recalls have been used recently by Philp (2003) and Egi (2004) in explorations of what learners notice about conversational feedback. Their studies are briefly described in Box 3.5.

Box 3.5: Two Studies Using Immediate Recall

Philp, J. (2003). Constraints on noticing the gap: Nonnative speakers' noticing of recasts in NS-NNS interaction. *Studies in Second Language Acquisition, 25,* 99-126.

Philp used immediate recall in a study designed to examine the extent to which learners noticed native speakers' reformulations of their nontargetlike grammar. English question forms were chosen as the target structure. A total of 33 adult learners participated in the study, and each was partnered with a NS interlocutor to form a dyad. For each NS-NNS dyad, five 20-minute interaction sessions were administered, each of which contained three tasks: a warm-up task, a story-completion task, and a picture-drawing task. For the test sessions, two tasks were used: a story-completion task and a spot-the-differences task. During the interactions, the NS interlocutor provided recasts in response to nontargetlike utterances, especially English question forms, and then knocked on the table twice as a recall prompt. The NNSs were instructed to repeat the last thing that they had heard prior to those knocking sounds (i.e., the recast). These repetitions were coded as correct recall, modified recall, or no recall. Among the discoveries Philp was able to make using this method was that shorter recasts with fewer changes were more likely to be noticed and that noticing was also moderated by the learners' proficiency levels.

*****

Egi, T. (2004). Verbal reports, noticing, and SLA research. *Language Awareness, 13,* 243-264.

Egi utilized both an immediate verbal report technique (modified from Philp, 2003) and stimulated recall in order to examine the use of immediate recall as a qualitative measure of noticing during oral interaction. She also addressed the methodological issues of reactivity and veridicality (whether something accurately depicts its target). Although the same auditory stimulus was used as in Philp's study (i.e., two knocking sounds), the learners were asked to make a different sort of response. In Egi's study, as opposed to repeating the recasts, learners were asked to verbalize their thoughts on language episodes during a 10- to 15-second-long conversational turn. Upon completion of each immediate recall event, the learners resumed their conversation until the next recall event or the end of the task. Two one-way information-gap tasks were carried out during each of two treatment

(Box 3.5 Continued)

Box 3.5 Continued

sessions. The pre- and posttests focused on both production and recognition, and stimulated recall sessions were conducted for a stimulated recall group after the posttest. Finding a relationship between the learners' perceptions of recasts and their subsequent linguistic accuracy, Egi argued that the learners were more likely to learn from corrective feedback when they recognized it as such.

As with all recalls, immediate recall can be conducted in the learners' L1 to allow them to express their thoughts fully, or in the L2, which might be necessary when the researcher does not speak the L1 of the participant. Either way, training is often essential to help learners get used to the technique. Immediate recalls may suffer from fewer of the problems of memory decay that can be a problem with stimulated recalls when done at some distance from the event, yet immediate recall is arguably a more artificial task and may also interfere with task performance. This issue, known as reactivity, has been the focus of several studies. Leow and Morgan-Short (2004), for example, compared the performance of learners in a think-aloud group and a non-think-aloud group and found no significant differences, suggesting that reactivity did not play a significant role in their study. Similar results in terms of reactivity were found in Egi's (2004) study in comparing the performance of the immediate report and stimulated recall groups. Her study also provided evidence for the veridicality of the verbal report data. Leow and Morgan-Short argue, however, that the use of think-alouds still needs to be validated empirically with a greater variety of L2 tasks.

A major advantage in the use of learners' verbal reports is that researchers can often gain access to processes that are unavailable by other means. At the same time, uncovering information about cognition and learner strategies is not easy, and it is therefore important to be aware of ways to avoid compromising the validity and reliability of verbal report data. With self-report and self-observational data, researchers should attempt to keep the time between the event reported on and the reporting itself short. As discussed earlier in relation to stimulated recall, this leads to more accurate and complete data. Also, in all research that relies on participants' providing information about their own thought processes (whether through stimulated recall or think-alouds), researchers need to be cognizant of the fact that participants may not be aware of their thought processes and/or may not wish or be able to reveal them. Gass and Mackey (2000, chap. 4) provide more detailed information on the *dos* and *don't*s of recalls, particularly stimulated recalls. As with all techniques, one must pilot the procedures to ensure not only that they work with the particular group of learners to be studied, but also that they elicit the type of data needed.

3.3 PROMPTED RESPONSES

Prompted responses have been used in second language research to investigate a number of issues, including the cognitive resources and capacities that learners have available for L2 learning. These include aptitude and working memory, which are discussed next.

3.3.1 Aptitude Tests

The concept of aptitude covers a variety of cognitive differences that are argued to reliably predict subsequent language learning achievement. It first came to the attention of second language researchers when Carroll and Sapon developed the Modern Language Aptitude Test (MLAT) in 1959, followed shortly thereafter by the Pimsleur Language Aptitude Battery (Pimsleur, 1966). Variations on the MLAT are available for different populations of learners. For example, for younger children (ages 8-11), the Modern Language Aptitude Test-Elementary (MLAT-E), also created by Carroll and Sapon, is available (see also Sawyer & Ranta, 2001), and a newer version of this test in Spanish (the MLAT-ES) has recently been developed and released by Second Language Testing, Incorporated. The MLAT and the MLAT-E, along with other language versions of the MLAT, are commercially available through Second Language Testing, Incorporated (http://www.2lti.com/home2.htm—retrieved April 10, 2006). As is detailed below, the MLAT has five sections designed to test the following learner abilities: L2 phonetic coding ability, rote learning ability, grammatical sensitivity, and inductive language learning ability.

The Modern Language Aptitude Test (MLAT)

Part I: Number Learning (aural)—Listening to an audio recording of pseudo-words for numbers and then transcribing numbers of up to three digits.

Part II: Phonetic Script (aural)—Learning and then demonstrating recognition of correspondences between speech sounds and orthographic symbols.

Part III: Spelling Clues—Reading words that are spelled as they are pronounced and then choosing synonyms for them.

Part IV: Words in Sentences—Noting selected words in model sentences and then locating words that have similar functions in other sentences.

Part V: Paired Associates—Memorizing a lexicon of 24 words from another language, practicing them, and then being tested on them.

The following are excerpts from the instructions to Parts I and III, retrieved from the Web site of Second Language Testing, Incorporated, a private organization that holds the copyright to the MLAT and various other versions of the test, such as the MLAT-E and the MLAT-ES. Additional samples can be found at http://www.2lti.com/htm/mlat.htm#10.1 (retrieved April 10, 2006). Below we present Parts 1 and 3 from the MLAT.

Part I (Number Learning):

Now I will teach you some numbers in the new language. First, we will learn some single-digit numbers:

> "ba" is "one"
> "baba" is "two"
> "dee" is "three"

Now I will say the name of the number in the new language, and you write down the number you hear. Try to do so before I tell you the answer:

> "ba" — That was "one"
> "dee" — That was "three"
> "baba" — That was "two"

Now we will learn some two-digit numbers:

> "tu" is "twenty"
> "ti" is "thirty"
> "tu-ba" is "tweny-one" in this language — because "tu" is twenty and "ba" is one.
> "ti-ba" in "thirty-one" — because "ti" thirty and "ba" is one.

Now let's begin. Write down the number you hear. [You have only about 5 seconds to write down your answer.]

> a. ti-ba
> b. ti-dee
> c. baba
> d. tu-dee

After you write down the numbes, you will be told how to fill in the appropriate spaces on the answer sheet. Although this example was fairly simple, on the actual test you will have to learn one-, two-, three-digit numbers and combinations.

Part III (Spelling Cues)

Each question has a group of words. The word at the top of the group is not spelled in the usual way. Instead, it is spelled approximately as it is pronounced. Your task is to recognize the disguised word from the spelling. In order to show that you recognize the disguised word, look for one of the five words beneath it that corresponds **most closely in meaning** to the disguised word. When you find this word or phrase, write down the letter that corresponds to your choice.

1. kloz
    a. attire
    b. nearby
    c. stick
    d. giant
    e. relatives
2. restrnt
    a. food
    b. self-control
    c. sleep
    d. space explorer
    e. drug
3. prezns
    a. kings
    b. explanations
    c. dates
    d. gifts
    e. forecasts
4. grbj
    a. car port
    b. seize
    c. boat
    d. boast
    e. waste

Second Language Testing, Inc. (n.d.). MLAT sample questions. (http://www.2lti. com.htm/mlat.htm#10.1—retrieved April 10, 2006).

The MLAT is a secure test available only to governmental agencies, licensed clinical psychologists, and other selected groups or researchers who are deemed appropriate to administer the test for assessment, diagnostic, or research purposes. Further information can be found at http://www.2lti.com (retrieved April 10, 2006). Box 3.6 presents an example of a study using MLAT scores.

Box 3.6: A Study Using the MLAT

Ehrman, M., & Oxford, R. (1995). Cognition plus: Correlates of language learning success. *Modern Language Journal*, 79, 67-89.

Ehrman and Oxford examined the relationship between language learning success and aptitude, learning strategies, learning styles, personality traits, motivation, and anxiety. The participants were 855 U.S. government employees, their spouses, and their college-aged children in a foreign language training program. Of the 855 participants, 282 completed the Modern Language Aptitude Test (MLAT). The participants' MLAT scores were compared to their foreign language performance at the end of the language training. Results indicated that the MLAT was one of the variables that was strongly correlated with Foreign Service Institute ratings for speaking and reading.

Several issues have recently been raised in relation to the concept of aptitude and the elicitation of data. It has been argued, for example, that aptitude may predict rate of learning as opposed to ultimate success. Furthermore, the relationship between aptitude test scores and the construct of aptitude is not clear, nor is the relationship between aptitude test scores and intelligence (both the construct and in terms of test scores). Also being discussed is the idea that, rather than being a static ability that does not change over time, aptitude might be related to skill development. Drawing from Sternberg's work on human intelligence (described in Sternberg, 2002), Grigorenko, Sternberg, and Ehrman (2000) have put forward a test of L2 aptitude that they call the Cognitive Ability for Novelty in Acquisition of Language as Applied to Foreign Language Testing (CANAL-FT). The test emphasizes measuring how people cope with novelty and ambiguity in language learning. As Dörnyei (2005) points out, this test is still developing, but shows promise.

There are many components that might be responsible for the aptitude-learning relationship, either separately or in combination. Perhaps one of the most promising is working memory, and a number of SLA researchers have begun to focus their attention on working memory as a potential predictor of learners' second language achievement. However, the elicitation of working memory data is no less challenging than the elicitation of aptitude data.

3.3.2 Working Memory Tests

A number of studies have addressed the relationship between working memory and success in second language acquisition. Working memory is different from short- and long-term memory in that it involves not only storage capacity but also processing capacity, which most people agree is related to attentional control. Before talking about how to elicit information about working memory, it is important to understand that different tests are derived from different models that do not understand working memory the same way. For example, N. Ellis (2005) points out that one typical operationalization of working memory (e.g., Daneman & Carpenter, 1980; Daneman & Case, 1981; Just & Carpenter, 1992), which he refers to as the Canadian model, emphasizes a trade-off between storage and processing through working memory tasks. Individual differences in working memory capacity operationalized in this way have been found to be related to both the products and processes of L2 learning (see Geva & Ryan, 1993; Harrington & Sawyer, 1992; Miyake & Friedman, 1998). A number of tests of verbal working memory originate from research in cognitive psychology and three that have been used in SLA are operation span, counting span, and sentence span. Common to these three is that learners have to do something and then remember something later on. (For a more elaborated overview that includes both descriptions of these working memory tasks, and also a discussion of issues related to administration, item size, randomization of presentation versus ascending order, scoring procedures, reliability, and validity, see Conway *et al.*, 2005). The following is a brief description of three verbal-span tasks:

> • Operation-span tasks require that participants solve mathematical operations while they are trying to remember words. A mathematical operation is presented (sometimes a correct equation [e.g., $(9/3) - 2 = 1$] and sometimes not [e.g., $(9/2) - 2 = 1$]), and participants are required to read it and state whether or not it is correct. There is then a word following the operation that they need to recall after reading through a set of operations (generally, two, three, four, and five operations).
> • Counting-span tasks (Case *et al.*, 1982) involve counting shapes and remembering the total number of shapes for later recall. As N. Cowan *et al.* (2003) point out, the visual displays can be made more complex by placing shapes against a backdrop of distractors that share the same shape or color. At the end of a sequence of trials, the participant remembers the number of a particular shape/color from each display in the order presented.

• Sentence-span tasks are perhaps the most frequently used of the three in SLA research. They can be performed as either auditory listening-span tests or written reading-span tests, and within each of these categories there are numerous variations. A typical reading-span task presents sentences visually in groups ranging from two to six. The groups can be presented in ascending order or arranged randomly. Participants are generally asked to state whether each sentence is *true* or *false, plausible* or *implausible,* or *syntactically/semantically correct* or *incorrect.* Then they are asked to remember something. There are numerous variations on what is to be remembered. Sometimes it is the last word of each sentence, sometimes a letter following the sentence, or sometimes an unrelated word following the sentence.

One example of a frequently used sentence-span test comes from Daneman and Carpenter (1980), modified by Waters and Caplan (1996). In typical adaptations of this test, learners are asked to make an acceptability judgment on each sentence in a set while at the same time remembering the final word of each. Their reaction times (when done as a computer-based test) and the accuracy of their acceptability judgments and sentence-final word recalls are then analyzed to determine working memory capacity.

Another model of working memory (e.g., Baddeley, 1986; Baddeley, Gathercole, & Papagno, 1998; Baddeley & Hitch, 1974; Gathercole & Baddeley,1989, 1993) is referred to by N. Ellis (2005) as the British model, and includes a phonological loop and a visuospatial sketch pad, along with a supervisory attentional system and an episodic buffer. Several studies have elicited test scores related to phonological loop capacity, operationalizing phonological short-term memory (PSTM) as the ability to store and accurately recall novel verbal input immediately following its presentation. This novel verbal input is presented in the form of pseudo-words or nonwords that follow the phonotactics of either the L1 or the L2. Gathercole and her colleagues have claimed that nonword recall tests are a valid measure of PSTM in that long-term stored lexical knowledge is less likely to interfere with the results (e.g., Gathercole & Martin, 1996).

A number of SLA studies have associated scores on PSTM with success in language learning (e.g., Daneman & Case, 1981; N. Ellis & Schmidt, 1997; N. Ellis & Sinclair, 1996; Papagno, Valentine, & Baddeley, 1991; Papagno & Vallar,1992; Service, 1992; Service & Craik, 1993; Service & Kohonen, 1995; Williams, 1999; Williams & Lovatt, 2003). For example, in a recent study employing artificial microlanguages, Williams and Lovatt (2003) found that PSTM was related to the learning of grammar rules.

Some researchers, notably Miyake and Friedman (1998), have argued that word-span tasks and other measures of short-term storage capacity (e.g., digit span) are inappropriate for testing L2 learners' operational abilities because they do not involve dynamic, simultaneous processing and storage. They review studies (e.g., Harrington & Sawyer, 1992) showing that measures of learners' abilities to both maintain and manipulate information (as in sentence-span tasks) correlate better with L2 comprehension skills than do the more passive digit- and word-span measures. In fact, their own experimental research corroborates this finding. Interestingly, however, N. Ellis (2005) has pointed out that sentence-span tasks risk the danger of "circularity in interpretation and operationalization" (p. 339); that is, studies employing them may be showing that learners' performance on language processing tasks predicts their language processing ability. In summary then, although not much research has attempted to compare these tests of working memory for their appropriateness in the context of SLA research, both sentence- and non-word-span tests have been shown to be good predictors of L2 learning success. In Box 3.7, a study that utilized a listening-span test is described.

Box 3.7: A Study Using a Working Memory Test to Investigate the Noticing of Feedback and L2 Development

Mackey, A., Philp, J., Egi, T., Fuji, A., & Tatsumi, T. (2002). Individual differences in working memory, noticing of interactional feedback and L2 development. In P. Robinson (Ed.), *Individual differences and instructed language learning* (pp. 181-209). Philadelphia: John Benjamins.

Mackey *et al.* examined the relationship between working memory capacity and the noticing of interactional feedback. The participants in the study were 30 ESL learners whose L1 was Japanese. In order to test their verbal working memory, the researchers used a listening-span test, which presented the participants with prerecorded sets of sentences. The participants were asked to listen to the sentences and judge each for acceptability immediately after its presentation. They were also instructed either to remember all of the initial or final words of the sentences. They also carried out a short term test of phonological memory, which was based on a nonsense word test. The nonsense words followed the phonotactic rules of Japanese, their L1. Participants were divided into groups based on high, low, and medium scores on the working memory tests. Test scores for the sentence span and the phonological short-term memory tests were examined, as well as composite scores. The results of the study showed an interesting but complex relationship between working memory scores and noticing.

As noted earlier, aptitude and working memory tests clearly measure some abilities or capacities and have been found to correlate with learning. At this point, however, they are not well developed enough in second language research for us to know precisely what they are testing. There is great promise in work by researchers such as Skehan (2002) and Robinson (2005), who have attempted to link work on aptitude and working memory with second language instructional techniques so as to benefit learners directly. Still, such work needs to be elaborated further into a testable series of claims. Miyake and Friedman (1998) have pointed out that working memory may in fact be what is measured in current tests of language aptitude. This is an interesting proposal that may turn out to be true, and the methods for isolating, measuring, and collecting data to address these sorts of questions are the focus of the current book. Indeed, whereas it is important to know that aptitude and working memory tests can be found or devised to elicit data, it is also crucial to realize (as with any data collection technique) that the constructs they are intended to measure must also be carefully considered with respect to SLA theory.

3.4 CONCLUSION

The field of second language research is currently witnessing a good deal of interest in learners' cognitive processes, capacities, and strategies. This chapter has reviewed a variety of methods commonly employed to gain information about these phenomena, including observations of naturalistic data, introspective measures allowing access to learners' thought processes, and predesigned tests of such constructs as aptitude and working memory capacity.

CHAPTER 4

Linguistics-Based Research

This chapter focuses on research dealing with language representation, meaning that the focus is on language and linguistic analysis and not on how language is processed in real time or used in context. The methods described in this chapter are, for the most part, descriptions of offline techniques used in the study of linguistic knowledge. Second language learning is usually viewed by linguistics-based researchers as the acquisition of a grammar of a second language, as well as the acquisition of processing strategies relevant to learning and using a language.

The theory of language known as Universal Grammar (UG) has been the dominant formal linguistic approach in second language acquisition research that is linguistics-based. The motivation and guiding principle for UG-based first language acquisition research begins from the perspective of learnability. If we assume that children have an innate "blueprint" that they bring to the task of learning languages, we can invoke innateness to explain the uniformly successful and relatively speedy acquisition of native languages by normal children despite incomplete (or what UG researchers argue is "impoverished") input. The main concern of UG research in SLA is the characterization and explanation of "the linguistic systems that second language (L2) learners develop, considering in particular the extent to which the underlying linguistic competence of L2 speakers is constrained by the same universal principles that govern natural languages in general" (White, 2003, p. 1).

The notion of principles and parameters has been important in theories of UG. Principles are invariant requirements on the form of grammars (they are true for all languages), whereas parameters vary from language to language. In child language acquisition, it is assumed that children are equipped with UG before being exposed to primary linguistic data (input), that UG constrains the L1 acquisition process, and that native language grammars are correspondingly constrained by UG. In other words, in terms of both the dynamic devel-opment and the "static" form of mental representations (i.e., fully formed natural languages), UG is a guiding and constraining factor. In UG theory, universal principles shape part of the mental representation of language, and properties of the human mind are what make language universals the way they are. As Chomsky (1997) noted, "The theory of a particular language is its *grammar*. The theory of languages and the expressions they generate is *Universal Grammar* (UG); UG is a theory of the initial state S_o of the relevant component of the language faculty" (p. 167).

Briefly, within this characterization of acquisition, there are two main types of information that learners use when learning a language: positive evidence and negative evidence.[1] Positive evidence refers to the input, or the ambient language that a learner is exposed to, whether through the oral or written medium; negative evidence refers to information that an utterance or written form is incorrect. Importantly, whereas negative evidence informs the learner about incorrectness, it does not necessarily provide information about the location or nature of the specific problem or how to correct the form.

While the assumption that UG is the guiding force of child language acquisi-tion has long been maintained by some researchers and hotly debated by others, in this book the actual debate is not of concern. The question for second language research concerns the extent to which UG may be available to second language learners. Or, to put it differently, to what extent does UG constrain the kinds of second language grammars that learners can come up with?

There are methodological issues specific to the UG paradigm that have to do with the nature of the information being collected. UG SLA researchers are interested in understanding linguistic competence or, whether the linguistic competence of L2 acquirers is constrained by UG. However, given that com-petence is a theoretical abstraction and unconscious in the mind/brains of learners, it is impossible to tap directly. Researchers can infer competence through production, comprehension, or intuitional measures. What they must always keep in mind, however, is that all of these are performance mea-sures and not direct reflections of mental representations. Thus, as with other domains of SLA research, but perhaps even more so within UG-based re-search, multiple measures are important. When results from different

---

[1]A third type of evidence, indirect negative evidence, also exists, but is not included here given the lack of discussion of this evidence type in the SLA literature. Simply put, it is evidence that comes from the lack of a particular linguistic feature in the input. The lack of exemplars where something is expected, can be argued to provide information to the learner that that par-ticular feature is not possible in the L2.

elicitation measures converge, one can have a greater sense of confidence in the inferences that are made. The techniques exemplified in this chapter focus on learners' knowledge without focusing on what learners actually do while they are using language.

4.1 NATURALISTIC DATA

In order to gain information about learners' competence, researchers need to be able to infer not only what learners know is correct in the second language, but also what learners know is not possible. As a result, elicitation of naturalistic data is not often the method of choice because it provides information on the former, but not on the latter. There are times, however, when naturalistic data are useful in either UG-based research or research on formal linguistic systems in general. This may be the case, for example, when dealing with learners who are illiterate or have little formal education, because they may find the tasks typically used in UG-based research difficult to carry out. An example of a study using naturalistic data is given in Box 4.1.

Box 4.1: A Study Using Naturalistic Data Within a UG Framework

Lardiere, D. (1998a). Dissociating syntax from morphology in a divergent L2 end-state grammar. *Second Language Research, 14,* 359-375.

In this study, Lardiere raises a fundamental question from the minimalist perspective: What counts as UG-constrained knowledge? To this end, she pays close attention to optional verb movements in L2 grammars, where syntactic features encoded in morphology are assumed to trigger UG-constrained syntactic operations such as verb-raising (a type of movement that is observable in a given language in the placement of inflected verbs with respect to, for example, subjects in questions, negation, and adverbs). The raising of finite (tensed) verbs is said to be determined by the strength (strong and weak) of subject-verb agreement features.

Lardiere used a longitudinal design to investigate verb-raising in naturalistic data coming from an adult Chinese-speaking learner of English. A description of her subject, Patty, along with a description of the type of language recorded, can be found in Lardiere (1998b). Data collection occurred at three points. The first was when Patty was 32 years old and had been in the United States for 10 years. The second and third recordings were taped 8½ years later, 3 months apart. Information regarding the content of the recordings is given next:

(Box 4.1 Continued)

Box 4.1 Continued

> The first recording, about 34 minutes long, is the most spontaneous and naturalistic of the three conversations, and includes discussion by Patty of some of her philosophical and religious views. The second recording is about 75 minutes long and consists primarily of Patty's responses to somewhat more formal interview-like questions about her language background and life history, and her narrative of past events in her life. The third, about 31 minutes long, included Patty's husband in the conversation, during which they both provided details of events relating to how they met and decided to get married, and their observations about language learning in general and Patty's English in particular, among other topics. (1998b, pp. 13-14)

> Lardiere made two calculations: (a) agreement marking in all possible non-past, finite, third-person singular contexts for thematic main verbs and the auxiliaries *do* and *have*, as well as all finite contexts for the copula *be*, and (b) all obligatory finite contexts containing thematic verbs (in addition to utterances with *do* and modals) and negation and/or clause-internal adverbs. She found that, although Patty omitted verb agreement morphology in about 96% of obligatory contexts, no occurrences of thematic verb-raising over negation and adverbs were found in the audiotaped data. In other words, despite producing verbal morphology incorrectly, Patty did not demonstrate any optionality in verb-raising. These findings disconfirm the hypotheses, which directly associated verb-raising and morphological agreement, and Lardiere uses the data to argue that verbal morphology and the hypothetically consequent syntactic raising operation are in fact independent in an L2. She concludes that syntax and morphology in an L2 can therefore be dissociated.

Reference

Lardiere, D. (1998b). Case and tense in the "fossilized" steady state. *Second Language Research, 14,* 1-26.

Whereas the study in Box 4.1 dealt with theoretical aspects of UG, there are other studies that use naturalistic, longitudinal data to investigate formal aspects of grammatical knowledge that are not grounded in UG theory. Box 4.2 describes one such example.

Box 4.2: A Study Using Naturalistic Data to Investigate Tense/Aspect Systems

Kumpf, L. (1984). Temporal systems and universality in interlanguage: A case study. In F. R. Eckman, L. W. Bell, & D. Nelson (Eds.), *Universals of second language acquisition* (pp. 132-143). Rowley, MA: Newbury House.

Kumpf's goal in this study was to investigate the systematicity of a learner's interlanguage without reference to an external system (either the L1 or the L2). The study approached systematicity through a discourse-functional approach and examined the occurrence of tense and aspect forms in actual discourse, using the concepts of *foreground* and *background.* She used a narrative context for this purpose because of its inherent story line, considering the foreground to be the sequence of events while the background "consists of causes which set the scene, make digressions, change the normal sequence of events, or give evaluative remarks" (p. 133).

The participant in Kumpf's study, a native speaker of Japanese, had been in an English-speaking environment for 28 years when she provided the English narrative on which the study is based. She was fluent in the sense that her words came easily; however, her English was clearly non-native-like.

Kumpf departed from more traditional analyses in that she did not analyze the narrative on the basis of English categories. Rather, she imposed an interlanguage discourse structure on the narrative based on foregrounded and backgrounded clauses. This allowed her to discover regularity and systematicity that could not have been revealed using an English morphosyntactic analysis. Briefly, Kumpf found that her participant generally used the base form of a verb when material was being foregrounded. In the background, verbs (especially stative verbs) received tense marking. Active verbs in the background were marked for habitual and continuous aspect, but only irregularly for tense. In sum, because Kumpf analyzed naturalistic data, she was able to find a system in this speaker's interlanguage that would not have been obvious with prompted data.

As mentioned earlier, given that researchers have little control over what learners will produce, naturalistic data are often not useful when attempting to determine possible and impossible grammars. They are useful, however, when researchers want to look at the language development of individual learners or, as in the study by Kumpf, when they want to consider discourse features of language. Another, more controlled, means for eliciting linguistic data is through prompted production, and it is to this area that we turn next.

4.2 PROMPTED PRODUCTION

This section deals with structured data—that is, data that are guided in a particular direction. When researchers ask research questions specifically targeting particular areas of grammar, they need to devise tests or tasks that are likely to generate instances of those areas. The sections that follow deal with some typical ways of gathering production data. We continue to focus on structured data in a later section but do so through learners' responses rather than through their actual production.

4.2.1 Elicited Imitation

As discussed in chapter 2, elicited imitation is often used as a means to determine the nature of learners' grammatical systems. However, as Bley-Vroman and Chaudron (1994) point out, the process is not well-understood. Nonetheless, as noted by Chaudron and Russell (1990), the results from elicited imitation tasks and general proficiency measures correlate reasonably well.

Comparisons with native speaker data can be revealing. Bley-Vroman and Chaudron (1994) noted that, in a study by Merzenich (1989) on reflexive binding (what a reflexive pronoun refers to), non-native speakers would change sentences (e.g., *Jane wants Bill to scratch herself*) to their correct versions (i.e., *Jane wants Bill to scratch himself*), whereas native speakers repeated the deviant forms. Unfortunately, as they noted, this clouds the interpretations that can be given to non-native so-called corrections. Are they truly corrections, or are they inaccurate repetitions that turn out correct by coincidence? Although these are reasonable questions, one must also consider memory limitations because native speakers can generally hold a longer chunk of language in memory and repeat it verbatim than learners can. Even though everyone (native and non-native speakers alike) may truly have to generate the sentences if they cannot hold them in memory, the fact that the amount of language that non-native speakers can hold is less than that of native speakers suggests that their modifications are more likely to represent their grammatical knowledge.

Box 4.3 presents a study on the acquisition of English relative clauses that used elicited imitation. The focus of the study was methodological, comparing the results obtained using elicited imitation versus the results of acceptability judgments.

Box 4.3: A Study Comparing Elicited Imitation[2] with a Judgment Task

Munnich, E., Flynn, S., & Martohardjono, G. (1994). Elicited imitation and grammaticality judgment tasks: What they measure and how they relate to each other. In E. Tarone, S. Gass, & A. Cohen (Eds.), *Research methodology in second-language acquisition* (pp. 227-243). Hillsdale, NJ: Lawrence Erlbaum Associates.

This study is primarily concerned with comparing the results from two data elicitation techniques: elicited imitation and acceptability judgments. The participant pool consisted of 12 native speakers of Japanese who were learning English. They were initially given the Michigan Placement Test, a standardized test of English language proficiency; their range of scores was wide.

The treatment consisted of 12 sentences in each of four tasks: an elicited imitation task that was read to participants orally, an elicited imitation task that was pre-recorded, an acceptability judgment task in which the participants read a stimulus sentence and then stated whether they thought the sentence was grammatical, and an acceptability judgment task in which the participants heard a sentence read on tape and then had to determine the grammaticality of the sentence. In the elicited imitation tasks, each sentence was followed by a 10-second interval during which the participants were to repeat the sentence. In the acceptability judgment tasks, there was a 15-second interval between the sentences. The test sentences contained relative clauses with object-object order or with object-subject order (both grammatical and ungrammatical). The ungrammatical sentences included resumptive pronouns, as in *The man greeted the doctor who the actor introduced him.

The authors found convergence between the two types of tasks on the grammatical sentences. The general finding for the ungrammatical sentences was that, considering the frequency with which learners correctly identified ungrammatical sentences as ungrammatical, there was convergence on three of the four tasks. The exception was the acceptability judgment task in which the participants read the stimulus sentences. The authors' conclusion suggests that elicited imitation can differentiate between ungrammatical and grammatical sentences and can, therefore, be used to tap knowledge of ungrammatical sentences.

(Box 4.3 Continued)

---

[2]Along with this article by Munnich *et al.* (1994), the conclusions of Bley-Vroman and Chaudron (1994) should also be carefully considered. The latter authors deal with the particular issues raised by Munnich *et al.*, as well as with important methodological issues related to elicited imitation in general.

Box 4.3 Continued

Reference

Bley-Vroman, R., & Chaudron, C. (1994). **Elicited imitation as a measure of second-language competence.** In E. Tarone, S. Gass, & A. Cohen (Eds.), *Research Methodology in Second-Language Acquisition* (pp. 245-261). Hillsdale, NJ: Lawrence Erlbaum Associates.

As the study described in Box 4.3 suggests, and as Bley-Vroman and Chaudron (1994) point out, further research is needed to understand more clearly what is involved in doing an elicited imitation task and therefore how researchers can best interpret the results of such tasks. Nonetheless, a number of recommendations can be made for doing elicited imitation.

Recommendations for Elicited Imitation Tasks

- Ensure an appropriate length in terms of the number of words and syllables for all sentences. For example, a length of between 12-17 syllables might be appropriate, depending on proficiency level.
- Pre-record sentences for uniformity.
- Randomize all sentences.
- Include enough tokens of each grammatical structure so that you can make reasonable conclusions. This will depend on how many structures you are dealing with. As with other methodologies, researchers have to balance the need for an appropriate number of tokens with the necessity of not tiring the participants to the point that their responses are unreliable. Different randomizations help ensure that tiredness will not systematically affect the results.
- Ensure that sentences are of comparable complexity.
- Ensure that there is enough time between the end of each prompt and the moment when the learner begins to speak. (Researchers sometimes ask participants to count to 3 before beginning to speak to ensure that "echoic" memory is not being used; this is not critical as long as the sentences are long enough.)
- Pilot-test everything.

4.2.2 Picture Description

As mentioned earlier, it is often important for researchers to be able to elicit sufficient exemplars of a particular form. One way of doing this is through a picture-description task. Many different types of pictures can be used. For example, participants can be asked to describe a picture sequence designed to elicit a particular grammatical structure. In Box 4.4, we discuss a study that investigated the role of positive evidence in triggering a new parameter setting. This study used a single picture rather than a sequence of pictures.

Box 4.4: A Study Using a Picture-Description Task to Investigate the Role of Evidence Types

Trahey, M., & White, L. (1993). **Positive evidence and preemption in the second language classroom.** *Studies in Second Language Acquisition, 15,* 181-204.

This study focused on the type of input needed to modify second language grammars. In particular, Trahey and White were concerned with the extent to which positive evidence could trigger change in a UG-proposed parameter (verb-raising).

Their participants were 11-year-old Francophone children learning English in Quebec, and the treatment involved 2 weeks of intensive exposure to English adverbs used as naturally as possible. The students were tested immediately prior to the treatment, immediately after the treatment, and then again 3 weeks later.

There were a number of tasks used to elicit data (see also Box 4.11, which discusses this study as well), but here we focus on one: an oral production task. The children were given a single cartoon picture with an adverb written below it (e.g., a picture of a child watching TV with the word *quietly* written underneath) and were told to make a sentence using the adverb below the picture. Each picture had what could be construed as a subject (e.g., *child*) and an object (e.g., *TV*). There were four such pictures, two with adverbs of manner and two with adverbs of frequency.

The difference between the learners' pretest and first posttest scores was significant, but the difference between the first and second posttests was not. The learners increased their usage of the Subject-Adverb-Verb-Object sequence (grammatical in English), but they did not lose their Subject-Verb-Adverb-Object sentences (grammatical in French).

4.2.3 Structured Elicitation

This technique, based on child language research (notably, Berman, 1993, 2000), is a highly structured version of a picture description. The idea is to explore the creative abilities of learners (child or adult) when confronted with rule-based morphological processes. In these tasks, the researcher describes a picture, thereby providing the targeted verb. The research participant then describes a second picture using that verb. In a modification of the technique used by Berman, Zyzik (2006) used structured elicitation to study the acquisition of clitics in L2 Spanish. A description is given in Box 4.5.

Box 4.5: A Study Using Structured Elicitation to Investigate the Acquisition of Clitics in L2 Spanish

Zyzik, E. (2006). Transitivity alternations and sequence learning: Insights from L2 Spanish production data. *Studies in Second Language Acquisition, 28,* **449-485.**

This study examines the learnability problem associated with alternating verbs in Spanish (e.g., *quemar[se]* 'burn') from a sequence learning (i.e., 'chunking') perspective (N. Ellis, 1996, 2002). For verbs of this class, intransitives are obligatorily marked with the clitic *se*. Zyzik set out to investigate the overgeneralization of *se* to transitive event scenes.

Fifty native speakers of English learning Spanish as an L2 participated in this study. They were divided into four proficiency groups based on their institutional status and prior exposure to Spanish: beginning, intermediate, high intermediate, and advanced. In the study, each learner was presented with pairs of pictures that represented similar events, but from different perspectives. The researcher described the first picture in each pair, thereby providing the targeted verb, and then asked the participant to describe the event of the second picture. The verbs that were targeted could express both transitive and intransitive events (e.g., *dry*). There were eight target verb pairs (16 pictures) and four pairs of distractor pictures (e.g., a man carrying a suitcase vs. a woman carrying a baby). The following example illustrates the procedure. English translations are given below the source and target sentences:

Source: *Este hombre se pesa. ¿Y qué sucede en este dibujo?*[This man is weighing himself. And what is happening in this picture?]

Target: *El hombre pesa las manzanas.*[The man is weighing the apples.]

Two verb classes were tested: causative/inchoative alternation (e.g., *despertar[se]*, *esconder[se]*, *secar[se]*, *quemar[se]*—i.e., 'to wake up,' 'to hide,' 'to dry,' 'to burn') and transitive/reflexive alternation (*mirar[se]*, *pesar[se]*, *bañar[se]*, *afeitar[se]*—i.e., 'to look at,' 'to weigh,' 'to bathe,' 'to shave'). Directionality was manipulated between verb pairs. That is, in some cases, participants were given *mirar* ('to look at') as the source input in a transitive context and were expected to produce the reflexive *se mira* ('she looks at herself') in conjunction with a picture

---

that depicted such a reflexive event. In other cases, the source input was the opposite; learners were given the reflexive and had to produce the transitive version. The order of presentation was randomized for transitivity direction and verb type.

Scoring is always a difficult task when dealing with a range of response possibilities. In this study, responses were divided into two main categories: *appropriate* and *inappropriate*, with the appropriate category further subdivided into *correct* (i.e., making the expected transitivity alternation) and *acceptable* (i.e., producing a grammatically correct response without making the expected alternation). Examples are given here:

a.	correct	La ropa *se está secando*
		[The clothes are drying.]
b.	acceptable	La mujer *seca* la ropa afuera.
		[The woman is drying the clothes outside.]

The inappropriate responses were also further subdivided into *ungrammatical* and *irrelevant*. Examples of both types of inappropriate responses are given below:

a.	ungrammatical	*La ropa *seca* afuera.
		[The clothes are drying outside.]
b.	irrelevant	La ropa *está* afuera.
		[The clothes are outside.]

The results suggest that overgeneralization errors are indeed frequent, but that with greater proficiency, learners are eventually able to recover from them. Zyzik proposes that the acquisition of L2 morphosyntax is shaped by learners' familiarity with individual lexical items and the sequences in which they tend to appear.

References

Ellis, N. (1996). Sequencing in SLA: Phonological memory, chunking, and points of order. *Studies in Second Language Acquisition, 18,* 91-126.

Ellis, N. (2002). Frequency effects in language processing: A review with implications for theories of implicit and explicit language acquisition. *Studies in Second Language Acquisition, 24,* 143-188.

4.2.4 Story Telling

The elicitation technique of story telling uses a variety of sources as prompts. For example, learners can be shown short video clips or a series of pictures, or they can be asked to narrate a story. Similarly, a variety of "listeners" are possible. For example, researchers can tape-record learners' stories and have them tell the stories to a friend, to a researcher, or to another learner. The most crucial requirement is to ensure, through pilot-testing, that the structures or grammatical areas in question will be produced in sufficient numbers. Story telling leaves learners relatively free to select alternative constructions to express their meanings, either by preference or by avoidance. Box 4.6 provides information on a study that used story telling to elicit data on syntactic and pragmatic/semantic features of Spanish by Spanish heritage language speakers (i.e., learners with Spanish as a home language).

Box 4.6: A Study That Illustrates the Acquisition of Syntactic vs. Semantic and Pragmatic Properties Using a Picture-Description/Story Telling Task

Montrul, S. (2004). Subject and object expression in Spanish heritage speakers: A case of morphosyntactic convergence. *Bilingualism: Language & Cognition, 7,* 125-142.

Montrul conducted this study under the assumption that the language of Spanish heritage speakers represents a type of language loss. Her hypothesis, based on past research, was that although purely syntactic properties do not attrite, areas of language representing a syntax-related interface (e.g., discourse pragmatics and lexical semantics) can be lost.

To address this question, she elicited oral data from 24 intermediate and advanced heritage language speakers and 20 monolingual Spanish speakers, considering both syntactic properties of Spanish (null subjects and object clitics) and interface properties (the distribution of null vs. overt subjects, the *a* preposition with animate direct objects, and semantically based dative clitic-doubling). The task involved describing a set of colored pictures from the familiar story "Little Red Riding Hood" in Spanish. The narratives were tape-recorded for later transcription.

Montrul found that the oral production of the intermediate learners showed variable performance with the pragmatic and semantic features, suggesting convergence with English (the language of the environment) in these areas.

4.2.5 Sentence Combining

Sentence combining is a way of eliciting data on compound sentences; it has thus been put to profitable use in relative clause research, which investigates learners' embedding of one clause within another. Generally, participants are presented with two sentences (e.g., *That boy is my brother* and *That boy is running*) and asked to combine them, with the expectation that the resultant sentence will employ a relative clause (e.g., *That boy who is running is my brother*). The most challenging part of this technique is to ensure that the task instructions are unambiguous. For example, if a researcher is targeting sentences of the type *The man whom I love is out of the country*, it may not be sufficient simply to provide the sentences *The man is out of the country* and *I love the man* because learners could also use them to produce the sentence *I love the man who is out of the country*. If the researcher is trying to investigate differences between subject relative clauses and direct object relative clauses, there is no way of knowing whether learners who produce *I love the man who is out of the country* do so because they do not know how to produce direct object relative clauses or because they simply find subject relatives easier. It can thus be useful to provide learners with the first words of a desired sentence, as follows:

The man _____

Gass (1980), who did not use this sort of lead-in sentence frame, found interesting results based on when the instructions were or were not followed. This study is described in Box 4.7.

Box 4.7: A Study Investigating the Acquisition of Relative Clauses with a Sentence Combination Task

Gass, S. (1980). An investigation of syntactic transfer in adult L2 learners. In R. Scarcella & S. Krashen (Eds.), *Research in second language acquisition* (pp. 132-141). Rowley, MA: Newbury House.

This study investigated the acquisition of relative clauses using the accessibility hierarchy (Keenan & Comrie, 1977) as a theoretical framework. Gass predicted that second language data would follow the predicted orderings of the hierarchy.

In order to test this prediction, 17 participants were given three tasks: an acceptability judgment task and two tasks that were designed to elicit information about productive knowledge. The one focused on here is a sentence combination

(Box 4.7 Continued)

Box 4.7 Continued

task that was designed "to gather data on performance and to ensure enough tokens from which valid conclusions could be drawn" by "forcing" the participants to produce sentences containing relative clauses (p. 133). In this paper-and-pencil task, participants were given 12 pairs of sentences and were told to combine them using a relative clause. The combinations represented the following relative clause types (The first abbreviation represents the intended grammatical position of the relevant noun in the first sentence, whereas the second abbreviation represents its intended position in the subordinate sentence):

SU	SU	Example: *The boy* fell. *The boy* came.
SU	DO	Example: *The boy* fell. I saw *the boy*.
SU	IO	Example: *The boy* fell. I gave *the boy* cookies.
SU	OPREP	Example: *The boy* fell. I talked with *the boy*.
SU	GEN	Example: *The boy* fell. *The boy's* dog is cute.
SU	OCOMP	Example: *The boy* fell. I am taller than *the boy*.
DO	SU	Example: I saw *the boy*. *the boy* fell.
DO	DO	Example: I saw *the boy*. I like *the boy*.
DO	IO	Example: I saw *the boy*. I gave *the boy* cookies.
DO	OPREP	Example: I saw *the boy*. I talked with *the boy*.
DO	GEN	Example: I saw *the boy*. *The boy's* dog is cute.
DO	OCOMP	Example: I saw *the boy*. I am taller than *the boy*.

Key:

SU	=	subject
DO	=	direct object
IO	=	indirect object
OPREP	=	object of preposition
GEN	=	genitive
OCOMP	=	object of comparative

The results supported the predictions based on the accessibility hierarchy, and, interestingly, because the participants were given specific instructions on how to combine the sentences, Gass was also able to look at those cases where they did not follow the instructions. She found that the learners were more likely to display evidence of avoidance, producing easier structures instead, on those sentence combinations that were predicted by the hierarchy to be difficult.

Reference

Keenan, E., & Comrie, B. (1977). Noun phrase accessibility and universal grammar. *Linguistic Inquiry, 8,* 63-99.

The preceding sections have dealt with second language production data that, unlike naturalistic or spontaneous data, do have specific linguistic targets. Production data provide us with just that: production data. We can infer that they represent what learners believe is grammatical, but we do not know what is not allowed in the learners' grammars. The latter sort of information is an important aspect of competence because, as mentioned earlier, part of understanding what someone knows about language includes understanding what they consider impossible. The fact that this cannot be inferred from natural production alone is demonstrated by the following example.

Research question: Do learners know the third-person singular
-s in English?

Typical production: The man walks down the street.

If learners consistently produce sentences such as the previous one, then it might seem reasonable to assume that they have knowledge of the third-per-son singular. However, that conclusion would be based on insufficient evi-dence. It would be a valid conclusion only if we knew that the learners also ruled out *The boys walks down the street as a possible English sentence. In other words, it is necessary to ask whether they recognize that -s is limited to third-person singular as opposed to being a generalized present-tense marker. In addition, even if learners do not appear to use a form at all, it is not possible to assume that they cannot use the form unless they consistently do not use it in required contexts. As already discussed, researchers wishing to draw justi-fied conclusions might have to wait a considerable amount of time for enough required contexts to occur, and with time, of course, changes can occur in sec-ond language grammars. Thus, it is often the case that researchers have to "force" this sort of information through prompted responses, which is the area discussed next.

4.3 PROMPTED RESPONSES

Prompted responses are a common way of eliciting data within formal linguistic approaches to SLA. As discussed earlier, the theory underlying UG assumes that language is constrained by a set of abstract principles that characterize the core grammars of all natural languages. In addition to principles that are invariant (i.e., characteristic of all languages), there are parameters that vary across languages. UG-based second language research seeks to determine the extent to which second language learners have the same abstract representations as native speakers. Researchers thus need to determine not only what learners believe to be grammatical in the language being learned, but also what they consider ungrammatical. Importantly, second language input alone does not provide learners with this information (see Gass & Selinker, 2001, Chap. 7, for further details).

This section deals with some of the most commonly used elicitation measures in the second language literature, but, as with any other means of eliciting data, researchers must be innovative in their approaches to data collection. This often means adapting techniques from other disciplines (e.g., child language research) or modifying existing methods to suit a particular learner population. The sections that follow focus on acceptability judgments, magnitude estimation, interpretation tasks, and sentence matching, all of which are techniques whereby the data set to be examined is based on responses (e.g., "yes," "no," "ungrammatical," "grammatical") rather than on linguistic utterances.

4.3.1 Acceptability Judgments

Because the nature of abstract representations is inferable only from surface-level phenomena, UG researchers often find themselves in the position of needing to force learners into stating what is possible and what is not possible in their second language. Acceptability judgments, a common elicitation tool in linguistics, are often used for this purpose.[3] Box 4.8 presents an example of a study that uses acceptability judgments.

Box 4.8: A Study Using Acceptability Judgments to Investigate Small Clause Complements

Chen, M. Y.-c. (2005). English prototyped small clauses in the interlanguage of Chinese adult learners. *Second Language Research, 21,* 1-33.

In this study, Chen was concerned with English small clause complements, as in the sentence We *found [Mary intelligent]*. Noting that Chinese speakers do not have small clauses in their L1 grammar, she reasoned that Chinese-speaking learners of English might use only full clauses as a result of L1 transfer. Chen thus investigated small clauses with either noun-phrase or adjective/past participle predicates, looking at learners' preferences for these structures in relation to infinitival complements (*We found Mary to be intelligent*), tensed clause complements (*We found Mary was intelligent*), and clause complements introduced by that (*We found that Mary was intelligent*).

---

[3]The term acceptability judgment is often used interchangeably with the term grammaticality judgment. This is technically not correct. We make inferences about grammaticality based on judgments of acceptability, but because grammar is abstract, we cannot examine it directly in this way.

The data came from 26 native speakers of Mandarin Chinese and a control group of 26 native speakers of English. Production data were gathered through oral translations, and information on implicit knowledge was gathered through an acceptability judgment task (described earlier), in which Chen had the learners provide relative ranking judgments. Because the researcher was interested in the "composite nature of the participants' interlanguage" (p. 10), no pretest was given.

The participants were administered an acceptability judgment task via computer. Each set of sentences had an introductory sentence to provide some context, followed by four to five sentences that appeared on the screen for 30 seconds (although this could be extended by the participant). In all, there were 17 sets of test sentences, 4 of which were analyzed for this study. Because all of the sentences in a set were on the screen at the same time, comparison was built in as part of the task. An example of one such set is given here:

> After talking to Mary for a while,
> A. we found Mary to be interesting.
> B. we found Mary was interesting.
> C. we found that Mary was interesting.
> D. we found Mary as interesting.
> E. we found Mary interesting.

The participants were asked to respond to each sentence (on a separate piece of paper) on a 4-point scale: definitely acceptable, probably acceptable, probably unacceptable, and definitely unacceptable. No corrections were asked for because all of the sentences were grammatical in English.

Chen found that the learners tended not to prefer small clause complements or infinitival complements, instead preferring tensed clauses and clauses introduced by that. She takes the results to suggest a transfer influence from Chinese and difficulty based on universal development orders.

Over the years, there have been numerous challenges and controversies surrounding the use of acceptability judgments. Among them are questions relating to just what individuals are doing when they make judgments. In other words, what sort of knowledge is being tapped? For example, particularly with second language learners, we can ask whether their responses to sentences are truly representative of their knowledge of the second language or whether they are trying to remember what some teacher said should be the case. In fact, learners will often say that a particular sentence is not possible (as in *The boy walk down the street*), but will still continue to utter sentences like this. How does one reconcile their apparent "knowledge" with their practice? It is important to remember that native speaker judgments are tapping a system that the individual has automatized command over. This is not the case with nonnative speakers, who are being asked about the second language while inferences are being made about another system: their interlanguage.

The general procedure for using acceptability judgments is to give participants a list of target language sentences to be judged and to ask for corrections of any sentences judged to be incorrect. There are numerous practical considerations when dealing with judgment data, some of which are addressed next (see also Schütze, 1996).

4.3.1.1 Materials

Order of Presentation.   Judging sentences for their acceptability can become tiresome, and judgments may become unreliable due to participant fatigue. One way of countering this is to make sure that different participants are given different orders of sentence presentation—that is, the sentences that appear at the end for some individuals are in a different place in the sequence of sentences for others. Counterbalancing in this way reduces the possibility that ordering will affect the results. Box 4.9 presents a study in which each participant received a different sentence ordering on an acceptability judgment task.

Box 4.9:A Study Investigating Relative Clause Acquisition with Acceptability Judgments

Gass, S. (1994). The reliability of second-language grammaticality judgments. In E. Tarone, S. Gass, & A. Cohen (Eds.), *Research methodology in second-language acquisition* (pp. 303-322). Hillsdale, NJ: Lawrence Erlbaum Associates.

This study was designed to test the reliability of grammaticality judgments by giving the same test to participants two times at a 1-week interval. The linguistic structure being tested was relative clauses (see also Box 4.7).

Twenty-three ESL learners took acceptability judgment tests, each of which contained 30 sentences (24 relative clause sentences and 6 distractors). They were asked to judge each sentence categorically as grammatical or ungrammatical, after which they were asked to state how confident they were (definitely incorrect to definitely correct, on a 7-point scale). There was no time limit, but they were not allowed to go back and change their responses. They did not know that there would be a second administration 1 week later.

With regard to order of presentation, Gass developed a different randomly generated order of sentences for each participant. Thus, there were 46 different tests all together (23 for the first administration and 23 for the second). After the second administration, four of the participants were interviewed to learn more about the differences in their responses (if any) between the first and second

---

administrations. In general, the results demonstrated considerable consistency in judgments from Time 1 to Time 2.

Number of Sentences.   Another way to mitigate the effects of fatigue on acceptability judgment tasks is to limit the number of sentences given, balancing the number of grammatical and ungrammatical sentences. R. Cowan and Hatasa (1994) have argued that because longer tests result in greater reliability, acceptability judgment tasks should include a total of 60-72 sentences. Although studies have been carried out with as many as 101 (Hawkins & Chan, 1997) and 282 sentences (J. Johnson & Newport, 1989), we recommend no more than approximately 50-60. If more are necessary, then it would be advisable to follow J. Johnson and Newport's practice of presenting them in blocks with a break in between and letting the participants know that they can rest if they are tired. J. Johnson and Newport's (1991) study, in which they gave participants 180 sentences on an acceptability judgment task, is described in Box 4.10.

It is also important to make sure that an acceptability judgment test contains a sufficient number of filler, or distractor, sentences, so that the participants cannot easily guess what the study is about. This would be a threat to the study's internal validity. If a researcher is investigating a number of structures in one study, then it may be possible for the structures to serve as distractors for one another.

Box 4.10: A Study Using an Acceptability Judgment Test with a Large Number of Sentences

Johnson, J. S., & Newport, E. L. (1991). Critical period effects on universal properties of language: The status of subjacency in the acquisition of a second language. *Cognition, 39,* 215-258.

In this study, Johnson and Newport sought to determine whether and to what extent L2 learners have access to language properties that are thought to be innate. They investigated these questions with 23 native speakers of Chinese who had first entered English immersion environments after age 17 and with a control group of 11 native speakers of U.S. English. Their particular linguistic target was the principle of subjacency, which limits the movement of words over what are called bounding nodes. The subjacency principle restricts *wh*-question formation

(Box 4.10 Continued)

Box 4.10 Continued

in English (e.g., the question *What does Mary like how John does?* is ungrammatical), but it does not apply to *wh*-questions in Chinese, which do not involve movement.

The participants listened to a total of 180 recorded sentences, presented in two blocks, and were asked to make grammaticality judgments by circling yes or no. Each sentence was read twice by a female native U.S. English speaker with normal intonation at a slow to moderate speed. The repetitions were separated by a 1- to 2-second pause, and the next item followed after 6 to 9 seconds, which was enough time for the participants to make their judgments. They were told that they could ask the experimenter to stop the tape to take a break or to take more time whenever necessary.

The sentences included three types of syntactic structures that are affected by subjacency in English: noun phrase complements, relative clauses, and *wh*-complements. Twelve basic sentences were created for each of these structures, making a total of 36 items. Additionally, each of these 36 sentences was presented in four forms (a declarative sentence, a *wh*-question violating subjacency, a control sentence with grammatical *wh*-movement, and a question without subject-auxiliary inversion), making a total of 144 items.

In addition to the 144 test items, 12 simple grammatical *wh*-questions were included to ensure that the participants had enough competence to be evaluated on the more complex structures. Twenty-four filler items (half grammatical and half ungrammatical) were also added to increase the variability of the sentence types, but were not included in the analysis. Of the 156 analyzed items (144 test items + 12 simple *wh*-questions), 72 were ungrammatical and 84 (72 +12) were grammatical.

The sentences were presented in a pseudo-random order. An equal number of sentences from each of the three structures and from each of the four sentence types was included in each block, and one grammatical and one ungrammatical version of the same sentence were presented in each block. The sentences were also ordered to prevent the repetition of similar items or long runs of grammatical or ungrammatical sentences.

Although only the *b* sentences contain subjacency violations, all four conditions are critical for the interpretation of the results because the participants' judgments of them can rule out or confirm other explanations. Specifically, it is important to know whether the participants know enough about *wh*-movement and multiclause sentences to be evaluated on subjacency.

The L2 participants judged a significantly larger number of the sentences involving subjacency violations to be grammatical than the native speakers did, suggesting that their access to UG principles is qualitatively different. They also performed better on the ungrammatical no-inversion sentences than on the subjacency violations, suggesting that the subjacency principle is not privileged over language-specific structures. The learners performed better than chance on subjacency violations, however, leading Johnson and Newport to conclude that subjacency "survives in a weak and probabilistic form in adult learners" (p. 239).

Timing.   With tests given orally or via computer, the timing between sentences can be controlled. Questions about how much time should elapse have not been seriously addressed in the literature, but could potentially affect the results (see V. Murphy, 1997, in which participants were slower in an aural condition than in a visual one and slower to judge subjacency violations than other sentences). Another related issue to consider is whether participants should be allowed to go back and change their answers. In attempting to gain knowledge about a learner's "grammar" as opposed to formal rule knowledge, it is advisable to get "quick" responses without allowing a great deal of thinking time. With an orally administered test or with a computer-based test, this is relatively easy to control; with a paper-and-pencil test, a researcher could, for example, give everyone a pen with nonerasable ink so that answers cannot be changed. This does not necessarily eliminate the "thinking-time" problem, but it does make it more likely that learners will not change their responses on the basis of something later in the test.

Context.   Sentences can be embedded within predetermined situational contexts so that participants' imagination of other possible contexts does not enter into the picture, affecting their judgments. This is discussed in more detail in a later section on truth-value judgments.

Comparisons.   At times, researchers want to obtain sophisticated judgments of acceptability involving subtleties in language. In such instances, it might be advisable to ask participants to judge sentences as they relate to one another (e.g., *We didn't dare to answer him back* vs. *We didn't dare answer him back*—which is better?). An example of a study using a preference task is described in Box 4.11.

Box 4.11: A Study Using an Acceptability Preference Task

Trahey, M., & White, L. (1993). Positive evidence and preemption in the second language classroom. *Studies in Second Language Acquisition, 15,* 181-204.

As mentioned in Box 4.4, this study was focused on the type of input needed to modify second language grammars. In particular, Trahey and White were concerned with the extent to which positive evidence could trigger change in a UG-proposed parameter (verb-movement). Their participants were 11-year-old francophone children learning English in Quebec, and the treatment involved 2 weeks of intensive exposure to English adverbs used as naturally as possible. The students were tested immediately prior to the treatment, immediately after the treatment, and then again 3 weeks later.

Here we focus on another of the elicitation measures: a preference task. The children were given pairs of sentences, such as the following:

a. Anna carefully drives her new car.
b. Anna drives carefully her new car.

Below each pair, they were asked to circle one of the following: only *a* is right, only *b* is right, both are right, both are wrong, or don't know. Two versions of the test were created with mixed orders; each contained 32 pairs of sentences, 28 of which targeted adverbs. These were given randomly to each child.

Trahey and White again found that the difference between the learners' pretest and first posttest scores was significant, but the difference between first and second posttests was not. The results also suggested that the learners had learned the correct placement of the adverb (as in *a*), but that the input had not been sufficient to rule out the ungrammaticality of sentences such as *b*.

Modality. Should sentences be given orally, on paper, or via computer? Researchers need to be cognizant of potential differences in results due to methodology (see V. Murphy, 1997, for a review). Examples abound of each type; however, the paper-and-pencil task is probably the most common, with computer testing increasing in recent years. The least common modality for acceptability judgment tasks is oral administration, but its use can be justified. An example of a study using oral input on acceptability judgment tasks is presented in Box 4.12.

Box 4.12: A Study Using Oral Input on Acceptability Judgment Tasks in Child Second Language Acquisition to Investigate Agreement Morphology

Ionin, T., & Wexler, K. (2002). Why is "is" easier than "-*s*": Acquisition of tense/aspect agreement morphology by child second language learners of English. *Second Language Research, 18,* 95-136.

This study focused on the concept of functional categories and the omission of verbal inflection in L2 English. The participants were young Russian-speaking learners of English, ranging in age from 3 years and 9 months to 13 years and 10 months. Through production data, Ionin and Wexler observed that whereas the children omitted inflectional morphology on verbs, they rarely produced incorrect tense/agreement morphology (e.g., **I likes costumes for Halloween for Batman*). They also noted that suppletive inflections (e.g., forms of the auxiliary/copula *be*, e.g., *is* and *are*) were used more than affixal inflections (e.g., like*s*) and that the auxiliary *be* was used in contexts where it was inappropriate (e.g., in sentences such as *the lion is go down*—not to mark progressives without the *-ing* morpheme, but rather with generic/habitual meanings and stative verbs).

The authors argue, based on these production data, that these children did have intact functional categories in their grammars; the fact that they often produced suppletive forms correctly suggests that tense and agreement features were not impaired. On the other hand, affixal inflections were apparently more difficult for them to learn because *-s* and *-ed* are less accessibly related to tense and agreement in English. That is, whereas the auxiliary/copula be raises to tense, the lack of thematic verb-raising in English (e.g., for verbs such as *likes*) means that the third-person singular *-s* is separated from tense, where features are checked.

As a follow up to analyzing these production data, Ionin and Wexler elicited grammaticality judgments from 18 young Russian-speaking learners of English (ages 6-14), 12 of whom had participated in the production part of the study, in order to investigate how they treated suppletive versus affixal agreement morphology.

There were 56 test sentences. Due in part to the young age of the participants and in part to the difficulty some of them had in reading English, the task was presented in an oral format. Because a group format seemed inadvisable, the participants were given the test in their homes or individually at school. The instructions were given in Russian, and the investigator talked through practice sentences with each child to make sure that grammaticality rather than meaning would be the focus of their responses. (The practice sentences were in Russian or simple English, with the ungrammatical ones containing errors other than verbal inflection

(Box 4.12 Continued)

95

Box 4.12 Continued

errors.) The children had to respond "yes" or "no" according to the grammaticality. At times (unspecified by the researchers), the children were also asked to make corrections when they responded that sentences were ungrammatical.

The results, showing differences between suppletive and affixal morphology, supported the production data. Furthermore, the finding that the more advanced learners were able to learn both types of agreement suggests that this is not an enduring problem.

Pictures. Although not eliciting acceptability judgments per se, a slight variation on acceptability tasks involves the use of pictures. In these situations, learners might have to match a sentence with a picture or provide a judgment about a sentence in relation to an accompanying picture, as in a study by Montrul (2001), who used a picture judgment task to examine L1 transfer in the acquisition of L2 argument structure (namely, overgeneralization and undergeneralization errors with change-of-state and agentive manner-of-motion verbs). Information from these tasks may lead to inferences regarding grammaticality.[4] Box 4.13 describes a study in which a picture-selection task was used to investigate the interpretation of locative constructions by learners of English as an L2.

Box 4.13: A Study Using Sentence-Picture Matching to Assess Locative Constructions

Bley-Vroman, R., & Joo, H.-R. (2001). The acquisition and interpretation of English locative constructions by native speakers of Korean. *Studies in Second Language Acquisition, 23,* 207-219.

This study investigated the acquisition of English locative constructions, using a forced-choice picture-selection task to examine how Korean-speaking learners of English interpret locative alternations. The authors' focus was on sentences such as *John loaded hay onto the wagon* and *John loaded the wagon with hay*, in which a "figure" (*hay*) moves to a "ground" (*wagon*). Some verbs in English allow both of these sentence types, with different nuances of meaning (a "holism" effect), whereas others allow only a ground-object construction or a figure-object construction. For example, one can say in English *I sprayed*

---

[4]See Juffs (2001) for a discussion of the necessity of using pictures for some types of linguistic information and for an explanation of the drawbacks of using still pictures.

paint on the statue and *I sprayed the statue with paint* (alternating); however, other verbs, such as *fill* and *pour*, allow only one or the other, but not both: *I filled the glass with water* (ground-object) but **I filled water into the glass*, and *I poured water into the glass* (figure-object) but **I poured the glass with water*. The narrower constraints are thought to be more difficult to acquire.

The picture-selection task involved presenting participants (probably in writing, although this was not specified by the authors) with an English sentence of one of these verb types. Each sentence was accompanied by two two-picture story strips, as shown here (p. 211).

©Cambridge University Press. Reprinted with the permission of Cambridge University Press.

The first picture in each pair of picture strips was the same; it illustrated a person doing something (e.g., spraying). However, the second picture differed. In the figure, for example, the door is not completely covered with paint in the first picture strip, but it is wholly affected in the second. The assumption in this study was that native speakers of English, when presented with a sentence like *John sprayed the door with paint*, would select the picture showing the door completely covered, but would do so to a lesser extent with a sentence like *John sprayed paint on the door*. The participants (native speakers of English and Korean learners of English) were presented with a sentence and one of two pictures, one in which the ground argument is wholly affected (picture b) and one in which it is not wholly affected (picture a). They are told to match the sentence with the picture or to respond neither for sentences that did not reflect either picture (i.e., ungrammatical sentences).

The results showed that both the native speakers of English and Korean learners of English demonstrated evidence of the holism effect; however, the L2 learners did not show native-like knowledge of the narrow constraints on locatives.

4.3.1.2. Procedures

Corrections.   Certain assumptions that are often made with native speaker acceptability judgments cannot always be made with non-native speaker judgments. For instance, as alluded to earlier, one might reasonably be able to assume with native speakers that the area targeted by the researcher will also be the one targeted by the native speaker judge. With non-native speakers, on the other hand, this is not the case, because their grammars can be non-native-like in many ways. Thus, in order to ensure that the research focus of a study is the same as the focus of the non-native speaking participants, it is necessary to ask the learners to correct any sentences that they judge to be unacceptable. Given the sentence *She knows the woman whom is the sister of my friend*, for example, learners might judge this to be incorrect. But without their own correction of it, we cannot be sure what they think is incorrect about it. If our target is relative pronouns (*whom*) and they change the sentence to *She knows the woman whom is my sister's friend*, then we can make the assumption that they believe that *whom* is correct. This is an important consideration when contemplating scoring.

When should the participants make their corrections? This is generally done immediately following each judgment. In other words, participants judge a sentence as correct or incorrect and then immediately make corrections if the sentence has been judged incorrect. Instructions should generally include information about corrections as part of what the participants are expected to do, as shown in Box 4.14. This is an example of how a computer can be used to determine which sentences are to be corrected.

Box 4.14: A Study Using the Computer to Generate Sentences to Be Corrected with a Focus on Spanish Grammar and Lexicon

Gass, S., & Alvarez-Torres, M. (2005). Attention When?: An investigation of the ordering effect of input and interaction. *Studies in Second Language Acquisition, 27,* 1-31.

This study looked at the roles of input and interaction (in combination and alone) as factors promoting the learning of Spanish by native speakers of English. The study focused on gender agreement, the Spanish copula *estar* + location, and lexical items. A total of 102 learners participated and were assigned to one of five treatment conditions: input only, interaction only, input followed by interaction, interaction followed by input, and control. To determine the effects of these treatments, pre- and post-treatment acceptability judgments were collected from the participants via computer, using 24 sentences each time. At the end of the session, the computer

---

printed out all of the sentences that the participant had judged incorrect, at which point the participant was asked to make corrections. Instructions were as follows:

> In this exercise the computer will present a number of sentences in Spanish. Sentences will appear one at a time and for a specific period of time. On the lower part of the screen you will have two buttons: a button labeled "correcto" and a button labeled "incorrecto." Your task will be to decide whether the sentences are correct or incorrect and then hit the appropriate button. You will not be able to go back to the sentences that you have already completed. Before the exercise starts, you will have a practice session to familiarize yourself with the exercise format. Once you are done with the practice session, click start the test, type your ID and the appropriate number of the exercise (1 or 2), and hit enter.
>
> Once you have completed the exercise, the computer will print out a copy with those sentences that you have marked as incorrect. Please, write your user ID on the print-out and then make the appropriate corrections for those sentences.
>
> Results showed that, although the treatment effects were not identical for all language areas, the combination treatments (containing interaction and input in either order) were more effective than treatments with either input only or interaction only. The learners who engaged in interaction followed by input improved the most on gender agreement and *estar* + location constructions.

Instructions.   The idea of rating sentences for grammaticality/acceptability is novel to many participants, who often confuse "making sense" with judgments of grammaticality. For example, the sentence *The table bit the dog* is grammatical in the pure sense; there is a noun phrase and a transitive verb followed by another noun phrase. However, because the first noun is inanimate and the second is animate, the sentence does not make sense; tables cannot bite dogs. Instructions and the examples provided to participants, therefore, need to be carefully crafted.

Birdsong (1989, pp. 114-115) gives examples of some unsuccessful instructions:

- *Do the following sentences sound right?*
  This does not eliminate the problem of confounding grammaticality with sentences that are semantically anomalous.
- *Tell me if for you this makes a sentence.*
  A "sentence," such as "When will your grandmother arrive?," may be rejected because it is a *question* and not a *sentence*.

One of the most thorough sets of instructions, presented here, comes from Bley-Vroman, Felix, and Ioup (1988, p. 32) in their investigation of UG accessibility with a specific focus on *wh*-movement by Korean learners of English.

Sentence Intuitions

Speakers of a language seem to develop a "feel" for what is a possible sentence, even in the many cases where they have never been taught any particular rule.

For example, in Korean you may feel that sentences 1-3 sound like possible Korean sentences, whereas sentence 4 doesn't. (The sentences were actually presented in Korean.)

1) Young Hee's eyes are big.
2) Young Hee has big eyes.
3) Young Hee's book is big.
4) Young Hee has a big book.

Although sentences 2 and 4 are of the same structure, one can judge without depending on any rule that sentence 4 is impossible in Korean.

Likewise, in English, you might feel that the first sentence below sounds like it is a possible English sentence, whereas the second one does not:

1) John is likely to win the race.
2) John is probably to win the race.

On the following pages is a list of sentences. We want you to tell us for each one whether you think it sounds possible in English. Even native speakers have different intuitions about what is possible. Therefore, these sentences cannot serve the purpose of establishing one's level of proficiency in English. We want you to concentrate on how you feel about these sentences.

For the following sentences please tell us whether you feel they sound like possible sentences of English for you, or whether they sound like impossible English sentences for you. Perhaps you have no clear feeling for whether they are possible or not. In this case mark not sure.

Read each sentence carefully before you answer. Concentrate on the structure of the sentence. Ignore any problems with spelling, punctuation, etc. Please mark only one answer for each sentence. Make sure you have answered all 32 questions.

It is often beneficial if instructions can be translated into the native languages of the participants. The previous instructions would, of course, need to be modified according to the specific circumstances.

Scoring.   Scoring will depend on how the acceptability judgment task is set up. For example, researchers might ask for a dichotomous choice (i.e., the sentence is either good or not good), or they might ask for an indication of relative "goodness" on a Likert scale. There is little uniformity in the second language literature on this issue, but the choice will naturally influence scoring concerns. Consider a single issue of the journal *Studies in Second Language Acquisition*, in which two articles—both investigating L1 influence on the L2 acquisition of manner-of-motion verbs—use Likert scales for the participants' acceptability judgments, but with different ranges and numerical values. Inagaki (2001) uses a 5-point Likert scale (-2 = completely unnatural, 0 = not sure, +2 = completely natural), whereas Montrul (2001) uses a 7-point Likert scale (-3 = very unnatural, 0 = cannot decide, 3 = very natural).

In contrast to Inagaki and Montrul, some researchers elect not to allow the "not sure" or the middle of the road option and instead use a 4- or 6-point scale (see Hawkins & Chan, 1997). Juffs (2001) makes the important point that without a standard in the field, it is difficult to compare the results of studies. He also points out that having a positive and negative scale with a zero midpoint makes it unclear whether a zero response should be interpreted as a "don't know" or as a midpoint. His suggestion is to use a completely positive scale (e.g., ranging from 1-7). Another possibility is to put no numerical values on the scale itself, using only descriptors, as shown here.

x............x............x............x............x............,x............x
very natural   don't know   very unnatural

When scoring, it is also necessary for researchers to separate the grammatical from the ungrammatical sentences so that they can determine learners' knowledge of what is correct (i.e., grammatical), as well as their knowledge of what is ungrammatical (i.e., excluded by their second language grammar). For a researcher using a 5-point Likert scale, the following is a possible scoring scheme:

Grammatical sentences	Ungrammatical sentences
Definitely correct = 4	Definitely incorrect = 4
Probably correct = 3	Probably incorrect = 3
Don't know = 2	Don't know = 2
Probably incorrect = 1	Probably correct = 1
Definitely incorrect = 0	Definitely correct = 0

Researchers might also give partial credit for recognizing the location of errors even if the corrections themselves are not accurate (see Gass, Svetics, & Lemelin, 2003). In any event, before doing the actual scoring, it is important to consider the corrections that have been made. For example, assume that you are studying the acquisition of morphological endings and the following sentence appears: *The man walk to the subway.* If the learner marks this "incorrect," but then changes the second definite article on the test sheet to *a* without addressing the lack of inflectional morphology on *walk*, then you would want to ignore the correction and count the sentence as if the learner had said "correct" because the object of inquiry, morphological endings, was deemed to be correct.

Although acceptability judgments had their origins within formal linguistic approaches to the study of language and are most commonly used within the UG paradigm in SLA research, they are like many other elicitation techniques in that they are not limited to that paradigm. In adopting them as a technique, however, second language researchers must keep in mind that, whatever the research question, they may be difficult to use and interpret; they must therefore be used with caution and careful thought as well as with awareness of their advantages and limitations.

4.3.2 Magnitude Estimation

Magnitude estimation is a well-established research tool used in a variety of disciplines (see Bard, Robertson, & Sorace, 1996, for a detailed description and history). It is useful when researchers want to know not only how participants would rank items in relation to one another, but also how much better they would judge X to be than Y. It has recently been used in investigating grammatical knowledge as a matter of gradations (i.e., which sentences are more acceptable than others, and by how much) as opposed to absolutes (i.e., acceptable or not). People can easily rank a list of things in order, but magnitude estimation additionally provides perspective on whether each of the rankings is equidistant from the others and, if not, the degree of this dif-ference in rank. Two of the positive aspects of this method, as noted by Bard *et al.* (p. 41), are:

- Researchers do not set the number of values used to measure the property of interest. Because the categories are not predetermined and im-posed, the data produced are more informative as it is the participants who establish both the range and the distribution of the responses.

- Researchers can observe meaningful differences that directly reflect differences in the participants' impressions of the property being investigated. This is so because magnitude estimation allows researchers to subtract the score on one sentence from that of another and be confident about the magnitude of difference.

As mentioned previously, magnitude estimation is a ranking procedure whose scale is not imposed by the researcher, but rather is determined by the individual participants themselves. In order to elicit judgments in this way, a stimulus is presented (orally or visually) and each participant assigns it a numerical value. Each subsequent stimulus is then rated according to the basis established with the previous stimulus. Thus, if a rater gives a value of 20 for an initial stimulus, then a second stimulus that is perceived as being twice as good would be assigned a value of 40. It is common to train participants using the physical stimulus of line length. To do this, the raters are shown a line and asked to assign a numerical value to it. Following this, they are shown another line and asked to assign a number to it in comparison with the length of the previous line. To make sure that the participants understand the task, this can be repeated. It is best to tell them to begin with a scale larger than 10 so that subsequent ratings do not end up with small numbers with which it might be difficult to work. In other words, because ratings are multiples or factors of previous ratings, if a rater were to start with the value 2, giving the second stimulus half that value, the third stimulus, if smaller, would be a fraction, which can soon become unwieldy.

Box 4.15 describes the use of magnitude estimation in a second language study.

Box 4.15: A Study Using Magnitude Estimation to Investigate Unaccusativity

Sorace, A. (1993). Incomplete vs. divergent representations of unaccusativity in non-native grammars of Italian. *Second Language Research, 9,* 22–47.

This study investigates unaccusativity in near-native speakers of Italian, those whose native language is French, and those whose native language is English. Unaccusativity is a type of intransitivity. Unaccusative verbs are those where the surface subject is the underlying direct object. Sorace lists three types of verbs of this sort in Italian (p. 25):

(Box 4.15 Continued)

Box 4.15 Continued

1. verbs in regular alternation with a transitive alternant (*bagnarsi* 'get wet' and *aumentare* 'increase')
2. inherently reflexive verbs (*fidarsi* 'trust')
3. verbs with no lexicalized transitive alternant (*arrivare* 'arrive' and *correre* 'run')

Specifically, she considers the unaccusative hierarchy and auxiliary use in Italian (*essere* 'to be' and *avere* 'to have'). There are three properties investigated in this study:

1. *Essere*-selection with different types of unaccusative verbs reflected in the hierarchy (e.g., change of location, continuation of a state)
2. Optional auxiliary change (verbs that can use either auxiliary, e.g., *potere* 'to be able')
3. Instances of obligatory auxiliary change

Twenty-four English speakers and 20 French speakers, all near-native speakers of Italian, participated in the study.

Magnitude estimation was used to judge 48 sentences reflecting the grammatical constructions in this study and others that were not dealt with in this study. A complete description of the procedure is not available in this study (see Gass, Mackey, Alvarez-Torres, & Fernández-García, 1999, for an L2 study using magnitude estimation to investigate the role of practice in L2 learning). In the Gass *et al.* study, following work with line length as described earlier, the following instructions were given to raters who were asked to judge speech samples. Presumably, similar instructions were given in the Sorace study:

Instructions

You will hear nine tapes of different nonnative speakers of Spanish doing an on-line description in Spanish of a video they were watching. Your task is to rate their Spanish. Assign any number that seems appropriate to you to the first speech sample. This number will be your "base." Then assign successive numbers in such a way that they reflect your subjective impression (use a range wider than 10). For example, if a speech sample seems 20 times as good, assign a number 20 times as large as the first. If it seems one-fifth as good, assign a number one-fifth as large, and so forth. Use fractions, whole numbers, or decimals, but make each assignment proportional to how good you perceive the person's Spanish to be. (p. 581)

The results from the Sorace study suggest that near-native speakers are different from native speaker intuitions. Further, both groups of native speakers (French and English) are sensitive to the semantic categories of the unaccusative hierarchy. Finally, there are distinct differences between the two groups.

Reference

Gass, S., Mackey, A., Alvarez-Torres, M. J., & Fernández-García, M. (1999). The effects of task repetition on linguistic output. *Language Learning, 49,* 549-581.

4.3.3 Truth-Value Judgments and Other Interpretation Tasks

Truth-value judgments are a way of understanding how people interpret sentences; they have been used extensively in the study of L2 acquisition of reflexives. The following is an example of a truth-value token from Glew (1998):

Bill was sick and in the hospital. Nobody knew what was wrong with Bill. The hospital did a lot of tests on Bill to find out what was wrong. Bill had to wait a long time in his hospital room. Finally, a doctor came in to tell Bill why he was sick.

After the medical tests, the doctor informed Bill about himself.

True   False

Here, the appropriateness of the reflexive *himself* is determined by the context of the story. Provided with sufficient contextual information, participants are able to consider all possible referents (i.e., Bill or the doctor) in making their response. Creating stories of this sort is a difficult process, however, and all such stories should be piloted. To underscore the importance of pilot studies, consider another example that was created for a study on reflexives, but that was ruled out after preliminary testing because it produced multiple possible interpretations:

Sally drove Jane to a party. They had a good time, but Sally had too much to drink. Jane didn't want her to drive home so Jane offered to drive.

Sally was happy that Jane drove herself home.

True   False

This example was intended to elicit a response of "False" because the point was that Jane drove Sally home. Still, it is clear that the story could be interpreted as implying that Jane drove herself home as well. Needless to say, this example was not included in the final set of materials.[5] In Box 4.16, we present an example of a study that used truth-value judgments as a source of data collection.

Box 4.16: A Study Using Truth-Value Judgments to Investigate the Preterite-Imperfect Contrast in Spanish

Montrul, S., & Slabakova, R. (2003). Competence similarities between native and near-native speakers: An investigation of the preterite-imperfect contrast in Spanish. *Studies in Second Language Acquisition, 25,* 351-398.

This study is concerned with the L2 acquisition of tense and aspect. This area is known as one of the most difficult domains for L2 learners; however, some research (e.g., White & Genesee, 1996) has demonstrated that very advanced adult L2 learners can acquire tense and aspect successfully, even in cases where direct evidence from L1 knowledge is not available.

Montrul and Slabakova investigate whether the end state competence of advanced NNSs is comparable to the grammatical knowledge of NSs with respect to the interpretive properties of the preterite and imperfect past tenses in Spanish. They assume that tense-aspect is part of UG and that aspect is instantiated in a functional category. Their interest is in whether features of functional categories that are not selected when learning an L1 are subject to a critical period in SLA.

---

[5]Over the years, there have been other means of obtaining information about reflexives. This is a particularly difficult structure to investigate because many sentences are grammatical only given a particular context. Other than truth-value judgments discussed earlier, researchers have used multiple-choice formats. Lakshmanan and Teranishi (1994) have pointed out that a task such as the following is not satisfactory because we gain information about who *himself* can refer to, but not about who *himself* can<u>not</u> refer to.

> John said that Bill hit himself.
>> Who does *himself* refer to?
>> a. John
>> b. Bill
>> c. Either John or Bill
>> d. Another person
>> e. Don't know

They offer the following revision (see their original article for an interpretation of results):

> John said that Bill saw himself in the mirror.
>> a. 'Himself' cannot be John.   agree   disagree
>> b. 'Himself' cannot be Bill.   agree   disagree

For further discussion of methodological points with regard to the study of reflexives, see Akiyama (2002).

Twenty NSs of Spanish from various countries and 64 NNSs of Spanish (with advanced proficiency) participated in this study. First, the non-native speakers took tests of comprehension and oral production and were classified into three groups: near-native (n = 17, high scores in both), superior (n = 23, high scores in comprehension, low scores in production), and advanced (n = 24, low scores in both). Two tasks were then administrated to all participants: a sentence-conjugation judgment task, and a truth-value judgment task. We focus here on the truth-value judgment task.

In the truth-judgment task, three conditions were devised to assess meaning contrasts associated with perfective/imperfective distinctions: (a) stative predicates that shift to eventives with the preterite, (b) habitual versus one-time events in the past, and (c) generic versus specific subject interpretation of empty pronouns in impersonal *se* constructions. The participants read 80 stories followed by sentences which they were asked to judge as *true* or *false*. Forty sentences were in the preterite (PRET) and 40 in the imperfect (IMPF); twelve were distractors. An example from each of the three conditions (translated into English) is given here:

Change-of-meaning preterites with stative or eventive interpretations

Last Christmas Carmen gives a party for all her old high school friends. Among all the guests are Marcos and Susana, who don't see each other very often. When Marcos and Susana chat with each other, Marcos asks Susana about her family. Susana tells him that her family is now living in Barcelona.

Marcos met (*conoció*-PRET) Susana (for the first time).　　F
Marcos knew (*conocía*-IMPF) Susana.　　T

Habitual versus one-time events

Laurita had many friends and after school she would spend time at her neighbors' house. Yesterday Laurita stayed at home with her mother and had a very good time.

Laurita played (*jugaba*-IMPF) with her neighbors.　　T
Laurita played (*jugó*-PRET) with her neighbors.　　F

Generic versus specific subject interpretation

According to the newspaper, the restaurant on Jefferson Street was very good and customers were always happy with the service. Unfortunately, the restaurant closed last summer and we never got to go.

One ate (se *comía*-IMPF) well at that restaurant.　　T
We ate (se *comió*-PRET) well at that restaurant.　　F

(Box 4.16 Continued)

Box 4.16 Continued

Their findings in both tasks, in short, were that the near-native group performed like the NS group, whereas the advanced and superior groups were significantly different from the NS group. The results indicate that there can be competence similarities between NSs and NNSs in the ultimate attainment of semantic interpretations, at least within the realm of aspectual distinctions. In addition, the results support the idea that L2 learners can access (+/- perfective) formal features even after a critical age.

Reference

White, L., & Genesee, F. (1996). How native is near-native? The issue of ultimate attainment in adult second language acquisition. *Second Language Research, 12,* 233-265.

4.3.4 Sentence Matching

Sentence matching is a procedure that, like acceptability judgments, has its origins in another discipline, in this case psycholinguistics. We include sentence matching in this chapter because its use in second language research has typically been to determine what learners believe to be grammatical versus ungrammatical. Sentence-matching tasks are usually performed on a computer, where participants are presented with a sentence that is either grammatical or ungrammatical. After a short delay, a second sentence appears on the screen, with the first sentence remaining in place. The participants are asked to decide as quickly as possible whether or not the sentences are identical (i.e., whether or not they match), entering their decision by pressing specific keys. The time from the appearance of the second sentence to the participant's pressing of the key is recorded and used in the analysis. Research with native speakers has shown that participants in a matching task respond faster to matched grammatical sentences than they do to matched ungrammatical sentences (See Gass, 2001, for possible explanations of this phenomenon). In other words, the reaction time would be expected to be less for the following two sentences:

John stated his plan to steal the car.

John stated his plan to steal the car.

than for the following:

John stated his plan for steal his car.

John stated his plan for steal his car.

Box 4.17 presents an example of a study that used sentence matching to investigate L2 learners' knowledge of clitics in French.

Box 4.17: A Study Using Sentence Matching

Duffield, N., Montrul, S., Bruhn de Garavito, J., & White, L. (1998). Determining L2 knowledge of Spanish clitics on-line and off-line. In A. Greenhill *et al.* (Eds.), *Proceedings of the 22nd annual Boston University Conference on Language Development* (pp. 177-188). Somerville, MA: Cascadilla Press.

This study investigates knowledge of clitics in L2 Spanish among native speakers of English (n = 19) and native speakers of French (n = 13). There were also 10 native speakers of Spanish used as a control. Data were collected using grammaticality judgment tasks, as well as a sentence-matching task. Here, we focus on the sentence-matching task, which was administered using PsyScope (J. D. Cohen, MacWhinney, Flatt & Provost, 1993) on a Macintosh computer with a button box.

There were 10 conditions in this study representing different aspects of the use of accusative clitics. In each condition, there were 8 grammatical and 8 ungrammatical sentence pairs. Word frequency, sentence length, and plausibility were counterbalanced through the division of participants into two groups. For those sentences presented in ungrammatical versions for the first group, participants in the second group received grammatical ones, and vice versa. The sentence-matching results were analyzed in terms of response times of all of the matching pairs that had been correctly identified as the same. Individual learners were eliminated if they had an error rate greater than 12.5%. Additionally, test items were eliminated for having high error rates (the authors did not specify what this level was).

The results of this study showed that learners can indeed learn the word order possibilities of clitics in an L2. In addition, because the authors also administered an offline grammaticality judgment task, they were able to show that sentence matching can also be used to assess grammaticality (at least in the area of clitics). In other words, the sentences judged to be ungrammatical in the offline task were those that took longer to respond to in the sentence-matching task.

Reference

Cohen, J. D., MacWhinney, B., Flatt, M., & Provost, J. (1993). PsyScope: A new graphic interactive environment for designing psychology experiments. *Behavior Research Methods, Instruments and Computers, 25,* 257-271.

With regard to general design, there are many decisions to be made when creating a sentence-matching task, and researchers are not in agreement as to the best solutions. There are a list of variables that need to be weighed when designing a study using a sentence-matching task.

Things to Consider in Designing Sentence-Matching Tasks

- How long the two sentences remain on the screen
- The amount of delay time between the two sentences
- Whether or not the two sentences remain on the screen until the participant has responded
- Whether or not the screen goes blank after a predetermined time
- Whether standard orthography or uppercase letters are used
- The physical placement of the second sentence relative to the first
- Whether participants are provided with feedback after each response
- How the keys are labeled (same, different; different, same)
- The number of items included
- The number of practice items included
- Whether participants control the onset of each pair of sentences

---

Another consideration when using sentence-matching tasks relates to the question of which data should be kept in the final data pool. For example, a participant might simply press the "same" key with no variation. Given that this individual's data are probably not reflective of anything other than not being on task, a researcher might decide to eliminate these data.

4.4 CONCLUSION

This chapter has dealt with elicitation techniques that focus on eliciting data to reflect what learners know about language. We have considered techniques that elicit actual production data, as well as techniques that elicit responses to data in an effort to determine what learners know about an L2 at various stages of proficiency. These are known as offline measures. The next chapter focuses, in particular, on interaction-based research, an area of research that uniquely brings together a focus on linguistic knowledge (the current chapter) and psycholinguistic processing (Chaps. 2 and 3).

CHAPTER 5

Interaction-Based Research

Over the past 25 years, interaction research has come to play a dominant role in our explorations of how second languages are learned. Beginning with research in the early 1980s, scholars have considered how conversational interaction can facilitate acquisition. The interaction approach to second language acquisition research "takes as a starting point the assumption that language learning is stimulated by communicative pressure and examines the relationship between communication and acquisition and the mechanisms (e.g., noticing, attention) that mediate between them" (Gass, 2003, p. 224). Long (1996) specified this within the framework of the interaction hypothesis, explaining the interaction-L2 learning relationship as follows: "*Negotiation for meaning*, and especially negotiation work that triggers *interactional* adjustments by the NS or more competent interlocutor, facilitates acquisition because it connects input, internal learner capacities, particularly selective attention, and output in productive ways" (emphasis in original, pp. 451-452).

In a prototypical interaction study, learners' interactions are recorded, and instances of interactional modifications, such as recasts and negotiation (e.g., clarification requests, comprehension checks), are tallied and analyzed based on the hypothesis that these interaction routines result in some kind of change in second language knowledge (see Gass & Varonis, 1994; Mackey, 1999). The next sections provide more detailed information on the most common types of data collection procedures in interaction-based research, including naturalistic data, prompted production, prompted responses, and introspective data. As in other chapters, these categorizations will be helpful for the purposes of exposition, but readers should keep in mind that they are necessarily somewhat oversimplified. In many instances, there is overlap among task types, and flexible researchers can benefit from creative combinations of the features of multiple data collection techniques.

5.1 NATURALISTIC DATA

One method for studying the role of interaction in second language development is to audio- or videotape naturally occurring conversations, such as those that take place at school or in the workplace. Often the method of choice for researchers conducting longitudinal studies, naturalistic data collection has the potential to help researchers gain a deeper understanding of the social and contextual nature of language use—an understanding that might be difficult to obtain if the researcher were to rely solely on language elicited in experimental laboratory conditions. Noting that much SLA research uses "static snapshots" and experimental techniques to make inferences about L2 development, Ortega and Iberri-Shea (2005) emphasize the importance of such longitudinal studies. They point out that quantitative descriptive (i.e., non-experimental) studies have illuminated various aspects of L2 development over time, focusing, for example, on L2 learners' pronunciation or their mark- ing of tense and aspect. In addition, qualitative interpretive studies have inves- tigated sociocognitive and sociocultural dimensions of language development. An example of a longitudinal study using naturalistic data is provided in Box 5.1.

Box 5.1: A Study Using Naturalistic Data to Investigate Variation

Tarone, E., & Liu, G.-Q. (1995). Situational context, variation, and second language acquisition theory. In G. Cook & B. Seidlhofer (Eds.), *Principle and practice in applied linguistics: Studies in honour of H. G. Widdowson* (pp. 107-124). Oxford, England: Oxford University Press.

Drawing on naturalistic data from a 26-month longitudinal study, Tarone and Liu describe the social interactions and L2 development of a Chinese boy named "Bob" from approximately age 5 to age 7. The authors note that, because learners "may seem to have mastered a given target language (TL) form in one social context, yet in another social context systematically produce a quite different (and possibly inaccurate) variant of that form" (p. 107), it is important to attempt to explain not only why IL performance varies across interactional contexts, but also how this is related to SLA.

Over the course of the study, Bob's interactions were videotaped, transcribed, and coded for a variety of factors, including the number and complexity of his utterances and whether these utterances were initiations or responses. The researchers also analyzed Bob's development of question forms. Three main types of

---

social interactions were observed and defined in terms of Bob's "role relationships" with different interlocutors: namely, his primary school peers, his teachers, and the researcher.

Quantitative analyses of Bob's language in each of these settings showed differences in linguistic complexity, variety of speech acts, and proportion of initiations, among other things. With his teachers, Bob appeared to be concerned with doing well and getting good grades; he did not tend to initiate interactions or take linguistic risks with complex structures. With his peers, on the other hand, Bob was more assertive, speaking more fluently and incorporating his friends' modeling of particular forms. Finally, with the researcher, Bob used a wide variety of language functions as well as complex syntax—to the extent, in fact, that he seemed to be at a higher proficiency level when interacting with the researcher than in the other contexts. Tarone and Liu argue further that the interactional features of each context may have had differential impacts on Bob's linguistic competence. Using Pienemann and Johnston's (1987) framework to examine the development of question forms, they note that evidence for almost every new stage in the developmental sequence appeared in Bob's interactions with the researcher much earlier than in the other settings. They suggest that this may have had to do with the quality of the input and the production of comprehensible output, in which Bob was pushed to stretch his linguistic resources (Swain, 1995). In sum, they take the results to show that "a learner's participation in different kinds of social interactions can result in different patterns in the longitudinal development of IL grammars" (p. 109).

References

Pienemann, M., & Johnston, M. (1987). Factors influencing the development of language proficiency. In D. Nunan (Ed.), *Applying second language acquisition research* (pp. 45-141). Adelaide, Australia: National Curriculum Resource Centre, AMEP.

Swain, M. (1995). Three functions of output in second language learning. In G. Cook & B. Seidlhofer (Eds.), *Principle and practice in applied linguistics* (pp.125-144). Oxford, England: Oxford University Press.

Although a number of valuable interaction-based studies have made profitable use of naturalistic data, as with all data collection methods, some caveats need to be mentioned. The first concerns the researcher's goals: If a researcher is seeking to investigate a learner's use of a particular linguistic structure (e.g., questions), then there simply may not be enough instances to examine in a given sample of naturally occurring data. In order to address this, the researcher may have to invest a considerable amount of time in recording language samples of L2 learners in order to gather enough examples to analyze. For this reason, tasks that make production of the targeted structure *essential* (or at least highly useful) can help researchers to collect more data than they would be able to through relying on naturalistic data alone (see the task-natural/task-useful/task-essential distinction of Loschky, 1994, and Loschky & Bley-Vroman, 1993, as well as a later section on prompted production tasks). The second caveat concerns the effect of tape-recording "naturally occurring" conversations. When learners are aware that their conversations are being re-corded, this may make their conversations less "natural" than they would be without the presence of the recorder or the researcher. (The fact that the act of observing can impact what is being observed is known as the observer's para-dox, as discussed in Chap.3; Labov, 1972). Perhaps for these reasons, the use of naturalistic data in interaction-based research is less common than the use of prompted production data.

5.2 PROMPTED PRODUCTION

Simply put, prompted production refers to the use of tasks that encourage (or "prompt") learners to produce language. As mentioned earlier, such tasks are often designed to elicit particular language structures and can greatly facilitate the data collection process. This is especially important in interaction-based research, because the point of many studies in this area is to investigate rela-tionships among the various components of interaction and the learning of various types of linguistic targets. Prompted production represents a highly efficient means of manipulating the kinds of interactions that learners are in-volved in, as well as the kinds of feedback they receive, and examining the characteristics of the output that learners produce. This section covers several of the most common types of prompted production data collection proce-dures, including picture descriptions, spot-the-difference tasks, story-comple-tion activities, map tasks, consensus tasks, and consciousness-raising tasks.

5.2.1 Picture-Description Tasks

Picture-description tasks typically involve having a learner describe a picture to a partner who cannot see the picture. For example, a learner may have a pic-ture of a park scene to describe to a partner, who in turn attempts to draw the scene on a sheet of paper. This type of picture-description activity would be considered a "one-way" task because one learner holds all the information and that information flows in one direction (i.e., from the picture-holder to the lis-tener). An example of a study employing picture-description tasks (as well as spot-the-difference tasks, discussed later) is presented in Box 5.2.

There are some important considerations to keep in mind when having learners carry out picture-description tasks. First of all, it is necessary to ensure that the describer's picture cannot be seen by the person tasked with reproducing the illustration based on verbal instructions. One way to accomplish this is through the use of a barrier, which can be made of cardboard or even a simple file folder (see Figure 5.1). Incidentally, this setup can be used for any sort of task in which participants should not be able to view each other's materials. Second, learners should receive explicit instructions to the effect that they are not allowed to show their pictures to their partners. These instructions can be provided orally (by reading a script), in writing, or via audiotape. The latter two methods, in particular, ensure that the instructions provided to all learners in the study are identical. Additional considerations are outlined in a set of guidelines applicable to both picture-description and spot-the-difference tasks.

5.2.2 Spot-the-Difference Tasks

Spot-the-difference tasks utilize pictures that are identical except for a predetermined number of modifications. When asked to find the differences through verbal interaction, participants are often told how many differences there are so that they have a goal to work toward. Because spot-the-difference tasks require two (or more) participants, each of whom holds different

Figure 5.1.   Set-up for a picture-description task.

information, to exchange that information, they are considered "two-way" tasks (also known as "jigsaw" tasks).

Figures 5.2a and 5.2b are examples of pictures that can be used for spot-the-difference tasks between two or three participants, respectively. Figure 5.2a depicts an "underwater" scene that can be used to elicit locatives, plurals, and, as with most spot-the-difference tasks, questions. The vocabulary is somewhat difficult (e.g., *submarine, scuba diver, sea monster*), but feasible to use with advanced learners or after preteaching vocabulary. The picture is also rather "busy," but can be simplified to meet the needs of the learners at hand.

Figure 5.2a. Spot-the-difference underwater scene task. Drawn by Jamie Lepore Wright. Printed with permission.

Figure 5.2b shows a kitchen scene that can be used with three participants (or two, by using only two of the three pictures). Again, question forms, locative constructions, and plural forms may be produced and investigated, along with (easier) household vocabulary.

Figure 5.2b. Spot-the-difference kitchen. Courtesy of Jane Ozanich, printed with permission.

Box 5.2: A Study Using Picture-Description and Spot-the-Difference Tasks to Investigate Evidence Types

Iwashita, N. (2003). Negative feedback and positive evidence in task-based interaction: Differential effects on L2 development. *Studies in Second Language Acquisition, 25,* 1-36.

In a study employing both picture-description and spot-the-difference tasks, Iwashita divided 55 beginning learners of Japanese as a foreign language into two groups: one that participated in task-based interaction (TBI) with a native speaker of Japanese (the treatment group) and another that participated in free conversation with a NS of Japanese (the control group). Using a pretest, posttest, delayed posttest design, Iwashita measured the participants' performance on a variety of Japanese grammatical structures, including the Japanese locative-initial structure and a particular verb form known as the "*te*-form."

One of Iwashita's research questions addressed whether there was any significant difference between the treatment and control groups in terms of their performance on the posttest and delayed posttest. She found that those learners who had participated in task-based interaction significantly outperformed the control group on both posttests, leading her to conclude that TBI facilitates the short-term development of L2 grammatical competence. The likely reason for this, she argued, was that TBI "fostered the natural use of target grammar structures" (p. 27), whereas free conversation did not. Her study thus supports Loschky's (1994, Loschky & Bley-Vroman, 1993) claim that focused task-based interactions in which targeted linguistic structures are essential or at least useful for task completion can facilitate learning.

References

Loschky, L. (1994). Comprehensible input and second language acquisition: What is the relationship? *Studies in Second Language Acquisition, 16,* 303-323.

Loschky, L., & Bley-Vroman, R. (1993). Grammar and task-based methodology. In G. Crookes & S. M. Gass (Eds.), *Tasks and language learning: Integrating theory and practice* (pp. 123-167). Clevedon, England: Multilingual Matters.

Below we present guidelines that can be used for picture-description as well as spot-the-difference tasks.

Guidelines for picture-description and spot-the-difference tasks

- Find pictures containing items that are easy to describe, but also vocabulary that is likely to cause some lack of understanding (and, hence, some negotiation). This might also involve eliciting language regarding the placement of objects (e.g., *above, on top of*).
- Ensure that the locations of items in the pictures are appropriate for the desired level of difficulty. For example, a picture with a car placed on top of a house would add another element of difficulty to the task.
- Where relevant, make sure that the task elicits the linguistic structures or forms of interest.
- Ensure that the task creates sufficient opportunities for interactional modifications, feedback, and output based on the research question(s).
- Separate the participants with a barrier or at least ensure that partners cannot see each other's pictures.

  For picture-description tasks:
  > Make sure the participants understand that the person who is drawing should not see the picture being described until the task is completed.

  For spot-the-difference tasks:
  > Make sure that the participants do not show their pictures to each other. Inform them about the number of differences if necessary.
- As always, carefully pilot-test the task.

5.2.3 Story-Completion Tasks

Another example of a two-way task is the story-completion task (also known as a narrative task). In this type of task, learners are given different parts of a story in written or pictorial form with instructions to work together to make a complete story. Figure 5.3 provides an example of this sort of task.

In order to construct this story, the learners take turns describing their pictures and attempt to come to a consensus on how to sequence them. Learners given the pictures in Figure 5.3, for example, would most likely order them to construct a story such as the following: While two friends were away playing tennis, a robber broke into the house through a window to steal a wallet. The robber was chased by a dog, however, and dropped the wallet. Later, one of the tennis players found the wallet while gardening and was surprised because he did not know that the dog had buried it. Box 5.3 contains an example of a study that used a story-completion task (among others) to investigate the effects of planning and task type on learners' L2 use.

Figure 5.3. Story-completion task. Courtesy of Jenefer Philp, printed with permission.

Box 5.3: A Study Using a Story-Completion Task to Investigate Planning and Task Type

Foster, P., & Skehan, P. (1996). The influence of planning and task type on second language performance. *Studies in Second Language Acquisition, 18*, 299-323.

In an experiment employing tasks to study the effects of planning time and task type on L2 performance, Foster and Skehan divided 32 college students learning English as a foreign language at the pre-intermediate level into three groups: a control group and two experimental groups. All learners worked in pairs to carry out three tasks: a personal information-exchange task, in which the students gave directions on how to reach their own homes in order to turn off a gas cooker; a decision-making task, in which the students were required to dole out prison sentences; and a narrative (story-completion) task, in which the students were asked to sequence a series of pictures and construct a story. One of the experimental groups was simply told to use 10 minutes to plan, whereas the other experimental group, given the same amount of time, was given suggestions on how to make use of their planning time. The control group received no planning time before engaging in the tasks.

The researchers hypothesized that, because the tasks involved different levels of complexity and difficulty (the personal task being relatively easy as it involved familiar information, the narrative task being of intermediate difficulty as it required using some imagination to order new visual information, and the decision-making task being the most difficult as it required dyads to come to an agreement on complex issues), there would be task effects on the fluency, accuracy, and complexity of the language the learners produced. More specifically, it was hypothesized that easier tasks would require less cognitive effort and therefore facilitate greater attention to the language being produced (i.e., greater fluency, accuracy, and complexity).

Concerning the narrative task, Foster and Skehan found, as predicted, that it did not lead to the greatest levels of fluency; however, it did lead to the greatest levels of complexity and was in fact associated with the lowest levels of linguistic accuracy. This led the researchers to conclude that there are trade-offs between accuracy and complexity in cognitively demanding tasks and that learners with limited capacities to attend to all features of the target language may focus on one at the expense of the other. They found that planning time had the greatest effect on the narrative task.

The results of this study thus provide evidence that there are important interactions between task characteristics and task implementation that may significantly affect the language that L2 learners produce.

As with picture-description and spot-the-difference tasks, it is important to ensure that the pictures in story-completion tasks are appropriate for the level of the participants in terms of vocabulary. With regard to implementation, it is once again crucial that the participants not see their partners' pictures.

5.2.4 Map Tasks

A map task is another example of a jigsaw task. Here, participants are given a map of a section of a city. In one variation of this task type, each participant is provided (orally or in writing) with different information about street closings, and they must explain to each other which streets are closed and when. Once this portion is completed, they have to work together to determine a route from Point A to Point B by car, keeping in mind that certain streets are closed. An example of a map task is provided in Figure 5.4.

In another variation of the map task, learners are given similar maps, but with each map containing different place markers. For example, Participant 1 may be given a map marking the location of the library, city hall, and post office, whereas Participant 2 is provided with a map showing the location of the high school, pharmacy, and bank. Each participant is then given a list of locations to find and thus needs to ask a partner for those locations.

5.2.5 Consensus Tasks

Consensus tasks, another type of jigsaw task, generally involve pairs or groups of learners who must arrive at an agreement on a certain issue. For example, learners might be told that 10 individuals are stranded on an island, but only 5 can fit into a boat to get back to the mainland. Characteristics are provided for each individual, and the pair or group must decide which 5 people should be allowed to get on the boat. Box 5.4 provides an example of a study that employed this type of task.

Box 5.4: A Study Using a Consensus Task to Investigate Task Type

Slimani-Rolls, A. (2005). Rethinking task-based language learning: What we can learn from the learners. *Language Teaching Research, 9,* 195-218.

In a study using a consensus task, Slimani-Rolls recruited 20 students of French for Business Purposes to complete three tasks: (a) a consensus task, which required the students to reach an agreement on marketing strategies for a new Paris restaurant; (b) a one-way information exchange, which involved having the students describe an admired celebrity to a partner; and (c) a two-way information exchange, in which the students exchanged information in order to complete a table

---

on French household spending. Taking as her point of departure the argument sometimes made in SLA studies that two-way tasks engender more negotiation for meaning (referred to in this study as "conversational adjustments") than other types of tasks, she sought to determine whether this was, in fact, the case.

Slimani-Rolls did find that the two-way information exchange led to more conversational adjustments than either the consensus task or the one-way information exchange; however, she also noted that there was a considerable degree of individual variation on the two-way information exchange, with over half of the conversational adjustments stemming from only three learners, and with four learners producing no adjustments at all. To investigate this further, Slimani-Rolls employed interviews to determine why the learners did (or did not) make use of conversational adjustments. She found that many of the learners thought that completing the tasks (and, in particular, completing the table involved in the two-way task) was more important than achieving mutual comprehensibility and, furthermore, that they refrained from making clarification requests out of a sense of politeness. She suggests, therefore, that in addition to task characteristics, individual and social concerns need to be taken into account when making decisions about which tasks to use in interaction-based research.

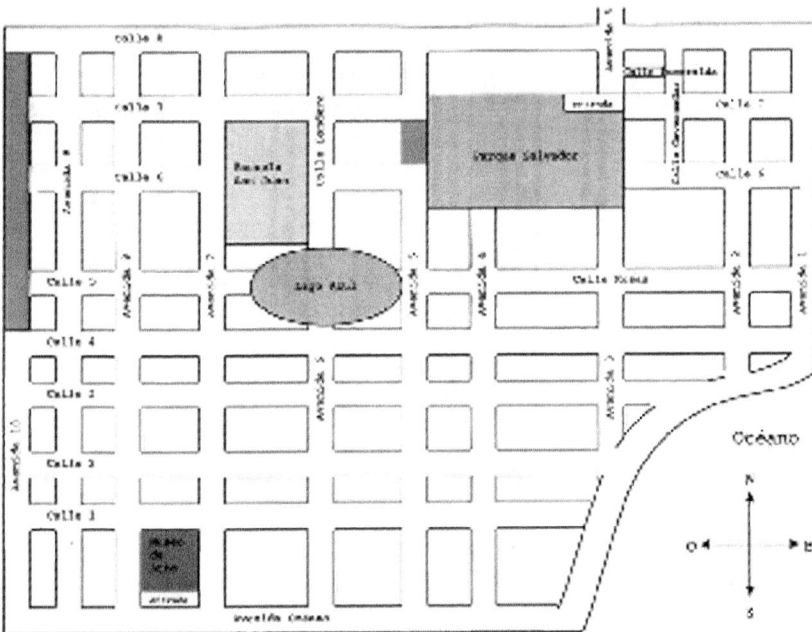

Participant 1	Participant 2
• La avenida 10 está cerrada entre la calle 4 y la calle 8.	• La avenida 5 está cerrada entre la calle 6 y la calle 7.
Avenue 10 is closed between Street 4 and Street 8.	*Avenue 5 is closed between Street 6 and Street 7.*
• La calle 5 está cerrada desde el Lago Azul hasta la avenida 10.	• La avenida 8 va en una sola dirección hacia el sur.
Street 5 is closed from the Blue Lake to Avenue 10.	*Avenue 8 goes in a single direction towards the south.*
• La avenida Oceano va en una sola dirección hacia el oeste.	• La avenida 2 estará cerradá todo el dia.
Ocean Avenue goes in a single direction towards the west.	*Avenue 2 will be closed all day.*

Figure 5.4. A map task. From "Task-Based Interactions in Classroom and Laboratory Settings," by S. Gass, A. Mackey, & L. Ross-Feldman, 2005, *Language Learning, 55*, p. 610.

Consensus tasks may perhaps allow for more open discussion than others do; however, as suggested by Slimani-Rolls's (2005) study in Box 5.4, they do not guarantee that there will be interaction. One individual might not participate, or, if the task is not engaging, then the learners might take only a few minutes to reach a decision without giving elaborate justifications for their arguments. As with other data collection methods, instructions are important to ensure that the learners understand the need to participate. Instructions could also stipulate that members of the group be assigned different roles; for instance, returning to our boat example, each participant could be assigned to support a different boat candidate and be required to argue for that person's suitability for rescue.

Another type of consensus task is a dictogloss task (see Box 5.5), a task that encourages learners to focus on form and meaning simultaneously. In this type of task, learners work together to reconstruct a text that has been read to them. Usually, the text is read aloud twice at normal speed (although this could be modified for the specific purposes of a study), which makes it so that the participants cannot write down everything they hear. Students listening to the text may be instructed to take notes on the first reading, the second reading, both, or neither, depending on the researcher's goals. Following the readings, participants can then work in dyads or small groups to reconstruct the text as faithfully as possible. The choice of text (e.g., based on its content, vocabulary, or particular grammatical structures) will naturally depend on the particular research goals at hand.

Box 5.5: A Study Using a Dictogloss Task to Investigate Task Type

Swain, M., & Lapkin, S. (2000). Task-based second language learning: The uses of the first language. *Language Teaching Research, 4(3),* 251-274.

In this study, Swain and Lapkin sought to compare L1 use by eighth-grade French immersion students engaged in two types of task: a dictogloss task and a picture-sequencing task. In the former, the students listened to a native-speaker rendition of a story involving an alarm clock; pairs of students were then asked to create a written version of the story. In the latter, dyads were given a sequence of pictures depicting the same story and were required to produce a written text. Swain and Lapkin found that the students used comparable amounts of English while engaged in the two different tasks. However, they also report that students engaged in the picture-sequencing task used considerably more of their L1 turns to search for L2 vocabulary items (27%), whereas students engaged in the dictogloss task devoted fewer of their L1 turns (14%) to this purpose. This result, the researchers explain, may be due to the fact that the dictogloss task provided the students with the necessary lexical items, whereas the picture-sequencing task required them to come up with appropriate L2 vocabulary on their own. Swain and Lapkin also investigated whether there was a link between L1 use and the quality of the written texts that the two groups of students produced. For both tasks, it appeared that students producing texts judged to be of higher quality tended to use the L1 less. However, this trend was statistically significant only for the students engaged in the picture-sequencing task. Commenting on this finding, as well as on the considerable individual variation that was observed, the researchers note that there are important interactions between task characteristics (e.g., whether the input is provided orally or visually) and task performance. They also conclude that other variables, such as social and affective factors, can play a significant role as well.

5.2.6 Consciousness-Raising Tasks

As the name implies, consciousness-raising tasks are intended to facilitate learners' cognitive processes in terms of their awareness of some linguistic structure or area of language. In these tasks, learners are often required to verbalize their thoughts about language on their way to a solution. An example of such a task is provided in Box 5.6.

Box 5.6: A Study Using a Consciousness-Raising Task to Investigate Instructional Tasks

Fotos, S., & Ellis, R. (1991). Communicating about grammar: A task-based approach. *TESOL Quarterly, 25*, 605-628.

In this study, the researchers employed a pretest, posttest, delayed posttest design to compare a consciousness-raising task with a more traditional, teacher fronted grammar lesson. Using two groups of Japanese university students (intermediate-level English majors at a women's college and business administration majors studying English at the basic level at another university), the researchers had half of the learners in each group complete a consciousness-raising task involving dative alternation (*I gave books to my friends* vs. *I gave my friends books* and *I suggested a plan for her* vs. **I suggested her a plan*). These learners were further divided into small groups, and each member of the group was given a different task card, which listed a number of grammatical and ungrammatical sentences involving dative verbs. Learners in the consciousness-raising task groups were required to exchange the information on the task cards in order to complete a chart and come up with three rules governing dative alternation in English. The remaining learners participated in a traditional grammar lesson, in which the teacher wrote on the board the sentences that had been provided on the task cards, pointing out the positions of the indirect objects. At the end of the lesson, the teacher wrote out three rules concerning dative alternation.

The researchers found that for both the intermediate and basic learners of English, and for both the consciousness-raising (CR) group and grammar-lesson (GL) group, there were significant improvements from pretest to posttest (each of which consisted of a grammaticality judgment test). However, Fotos and R. Ellis also report that the mean score received by the intermediate-level CR group on the delayed posttest (which was administered 2 weeks after the first posttest) was significantly lower than that obtained by the GL group. For the basic-level learners, the results also favored the traditional grammar lesson, as the difference between the pretest and posttest for the CR group was significantly smaller than that seen in the GL group. The researchers speculate that these results may have been due to the basic-level Japanese learners' relative lack of familiarity with pair/group work and their imperfect understanding of task requirements and procedures, although they might also be due to the fact that the teacher gave the GL group rules, whereas the rules in the CR group were learner generated.

Nevertheless, based on the fact that learners in the CR group did make notable gains in performance on the grammaticality judgment test, the researchers argue that tasks that encourage communication about grammar may have a significant role in the acquisition of the L2.

5.3 PROMPTED RESPONSES

In addition to prompted production tasks, interaction researchers have also made use of prompted response tasks to collect data. In this type of task, learners are not asked to produce language, but rather to manipulate objects in response to an interlocutor's instructions. For this reason, prompted response tasks may be said to be primarily designed to assess students' *comprehension* of the target language. In one typical prompted response task, a kitchen object placement task (see Figure 5.5 and Box 5.7), a learner is given a picture of a kitchen scene and several small cut-out objects, such as kitchen utensils and appliances. After listening to an interlocutor's instructions (e.g., "Place the toaster to the right of the refrigerator"), learners carry out the in structions to the best of their ability.

Box 5.7: A Study Using a Prompted Response Task to Investigate Instructional Treatment

Ellis, R., Tanaka, Y., & Yamazaki, A. (1994). Classroom interaction, comprehension, and the acquisition of L2 word meanings. *Language Learning, 44*, 449-491.

In one study making use of a prompted response task, R. Ellis, Tanaka, and Yamazaki investigated the relationship between different types of input and the acquisition of English lexical items by Japanese high school students. Students receiving "baseline input" were required to listen to instructions on the placement of various kitchen objects and to mark the correct locations on a sheet of paper; these students were not allowed to ask for clarification if they did not understand the instructions. Students receiving "premodified input" were also forbidden from asking for clarification; however, the instructions they received were spoken at a slower rate and contained greater redundancies. For example, whereas students in the baseline group heard, "We have an apple. And I'd like you to put the apple in the sink" (p. 462), the students in the premodified group received the instructions, "I have an apple. And I'd like you to put the apple in the sink. A sink is a hole and you wash dishes inside it and you fill it with water. It's a hole in the counter to put water and dishes" (p. 463). Finally, students receiving "interactionally modified input" listened to the baseline instructions, but were allowed to ask their interlocutor for clarification.

(Box 5.7 Continued)

Box 5.7 Continued

> The researchers found that the students who had received the interactionally modified input generally outperformed the other groups on the task itself, as well as on a posttest 2 days later, a delayed posttest 1 month later, and a follow-up test 6 weeks later. At the same time, the results of the study suggested that premodified input may also promote lexical acquisition, but not to the same extent as interactionally modified input. Based on these results, Ellis *et al.* concluded that opportunities to solve communication problems via interaction have the potential to promote both the comprehension and acquisition of lexical items.

5.4 INTROSPECTIVE DATA

An increasingly common method of collecting data for interaction-based studies in recent years is that of introspection (discussed in chap. 3). Introspective data generally take one of two forms. In the first, students are asked to verbalize their thoughts while they are engaged in a particular activity. These online think-alouds contrast with retrospective data collection methods, generally known as stimulated recalls, in which learners are asked to verbalize the thoughts they had while they were carrying out a previous activity. As discussed in chapter 3, in stimulated recalls, learners often watch a videotape of themselves completing an activity; the researcher (and/or the learner) stops the tape at certain critical moments (e.g., when the learner looks confused), and the researcher asks the learner what she was thinking *at that point in time*. Both methods are designed to gain access to the learner's internal thought processes—information that might remain unavailable to researchers relying on observation alone. An example of such a study is provided in Box 5.8.

Figure 5.5. A kitchen object placement task, drawn by Jamie Lepore Wright. Printed with permission.

Box 5.8: A Study Using Introspective Data to Investigate Learners' Perceptions

Mackey, A. (2002). Beyond production: Learners' perceptions about interactional processes. *International Journal of Educational Research, 37,* 379-394.

Making use of introspective data from stimulated-recall sessions, Mackey investigated whether and to what degree researchers' claims concerning interaction and learners' perceptions of those interactions overlapped. To this end, 46 ESL learners from various L1 backgrounds participated in task-based activities. These activities were videotaped, and episodes of interaction were coded as to whether their primary focus was comprehensible input, feedback, pushed output, or hypothesis testing. After the activities, the learners participated in stimulated-recall sessions, which consisted of watching the videotapes and being asked to introspect on their thoughts at the time of the original activities. For example, one learner was shown a video excerpt that contained the following interaction (pp. 389-390):

NNS:	And in hand in hand have a bigger glass to see
NS:	It's, err. You mean, something in his hand?
NNS:	Like spectacle. For older person.
NS:	Mmm, sorry I don't follow, it's what?
NNS:	In hand have he have has a glass for looking through for make the print bigger to see, to see the print, for magnify
NS:	He has some glasses?
NNS:	Magnify glasses he has magnifying glass
NS:	Oh, aha, I see, a magnifying glass, right that's a good one, ok.

This interaction was coded as an instance of pushed output, as the NS's clarification requests forced the NNS to modify her output to produce a more target-like lexical item. Upon viewing the videotape, the NNS in this example provided the following comment:

> In this example I see I have to manage my err err expression because he does not understand me and I cannot think of exact word right then I am thinking thinking it is nearly in my mind, thinking bigger and magnificate and eventually magnify. I know I see this word before but so I am sort of talking around around this word but he is forcing me to think harder, think harder for the correct word to give him so he can understand and so I was trying, I carry on talking until finally I get it, and when I say it, then he understand it, me.

Thus, in accordance with the researcher's coding, the learner indicated that her interlocutor was "forcing [her] to think harder" to produce the right word—that is, to modify her output. Overall, Mackey found that there was considerable overlap between the learners' insights and researchers' claims about interaction.

Arguably one of the most controversial of the data collection methods reviewed in this chapter, introspective methods have generated considerable debate. Some researchers have maintained, for instance, that the process of verbalizing one's thoughts while simultaneously trying to complete a task may compromise or otherwise impact the ability to carry out the task, especially if the learner is required to think aloud in the L2 (see Gass & Mackey, 2000). Stimulated recalls also need to be carried out carefully in light of concerns that as an event becomes more distant in time and memory, learners may (often unintentionally) create a "plausible story" concerning their thought processes during that event. Introspective methods, along with guidelines for employing them, are described in greater detail in Chapter 3. The flexibility of stimulated recalls and the different ways in which data can be interpreted is also something to consider. For example, in Chapter 3, we treated stimulated recalls as a prompted production method.

5.5 CONCLUSION

This chapter has reviewed some of the most common methods for collecting data in interaction-based research, including naturalistic, prompted production, prompted response, and introspective data. Although the sample tasks described here are certainly not exhaustive (see R. Ellis, 2003, and Pica, Kanagy, & Falodun, 1993, for additional examples), they represent some of the commonly used task types in interaction-based research. As can be seen, the tasks have many different characteristics—characteristics that need to be kept in mind when choosing which task(s) to use for investigating particular research questions. For example, some tasks are one-way tasks, in which the flow of information is unidirectional; others are two-way (jigsaw), as they involve having the learners interact in order to exchange information. Likewise, some tasks have only one correct outcome (e.g., in a closed task where participants need to identify exactly five differences between two pictures), whereas other tasks can be considered more open, because they require the participants to agree on a common outcome or conclusion. Other considerations that must be borne in mind include the difficulty of the task, the time required to complete it, whether the task is likely to be found engaging by the learners, and, of course, whether the task prompts the learners to use the particular linguistic form of interest (e.g., questions). In addition, researchers must understand that individual and social factors may also significantly impact learners' performance on a particular task. Pilot-testing is crucial in these respects because it allows researchers to determine whether tasks are appropriate for the particular groups of learners being investigated and the particular questions being addressed.

CHAPTER 6

Sociolinguistics and Pragmatics-Based Research

Both sociolinguistics and pragmatics involve the study of language in context. Thus, they emphasize social and contextual variables as they affect the learning and production of a second language. The underlying assumption of sociolinguistically oriented SLA research is that second language data do not represent a static phenomenon; rather, L2 production is affected by such external variables as the specific task required of a learner, the social status of the interlocutor, and gender differences. The resultant claim is that learners may produce different linguistic forms that are dependent, to a certain extent, on external variables. Second language research in sociolinguistics and pragmatics deals with both the acquisition and use of L2 knowledge.

Sociolinguistic and pragmatics-based research studies (see Kasper & Rose, 2002, for an overview) are difficult to conduct using forced-elicitation techniques, given that both consider language in context; yet, as in many other areas, it is often necessary to induce or provoke examples in order to collect sufficient data to draw conclusions. If, for example, a researcher wanted to gather data on learners' invitations to others, either in terms of production or interpretation, then it might be difficult to collect enough tokens to draw reasonable generalizations. Second language researchers must therefore create contexts that require the necessary tokens. There are certain methods commonly used for doing this, and they are discussed in the following sections.

6.1 NATURALISTIC DATA

There are many naturalistic settings in which second language data can be collected. This section deals with oral data and with written diary studies.

6.1.1 Oral Data

Researchers studying sociolinguistics and pragmatics in SLA often attempt to set up situations in which certain language events are likely to occur and recur. This can often involve manipulating or holding constant the setting or context. The example that follows in Box 6.1 comes from research on advising sessions between professors and students.

Box 6.1: A Study Using Naturalistic Oral Data from Advising Sessions to Investigate Pragmatic Behavior

Bardovi-Harlig, K., & Hartford, B. (1993). Learning the rules of academic talk: A longitudinal study of pragmatic change. *Studies in Second Language Acquisition, 15,* 279-304.

The focus of this study by Bardovi-Harlig and Hartford is the context of academic advising sessions for graduate students in an applied linguistics program. As the authors note, these involve unequal status encounters. Their concern is to understand how non-native speakers learn appropriate pragmatic behavior when the second language data are limited; in other words, the advising context is one that NNSs find themselves in only a few times a year. The research problem is to discover how this facet of institutional talk is acquired.

Six native speakers and 10 relatively advanced non-native speakers participated in advising sessions at the beginning and end of one semester with a faculty member from their graduate program. The graduate students came from a range of language backgrounds (Korean, Japanese, Chinese, Indonesian, Arabic, Catalan/Spanish). The sessions were audiotaped, and comparisons were made between the NSs and NNSs in such areas as suggestions and rejections, focusing on frequency, form, and success.

The researchers found that the NNSs evidenced change toward NS norms in that they used more suggestions and fewer rejections in the second advising session compared with the first. However, the NNSs did not show changes in the language forms they used. They used fewer mitigators and more aggravators (e.g., *I will take, I'm going to take, I just decided*) than the native speakers. Bardovi-Harlig and Hartford argue that the reason for the successful learning of speech acts, but not appropriate language forms, was due to the fact that the NNSs received feedback about the appropriateness of the speech acts, but not about the appropriateness of the forms.

In the next two examples, presented in Boxes 6.2 and 6.3, the data were also collected in naturalistic settings. The first study examined the acquisition process of sociocultural L2 knowledge in children, whereas the second compared the English intonation of native and non-native English-speaking teaching assistants.

Box 6.2: A Study of Sociocultural Competence in a Classroom Setting to Investigate the Use of Routines in L2 Learning

Kanagy, R. (1999). Interactional routines as a mechanism for L2 acquisition and socialization in an immersion context. *Journal of Pragmatics, 31,* 1467-1492.

In this study, Kanagy investigates how children in immersion kindergartens acquire sociocultural knowledge of their second language. The learners were 5-year-old native English-speaking children who had (with one exception) no exposure to Japanese prior to the study. In school, they received exposure to Japanese for about 90% of the school day. Data were collected twice monthly over an academic year through observations in which naturally occurring classroom interactions were audio- and videotaped. These interactions were naturalistic in the sense that no special tasks were carried out for the purpose of the study. To investigate the children's acquisition processes and products, their daily routines were analyzed, focusing on teacher-student participation patterns as well as "form, content, timing, and nonverbal aspects of children's participation" (p. 1471).

Through her analysis, Kanagy was able to show how L2 sociocultural competence is acquired through scaffolding by peers and the teacher, who provided models with repetitions, praise, and even nonverbal information. Through this modeling and repetition, the children eventually moved toward independence in their production of L2 scripts and routines. This was the case even though their abilities to express their own meanings remained at the one-word level.

Box 6.3: A Study Using Naturalistic Data to Investigate the Use of Intonation in Establishing Rapport in a University Classroom

Pickering, L. (2001). The role of tone choice in improving ITA communication in the classroom. *TESOL Quarterly, 35,* 233-255.

This study has its basis in the need to understand how native-speaking and non-native-speaking teaching assistants use intonation in the classroom. The assumption is that international teaching assistants (ITAs) need to understand and use features of language appropriate to the context in which they are teaching. This study investigates one intonational feature, tone choice, as a way of understanding differences between native and non-native speakers in the classroom.

(Box 6.3 Continued)

Box 6.3 Continued

Six ITAs (native speakers of Chinese, a language that uses tone as one way of encoding meaning) and six other teaching assistants (native speakers of English) were audio- and videotaped. The data for the study were drawn from 2- to 4-minute extracts of the opening sections of pre-lab presentations (all classes were in the sciences or engineering). The analysis consisted of coding falling, rising, and level tones, as well as the functions associated with each.

Among the differences found, the ITAs showed mismatches between syntactic and prosodic cues, which decreased the degree of redundancy in the discourse and increased the processing load for the hearers (native speakers of English), thereby leading to the possibility of miscommunication. Additionally, the ITAs' underutilization of the pragmatic functions inherent in tone choice was found to increase the distance between teacher and student and may even have contributed to interpretations of disinterest and lack of involvement.

6.1.2 Diary Studies

Chapter 3 discussed the use of diary studies as a way of gaining information about learners' internal processes. This chapter uses them to exemplify another facet of language learning: namely, their usefulness in gaining insight into language learners' affect, which is an important contextual variable. They are often revealing about attitudes toward language learning contexts and groups of people, and they may even display learners' reflections about language learning in general. The examples in Box 6.4 provide information about two diary studies in which the researchers themselves are the diarists. In the first, we learn about individual affective variables and their role in learning an L2 in different contexts. In the second, the author explores issues relevant to classroom learning. Diaries can provide insights that are not often available from the diaries of language learners without training in SLA.

Box 6.4: Two Studies Using Diaries to Focus on Individual Affective Variables

Schumann, J., & Schumann, F. (1977). Diary of a language learner: An introspective study of second language learning. In H. Brown, C. Yorio, & R. Crymes (Eds.), *On TESOL, 77* (pp. 241-249). Washington, DC: TESOL.

This study is a report on diaries kept by the two researchers as they attempted to learn languages in three settings: Arabic at the introductory level in North Africa,

---

Persian (Farsi) in a U.S. university setting, and Persian at the intermediate level in Iran. The authors note that the diary itself is "a possible vehicle for facilitating the language learning process" (p. 241). They also point out that the detailed records of emotional issues, such as transition anxiety, found in their diaries suggest that individual affective variables can promote or inhibit L2 learning. On the topic of transition anxiety, one of the diary entries reveals:

> I found one reasonably effective way to control this stress during travel to the foreign country. En route to Tunisia and during the first week or so after arrival, I devoted every free minute to working through an elementary Arabic reader. ... Learning more of the language gave me a sense of satisfaction and accomplishment that went a long way toward counter-acting the anxiety. (p. 246)

The diary writers' reflections thus provide insight into the way emotional factors may influence second language learning.

*****

Bailey, K. (1983). Competitiveness and anxiety in adult second language learning: Looking at and through the diary studies. In H. Seliger & M. Long (Eds.), *Classroom oriented research in second language acquisition* (pp. 67-103). Rowley, MA: Newbury House.

In this study, Bailey chronicles her university-level French language studies in a course of French for reading purposes. Her comments provide detail on three predominant themes: her responses to the language learning environment, her preference for a democratic teaching style, and her need for success and positive reinforcement. Entries regarding the first theme relate to her desire to move tables around in the classroom so that she would not feel isolated from the other students and the teacher. In relation to the second category, she noted that her teacher consistently sought the opinions of the students and did not retreat to an authoritarian position even in potentially confrontational situations (e.g., unfairness of an exam). Finally, Bailey refers on numerous occasions to her teacher's encouragement and even to her own structuring of the input to elicit positive feedback.

In these and many other diary reports, the research questions are not preestablished; the researchers act as participant observers, writing down their thoughts in a more or less systematic fashion. Bailey (1983) outlines five steps for carrying out diary studies (pp. 72-73):

1. The diarist provides an account of his or her personal language learning history.
2. The diarist/learner/researcher systematically records events, details and feelings about the current language-learning experience in a confidential and candid diary.
3. The journal entries are revised for public perusal. Names are changed and information damaging to others or extremely embarrassing to the learner is deleted.
4. The researcher studies the journal entries as data, looking for "significant" trends.
5. The factors identified as important to the language-learning experience are discussed, with or without illustrative data.

Because these are highly personalized accounts, there are times when personal information must ultimately be eliminated; however, Bailey emphasizes the importance of writing candidly, even regarding sensitive topics. Diaries can always be revised later, but in order to gain the maximum amount of insight, diarists should not censor themselves while writing.

6.2 PROMPTED PRODUCTION

As noted in other sections of this book, naturalistic data are useful but often limited. In L2 sociolinguistic research, it is therefore common to establish a structured context and attempt to prompt learners for particular types of responses. This section deals with narratives and role plays.

6.2.1 Narratives

Second language data can be collected in the form of elicited narratives in a variety of ways. In the examples that follow, learners' production is prompted using narrative tasks. As pointed out elsewhere in this book, many data elicitation techniques can be used to address a range of questions within a variety of domains. For example, narratives were discussed in chapter 4 with regard to formal linguistic models. This chapter describes narratives as they relate to sociolinguistic issues. Research has shown that the discourse genre of a specific task (e.g., argumentation, description, narrative) can influence learners' linguistic choices to a certain extent (G. Brown & Yule, 1983; Bygate, 1999; Newton & Kennedy, 1996; Tarone & Parrish, 1988). As Bygate (1999) puts it, "Specific task types can create a need for clarity in particular areas of meaning, leading speakers to focus their attention on the use of particular formal features of the language, suggesting an ideational and interpersonal content to tasks" (p. 190). In order to convey accurate narrative information to an interlocutor, for example, a learner may have to access L2 pragmatic knowledge as a means of producing correct and interpretable nominal reference, article use, and time relations. In fact, in first language research (e.g., Smith & Leinonen, 1992), pragmatic disorders have been diagnosed by creating contexts in which speakers must use particular sorts of language to express pragmatic functions. Box 6.5 presents a study that concludes that communicative L2 tasks can be designed to encourage learners to use particular linguistic features.

Box 6.5: A Study Using Communicative Tasks to Elicit Particular Linguistic Features

Newton, J., & Kennedy, G. (1996). Effects of communication tasks on the grammatical relations marked by second language learners. *System, 24,* 309-322.

The purpose of this study is to investigate the grammatical consequences of having language learners engage in particular types of L2 tasks. Eight high-intermediate adult learners of English as a second language completed four different tasks in groups of four. Two of these tasks were "shared information" tasks, in which all of the learners possessed all relevant information. They had to discuss an issue and come to a consensus about priorities through reasoning and persuasion. The other two tasks were "split information" tasks, in which the learners possessed different sets of information that they had to exchange with each other in order to arrive at an accurate description of a situation.

The authors point out that, whereas the split information tasks could be expected to involve the functions of describing and checking the accuracy of information using the present tense with simple additive conjunctions, the shared information tasks (because of the learners' interpersonal needs to argue cases, expressing cause-effect and condition-result relationships) would include frequent markings of mental processes and the use of subordinating conjunctions. They did, in fact, find the shared tasks to encourage the marking of interpropositional relationships with conjunctions, and they conclude that the communicative purposes of shared information tasks can be used "to encourage reasoning, argumentation, conjecture and other pragmatic behaviors with consequent linguistic marking" (p. 321). Furthermore, and importantly, they note that the qualities of this discourse (in terms of accuracy, complexity, lexical richness, or sociolinguistic appropriateness, for example) are relevant to SLA.

Of course, even though asking learners to engage in a certain genre of communication may help to encourage particular sorts of language use, speakers do have the freedom to avoid using language with which they are not completely comfortable. Researchers cannot always assume that linguistic features will be "essential" for task completion (Loschky & Bley-Vroman, 1993), as was exemplified in chapter 1. Another important point to consider when eliciting narratives is planning time: Should researchers elicit narratives immediately after providing the learners with prompts, or should learners be given time to think about what they will say? In fact, as described in chapter 2, the issue of planning is relevant to many production tasks and has been the focus of much recent work in the second language field (see Box 2.2 in this book and the edited collection by R. Ellis, 2005, for a review). The following are some dimensions that researchers need to consider when eliciting narratives:

Considerations When Eliciting Narratives

- Should learners be given time to plan?
- If so, how much time?
- If planning time is allowed, should learners be allowed to make notes for themselves?
- If so, can these notes be used during the narrative telling?
- If relevant, how can the use of a particular linguistic form be elicited?

6.2.1.1 Interviews. Interviews are one of the most common methods for eliciting narratives in sociolinguistic research. They are usually one-on-one exchanges conducted in person, and one of their advantages is that they provide researchers with unscripted, conversational data.[1] When researchers conduct interviews to elicit narratives, there are several points to consider. First of all, it is important to know, prior to conducting an interview, how much time will be needed to collect a sufficient amount of data. Depending on what kind of data needs to be elicited, the length of the interview may vary. Second, if the purpose is to elicit a lengthy narrative, then the questions must be carefully chosen by considering which topics the participants are most likely to be interested in. Of course, not all questions will work for all interviewees; individual differences such as age and cultural background need to be considered. Finally, researchers need to be aware that interviews, which

---

[1]Milroy and Gordon (2003) have questioned the claim that data elicited in interviews represent the "natural" speech of the interviewees. Because interviews are done by researchers who are usually strangers to the interviewees, elicited narratives might not reflect the natural speech patterns of the interviewees.

elicit a wide variety of content, may be less effective than narrative elicitation techniques, such as video story retellings. Even when interviewers use the same questions, people's responses can vary considerably when they are telling personal stories, especially given that such narratives are also a means of conveying evaluative information and expressing identity (Schiffrin, 1996).

6.2.1.2 Silent Films.   Another way to elicit data is through learners' oration of a silent film, which provides them with a uniform prompt from which to speak. In SLA research, these film clips are usually relatively short (about 2-4 minutes) and allow the researcher to keep information constant. Nonetheless, there are several other considerations to bear in mind, as outlined below.

Considerations When Eliciting Language Based on Silent Films

- Films must be as culturally neutral as possible if researchers intend to use them for a wide range of learners.
- Films should not be too long or too short. If they are too short, then there will not be a sufficient quantity of data. If they are too long, then learners might get embroiled in the recall of events.
- More authentic data may be obtained if learners believe that they are relating the plot line to a person who has never seen the film.

Questions Regarding Task Administration

- Should the participants tell the story while the film is playing, after the entire film has been shown, or in segments?
- Should they write their stories or tell them orally?
- If they tell their stories orally, should they tell them to a tape-recorder or to someone who has not seen the film?

Box 6.6 provides an example of a study that employed a silent film to elicit narratives from participants.

Box 6.6: A Study Using a Silent Film to Elicit Cross-Cultural Narratives

Von Stutterheim, C., & Nüse, R. (2003). Processes of conceptualization in language production: Language-specific perspectives and event construal. *Linguistics, 41*, 851-881.

This study examines how individuals from different language backgrounds retell the story of a silent film (*Quest*). The participants were native English, German,

(Box 6.6 Continued)

Box 6.6 Continued

and Algerian Arabic speakers. The film used for the study was 7 minutes long, and the participants told the story to their interlocutors, who could not see the film, while the film was playing. In a second part of the study, the participants had to describe what was happening in computer animations.

The first analysis of the data focused on differences between German and English speakers. It was found that English speakers mentioned phasal segments of events (ongoing activities), whereas German speakers also included the endpoints of the events. Whereas in English narratives the observer serves as a "temporal anchor point," relating events to one another, German speakers use an event-based perspective in which events are linked to one another with the narrator in the background. A third, culturally different, group of Algerian Arabic speakers was found to resemble the English speakers more than they did the German speakers. The authors conclude that different languages organize information based on different perspectives.

6.2.1.3 Film Strips with Minimal Sound. Some films with minimal dialogue can be used to elicit language in the same way as silent films by turning the sound off (see Gass *et al.*, 1999, discussed in Box 6.7, and Skehan & Foster, 1999, for examples). This is done to ensure that the learners are not influenced by the speech of either their native language or the target language. At the same time, it is also important that no essential dialogue be removed that would prevent participants from fully understanding the story.

Box 6.7: A Study Using a Film Strip with Minimal Sound to Elicit Narratives

Gass, S., Mackey, A., Alvarez-Torres, M., & Fernández-García, M. (1999). The effects of task repetition on linguistic output. *Language Learning, 49,* 549-581.

This study examined how task repetitions affect participants' retelling of a film strip with little audio. The film was a short vignette of Mr. Bean, whose protagonist often finds himself in unusual and comical situations. Some episodes contain spoken language, but the authors selected examples in which the sound could be removed without affecting learners' overall comprehension of the events.

English-speaking learners of Spanish (fourth semester) participated in the study. There were two experimental groups and one control. The first experimental group watched the same episode three times and a different episode the fourthtime, whereas the second experimental group watched four different episodes, and the control group watched only the first and fourth videos. The task in all cases involved a simultaneous telling of the story in Spanish, which was taperecorded. The analysis examined holistic measures, changes in morpho-syntactic accuracy, and lexical sophistication, all focusing on change over time. The results provide some evidence that task repetition affects the measures considered, although improvement did not always generalize to a new context.

6.2.2 Role-Plays

In general, there are two types of role-plays: open and closed. Closed role-plays are similar to discourse completion tests (to be discussed later) but are performed in the oral mode. Participants are presented with situations and are asked to give one-turn oral responses. They therefore suffer from the possibility of not reflecting naturally occurring language. Open role-plays, on the other hand, involve interactions played out by two or more individuals in response to particular situations and do not involve the limits specified in closed role-plays to any significant degree. Open role-plays reflect natural data more closely, although one must recognize that they are still collected in a non-natural environment and so are subject to some of the same difficulties as found with all non-naturally occurring data. Box 6.8 provides a description of an open role-play.

Box 6.8:A Study using an Open Role-Play in Evaluating the Appropriateness of Pragmatic Elicitation Techniques

Turnbull, W. (2001). An appraisal of pragmatic elicitation techniques for the social psychological study of talk: The case of request refusals. *Pragmatics, 11*, 31-61.

Turnbull collected data on refusals using several different methods in order to assess the relative appropriateness of various pragmatic elicitation techniques. Hypothesizing that more work to save face would occur in refusing a request made by someone of high status, he manipulated requester status through oral and written discourse completion tests, role-plays, and an experimental elicitation technique.

In the role-play situation, the participants engaged in individual open role-plays with the researcher in which they were asked to imagine themselves in a given situation and respond naturally. There was a screen between the participant and

(Box 6.8 Continued)

Box 6.8 Continued

the researcher, and both had a disconnected telephone. The researcher made a pretend phone call to the participant and made a request. Their dialogue was tape-recorded and transcribed for analysis. Turnbull then made comparisons between the refusals generated in this manner and naturally occurring refusals.

Results showed that the refusals made in the discourse completion tests were not representative of natural language. On the other hand, although the refusals in the roleplays tended to be long-winded and repetitive, they were found to be similar to authentic ones, as were refusals produced through the experimental elicitation technique. Turnbull proposes that the best pragmatic elicitation techniques ensure that the speakers are able to talk freely without being aware that aspects of their speech are under investigation.

6.3 PROMPTED RESPONSES

6.3.1 Discourse Completion Test (DCT)

Perhaps the most common method of doing pragmatics-based research in SLA has been through the use of a discourse completion test (DCT), a type of instrument that has been used for many years. DCTs are implemented most frequently in writing, with the participants being given descriptions of situations in which certain speech acts occur. After each description, there is usually a blank space where a response is required. The following example (Beebe & Takahashi, 1989, p.109) illustrates a situation in which a difference in status may be a factor when trying to convey embarrassing information to someone.

You are a corporate executive talking to your assistant. Your assistant, who will be greeting some important guests arriving soon, has some spinach in his/her teeth.

_____

_____

This technique is particularly useful for investigating speech acts such as apologies, invitations, refusals, and so forth. Researchers can relatively easily manipulate such factors as age and status differences between interlocutors. What is lacking, however, in this particular example is the option to ignore the spinach and say nothing.

Another means of forcing responses is to sandwich the response space between the stimulus and a reaction to the response. For example, Beebe, Takahashi, and Uliss-Weltz (1990, p. 69) provide the following discourse to elicit refusals:

Worker: As you know, I've been here just a little over a year now, and I know you've been pleased with my work. I really enjoy working here, but to be quite honest, I really need an increase in pay.

_____

_____

Worker: Then I guess I'll have to look for another job.

DCTs are useful because of the ease with which they can be administered; furthermore (in contrast to Turnbull, 2001), Beebe and Cummings (1995) have found the data to be consistent with naturally occurring speech, although they often produce shorter and less redundant language without capturing the full range of formulas that might be found in natural spoken data. Moreover, DCTs may not allow participants to access the interpersonal and contextual factors that are present in natural conversation. In order to address this criticism, DCT prompts may be enhanced by including social information, as in a study by Billmyer and Varghese (2000), presented in Box 6.9.

Box 6.9: A Study Using a Discourse Completion Test to Investigate the Use of DCT as an Elicitation Instrument

Billmyer, K., & Varghese, M. (2000). Investigating instrument-based pragmatic variability: Effects of enhancing discourse completion tests. *Applied Linguistics, 21,* 517-552.

This study is concerned with methodological issues of authenticity surrounding DCTs. The specific question being investigated concerns the effects of systematically modifying and enriching the content of prompts. To answer this question, the authors created two versions of a DCT. An example of version 1 is as follows:

You are trying to study in your room and you hear loud music coming from another student's room. You don't know the student, but you

(Box 6.9 Continued)

Box 6.9 Continued

> from another student's room. You don't know the student, but you decide to ask them to turn the music down. What would you say? (p. 522)

The second version elaborates on this situation considerably, providing the time and place, the name of the student, and a description of events preceding the incident, as shown here:

> It is 10:30 p.m. on a Wednesday night, and you have a paper due the next day. You are trying to finish the paper and you can't concentrate because you hear loud music coming from another student's room down the hall. You decide to ask her to turn the music down. The music has been on at this volume for half an hour. You have occasionally seen the student, Lucy Row, in the same dorm during the past 6 months. She is a student like you but you have never spoken to her. You have heard other people in the dorm complaining about the volume of her music on several occasions although you never have because you usually study in the library. However, today the library closed early. You are only half way through and you know the professor for this class is very strict and does not give extensions. What would you say? (p. 523)

Participants in this study were 39 native speakers of English and 49 learners of English with a variety of native languages (Korean, Japanese, Turkish, French, Chinese, Polish, and Kazakh). There was an approximately equal number of males and females in each group. About half of the participants in each group was given version 1, whereas the other half was given version 2. Coding was based on level of directness, supportive modification of the head act, and the length of the entire speech act. Results showed that the context-enriched version led to significantly longer and more elaborated request acts in both groups. The authors note that, although justified concerns have been raised regarding the authenticity of data produced by DCTs, no other data collection instruments for this sort of sociolinguistic research enjoy as many administrative advantages.

Researchers can also ask learners for a series of judgments of appropriateness following a description of scene-setting information, as in the following hypothetical example:

> Yesterday everything went badly. You were flying from Dayton, Ohio, to New York for a job interview. You were pleased because

you were one of the final candidates. On your way to the airport, there was a water main break and the highway was flooded,
which caused a closure of the highway. You had to take back
roads to the airport (an area of town you were not familiar with),
and arrived too late for your flight. You were going to call the
personnel manager to tell her of your predicament, but your cell
phone was not charged. Just then you realized that there was
another plane to NY that would still get you there in time. You
boarded the plane, but because of storms in the NY area, your
plane circled and circled, and when you landed, you were late for
your appointment. The office is closed and you have to wait until
the next morning to talk to the personnel manager.

What would you say?

1. I would like to take this opportunity to apologize for missing the
scheduled meeting. I'm sure I'll never let you down again.

__ yes   __ no

2. I would like you to give me another chance.

__ yes   __ no

3. I'm sorry that I didn't call earlier, but I was tired and so I slept late.

__ yes   __ no

4. I really, really want to work in your company. I want to make good
use of my studies.

__ yes   __ no

5. I sincerely apologize for not making the interview. Because of the
storms, my plane circled for over an hour and I couldn't call you. We
didn't land until after 5. I would appreciate it if I could reschedule my
interview.

__ yes   __ no

Judgments can be dichotomous, as in the previous example, or they can be scalar. A word of caution is in order, however. Such responses represent what learners believe they would say in particular contexts. This may or may not correspond to what would actually be said. Thus, results such as these need to be interpreted cautiously and verified against real situations whenever possible.

6.3.2 Video Playback for Interpretation

In pragmatics-based SLA research, we are sometimes interested in how people react to pragmatic infelicities. For example, how might a native speaker professor have reacted in the following situation and why? (from Goldschmidt, 1996, p. 255)

NNS (student):	I have a favor to ask you.
NS (professor):	Sure, what can I do for you?
NNS:	You need to write a recommendation for me.

If this situation had occurred naturally, a researcher might have been able to ask the professor how she interpreted this somewhat abrupt request for a letter of recommendation. Another possibility would be for the researcher to stage scenarios according to variables of interest, videotape them, and prepare specific questions for observers. Box 6.10 describes a study in which videos are used to determine learners' reactions to errors of pragmatics and grammar.

Box 6.10: A Study Using Video Interpretation to Obtain Pragmatic Information

Bardovi-Harlig, K., & Dörnyei, Z. (1998). Do language learners recognize pragmatic violations? Pragmatic versus grammatical awareness in instructed L2 learning. *TESOL Quarterly, 32,* 233-262.

This study represents an attempt to determine reactions to pragmatic and grammatical errors by videotaping staged clips of non-native speakers making both error types. Viewers (ESL and EFL learners and teachers) were given a questionnaire and asked to rate each episode. The following example describes a video stimulus with a grammatical error along with the question that was asked:

Context:	Peter has borrowed a book from his friend, George. George needs it back, but Peter has forgotten to return it.
Stimulus from Video:	
George:	Peter, do you have the book that I gave you last week?

Peter: I'm really sorry but I was in such a rush this morning and I didn't brought it today.

Was the last part appropriate/correct?   Yes   No

If there was a problem, how bad do you think it was?

Not bad at all _____:_____:_____:_____:_____Very bad

The following example shows a pragmatic error.

Context: It's Anna's day to give her talk in class, but she's not ready.

Stimulus from Video:

Teacher: Thank you, Peter, that was very interesting. Anna, it's your turn to give your talk.

Anna: I can't do it today but I will do it next week.

Was the last part appropriate/correct?   Yes   No

If there was a problem, how bad do you think it was?

Not bad at all _____:_____:_____:_____:_____Very bad

The participants in this study were 543 learners of English in Hungary (EFL) and the United States (ESL). Among the results was the finding that the ESL and EFL groups differed from one another in their sensitivity to pragmatic and grammatical errors. The EFL learners were less able to recognize pragmatic errors as such and judged them less severely, whereas the ESL learners judged pragmatic errors as being more serious than grammatical errors. The ESL group's greater degree of pragmatic awareness was likely due to their more extensive interactions with native speakers of English.

Another use of video is for purposes of evaluation. Yule and Hoffman (1993) assessed U.S. undergraduates' abilities to provide reliable evaluations by having them watch 10-minute videotaped presentations of international graduate teaching assistants. The following is the evaluation sheet used in this study, with the score corresponding to each answer given in parentheses:

1. Pronunciation

Generally clear _____(2)

Sometimes unclear _____(1)

Not clear at all _____(0)

2. Vocabulary

Easily understood _____(2)

Sometimes difficult to understand _____(1)

Very difficult to understand _____(0)

3. Rhythm of Speech

Close to American English _____(2)

Sometimes too fast or too slow _____(1)

Very different from American English _____(0)

4. Blackboard Drawing/Writing

Very clear _____(2)

Sometimes confusing _____(1)

Very confusing _____(0)

5. Contact with Audience

Frequently looked at audience _____(2)

Sometimes looked at audience _____(1)

Rarely looked at audience _____(0)

6. Overall Presentation

Easy to follow _____(2)

Sometimes difficult to follow _____(1)

Very difficult to follow _____(0)

7. Would you like this assistant as your instructor?

Strong Yes _____Weak Yes _____Weak No _____Strong No _____

8. Comments:

6.3.3 Matched Guise

Another technique often used in sociolinguistic research is the matched guise, which allows researchers to eliminate individual speech characteristics. In a matched-guise experiment, speakers who are fluent in two languages or two dialects are tape-recorded. Listeners are then asked various questions about the speakers in each of their "guises." Questions often relate to attitudes, such as "Do you think you would like this person?," "Is this person intelligent?," and "Would you want this person as a friend?" An example of such a study is given in Box 6.11.

Box 6.11: An Example of a Matched-Guise Study to Investigate Language Attitudes

Lambert, W., Giles, H., & Picard, O. (1975). Language attitudes in a French-American community. *International Journal of the Sociology of Language, 4,* 127-152.

This study investigated the reactions of bilingual groups to controlled speech samples, some of which were samples from the same bilingual individuals in two guises (i.e., their two languages), hence the term matched guise. There were three studies, made up of three listener groups: 27 bilingual French-American college students and 26 monolingual English college students, 55 French-American high school students of two age groups (13- and 17-year-olds), and 68 French-American 10-year-olds. The setting for the research was a peninsula in northern Maine that protrudes into the two Canadian provinces of Quebec and New Brunswick. There were seven varieties of speakers, each represented by two male and two female speakers. The variables of interest were class (middle and lower) and language (European French, French Canadian, Madawaskan French, Madawaskan English, and English from outside the local region). Of these, the middle-class Madawaskan English and middle-class Madawaskan French speakers were the same.

The researchers led the participants to believe that the focus of the experiment was their ability to infer personality characteristics using only cues from speech, much as they might do in a phone conversation or based on overhearing an unseen communicator. They were instructed to overlook the languages and dialect variations they heard, as these were insignificant to the task. The participants listened to the speech samples and rated the speakers on a number of variables. A sample from the rating scales for the college-level and high school listeners are given next.

What do you think of this person?

1. intelligent	___:___:___:___:___:	not intelligent
2. active	___:___:___:___:___:	passive
3. unfair	___:___:___:___:___:	fair
4. truthful	___:___:___:___:___:	untruthful
5. good-looking	___:___:___:___:___:	ugly
6. not comical	___:___:___:___:___:	comical
7. not courageous	___:___:___:___:___:	courageous; brave
8. unsure	___:___:___:___:___:	confident
9. likeable	___:___:___:___:___:	hateful
10. reliable	___:___:___:___:___:	unreliable

...

(Box 6.11 Continued)

Box 6.11 Continued

21. How much do you feel you resemble this person?

    Very Much   _____:____:____:____:____: Not At All

22. How much would you want to be like this person?

    Very Much   _____:____:____:____:____: Not At All

23. In your opinion, what would likely be the occupation of this person? Choose one of the following:

    _ Radio Announcer

    _ Lawyer

    _ Maid or Janitor

    _ Bus driver

    _ Bank Clerk

    _ University or High School Teacher

Among the findings was a difference between the high school and college-level students in their sensitivity to differences in language usage; the college-level group had a more balanced view of the bicultural situation in which they lived. As for the younger children, there were two groups: those who had been in a bilingual education program and those who had not. The former group preferred the middle-class French Canadian group overall and preferred the upper-class version of their local French variety to English. Those children who had not been in a bilingual program preferred the English-speaking models and, of the French varieties, the lower class variety of the local dialect.

The questionnaire used in the Lambert *et al.* study described in Box 6.11, or variations thereof, can also be used without aural input to investigate stereotypes. Likert-style questionnaires can also be used to gain information about language learning attitudes.

6.4 CONCLUSION

This chapter has dealt with language in context, focusing on a wide range of elicitation techniques. It is important to note that there are many second language researchers (e.g., ethnographers) who would argue that only language collected in its natural context will aid in our understanding of language learning. This may be the optimal situation, but it is also impractical in many instances given time constraints and the training necessary for collecting such data. Researchers who allow for a more practical approach may find some of the techniques discussed in this chapter useful for eliciting both sociolinguistic and pragmatic data.

CHAPTER 7

Survey-Based Research

In outlining the use of surveys in educational and social science research, Krathwohl (1998) notes that "while highly sophisticated interviewing and/or instrumentation is often involved, basically surveys involve getting reactions to questions or other stimuli from a representative sample of a target group, to which the researcher expects to generalize" (p. 352). In fact, a variety of data elicitation methods can be used to conduct survey-based research with second language learners, including open-ended questionnaires, closed-item questionnaires, interviews, or any combination of these. Thus, the data elicited may be categorized as either qualitative or quantitative. This chapter discusses questionnaires and interviews, briefly describing them as instruments before going on to discuss them in terms of the naturalistic data, prompted production, and prompted responses they can elicit. A range of different topics addressed through survey-based research is also discussed.

Questionnaires are one of the most common methods of collecting data on attitudes and opinions from large groups of participants. There are a number of different types of questionnaires, and they have been used to investigate a wide variety of questions in second language research. Questionnaires are generally written instruments that present all participants with the same series of questions or statements, which the participants then react to either through providing written answers, making Likert-style judgments, or selecting options from a series of statements. In addition to directly targeting learners' linguistic knowledge, some questionnaires allow researchers to gather information that learners are able to report about themselves, such as their beliefs and motivations about learning or their reactions to classroom instruction and activities—information that is typically not available from production data alone.

Interviews are another survey-based method of eliciting L2 data, commonly used to obtain information about language learners and their language use. As with questionnaires, there are many different types of interviews, ranging from highly structured encounters to those that resemble casual conversations. Data collected via interviews, whether structured or unstructured, have been exploited in a great deal of research, often providing contexts in which target linguistic structures may be elicited to answer particular research questions.

Generally speaking, questionnaires and interviews can be employed to collect three types of data about language learners: factual, behavioral, and attitudinal.[1] Factual questions may include information about age, gender, socioeconomic status, language learning history, and a variety of other types of background information that can help researchers to interpret research results more accurately. Most studies in SLA include a background questionnaire of this type for learners (often known as a biodata questionnaire), and researchers sometimes follow up on this source of information by using interviews to expand on particular topics or to clarify details (e.g., about the sorts of instruction learners have experienced previously). Behavioral questions, in turn, are utilized to collect data related to learners' lifestyles, habits, and actions (e.g., their strategies for learning vocabulary). Finally, attitudinal questions are used to elicit data on learners' attitudes, beliefs, opinions, interests, and values. For example, researchers may ask about learners' attitudes toward classroom instruction or toward the language they are learning.

Specialized types of questionnaires have also been developed to address specific research areas or questions. For example, as discussed in Chapter 6, discourse completion tasks have been used to investigate interlanguage pragmatics. In order to complete them, learners are asked to provide written responses that convey what they would say in a variety of situations requiring L2 pragmatic knowledge. The sections that follow discuss the types of data that can be gathered through survey-based research in naturalistic settings, from prompted production items, and from prompted responses.

7.1 NATURALISTIC DATA

As discussed in previous chapters, naturalistic data in second language research are defined as observations and recordings of learners' speech (or body

---

[1]Dörnyei (2003) describes these three types of information in his comprehensive text on questionnaires, which includes a classification of different types and provides examples of how questionnaires are utilized in research.

language) in naturalistic settings. Situations for naturalistic data collection may involve spontaneous interactions between learners and their peers, families, friends, and others outside the classroom, but they may take place inside authentic classrooms as well. Observations are sometimes carried out as a means of triangulating data collected through surveys, and vice versa. This process is illustrated in Box 7.1, which describes a study that used interviews and questionnaires to triangulate data gained through observations.

Box 7.1: A Study Using Participant Observation, Unstructured Interviews, and Questionnaires

Jasso-Aguilar, R. (1999). Sources, methods and triangulation in needs analysis: A critical perspective in a case study of Waikiki hotel maids. *English for Specific Purposes, 18,* 27-46.

This study describes the process of conducting a needs analysis for English lessons for hotel maids. The author utilized participant observation, unstructured interviews, and questionnaires to triangulate diverse sources of data related to the maids' English-language needs on the job.

Five participant observations were conducted in which the researcher observed the tasks and situations that the hotel maids routinely faced while carrying out their duties. The main data collection methods during these observations were tape-recording and note-taking. In order to experience the workers' language needs for herself, the researcher also chose to be trained as a new housekeeper at the onset of the observation process. In the unstructured interviews that Jasso-Aguilar conducted and tape-recorded, she asked questions about any issues that tended to arise in relation to the maids' low English proficiency and also talked with the participants about their families and lives outside the workplace. Additionally, housekeepers and their co-workers filled out questionnaires that asked about their English proficiency, whether they spoke English at work, and what they would like to learn in an English class, for example. The following is an excerpt from one of the unstructured interviews:

Researcher:	Do you think that ... to do your work, you need to speak English very well?
Josy:	No (without hesitation) ... you mean the housekeepers?
Researcher:	Yes, for example, for your job ... how much do you use English?
Josy:	Ah ... (she keeps working while she seems to be thinking).

(Box 7.1 Continued)

Box 7.1 Continued

Researcher:	That you have to use ... English.
Josy:	You have to (repeating my words) ... Ah! (seems to suddenly remember) because talk ... the guest yeah? But ... they don't understand too English yeah? They say "yes yes yes" ... you know the Chinese, like that ...
Researcher:	And does that sometimes create problems?
Josy:	Yeah problem ... because they don't understand the ... (p. 40)

Through her triangulation of data collection methods, Jasso-Aguilar discovered that different sources revealed different perceptions about the need for English. Whereas participant observation was crucial for gaining insights, the questionnaires used in this study turned out to be less useful in terms of providing information on the housekeepers' actual tasks and language needs. In addition, in comparing her findings with the predictions of a hotel task force (also in the process of performing a needs analysis to design an English course for the hotel maids), Jasso-Aguilar found that some of the task force's intuitions about hypothetical situations and language needs could not be confirmed.

7.2 PROMPTED PRODUCTION (OPEN-ENDED ITEMS)

Just as types of questionnaires may differ, so too do the items that appear on them. At least two types of questionnaire items can be identified: open-ended and closed-ended. Open-ended questions allow respondents to answer in any manner they see fit, letting them express their thoughts and ideas in their own manner, and thus potentially resulting in less predictable and more insightful data. An example of an open-ended question might be: "Describe ways that you have found to be successful in learning a second language." Box 7.2 describes a survey-based study that employed a questionnaire with open-ended questions. Closed-ended questions and some of the overall characteristics of both types of questionnaires are discussed in the next section.

Box 7.2: A Study Using Interviews and a Questionnaire Containing Open-Ended Items

Graham, S. J. (2004). Giving up on modern foreign languages? Students' perceptions of learning French. *The Modern Language Journal, 88,* 171-191.

In a study designed to investigate English students' attitudes toward French, as well as their perceptions about the reasons for students' levels of achievement in French, Graham used questionnaires containing both open-ended and closed-ended items, followed by interviews in which the students elaborated on their responses.

Learners of French (N = 1,188) in three academic year groups from 10 educational institutions in the south of England participated in the study. The students ranged in age from 16 to 19, and a slightly different questionnaire was developed for each year group in consideration of the British examinations that they had taken or were about to take. In the questionnaire, the participants were asked to respond in one of the following three ways, depending on each individual question: (a) by circling a number on a 6-point scale (closed-ended), (b) by circling an appropriate response to a Yes/No/Not Sure item (closed-ended), or (c) by providing explanations or reasons in their own words (open-ended). Data from the interviews were used to triangulate the findings indicated in the analysis of the questionnaire data. The following are some examples of the open-ended items employed (pp. 190-191):

Items common to Year 11, 12, and 13 questionnaires

 2. Please complete the following statements.

 (a) When I do well in French, it's usually because _____

 (b) When I don't do so well in French, it's usually because

 _____

Items from the Year 11 questionnaire

 9a. Do you hope to study French at AS-or A-level? Yes/No/Not Sure
 (ring one)

 9b. Please explain your reasons.

Item from the Year 12 questionnaire

 14. Why did you choose to study French at AS-level?

(Box 7.2 Continued)

Box 7.2 Continued

In addition to Item 9b, there were other open-ended questions that required the participants to provide reasons for their choices of answers on particular closed-ended items. For instance, one Year 11 female student circled the Number 4 on a 6-point scale regarding her level of achievement in French and explained her choice as follows: "I know even tho [sic] I am achieving [sic] high grades that I have v. poor ability in writing/speaking/understanding French" (p. 179). She then elaborated on this in her interview.

In brief, Graham was able to find through these survey-based methods that there were relationships between students' attributions of success and their levels of achievement. For instance, students who saw their success as being due to effort, ability, and learning strategies tended to achieve at higher levels, whereas students who did not succeed in their French studies tended to overlook the possible role of learning strategies, instead attributing their lack of achievement to low ability and task difficulty.

7.3 PROMPTED RESPONSES (CLOSED-ENDED ITEMS)

In a closed-ended item on a questionnaire, it is the researcher who determines the possible range of responses. Closed-item questions lead to answers that can be easily quantified and analyzed. They typically involve greater uniformity of measurement and therefore greater reliability in terms of the data obtained. An example of a closed-item question might be: "How many hours a week did you study to pass this test? Circle one: 2 or less, 3, 4, 5, or 6 or more." An example of a questionnaire with closed-ended items comes from a study by Takahashi (2005), as summarized in Box 7.3.

Box 7.3: A Study Using Questionnaires with Closed-Ended Items

Takahashi, S. (2005). Pragmalinguistic awareness: Is it related to motivation and proficiency? *Applied Linguistics, 26,* 90-120.

In a study designed to explore Japanese EFL students' awareness of L2 pragmalinguistic features, Takahashi made use of awareness retrospection questionnaires as well as a motivation questionnaire. Through these survey-based methods, Takahashi was able to investigate the relationships between learners' awareness of target features (biclausal request forms, which had been provided as implicit input) and two other variables of interest: motivation and proficiency.

The data collection process, involving 80 Japanese EFL students, included a motivation questionnaire, a proficiency test (the listening- and reading-comprehension sections of the General Tests of English Language Proficiency), three treatment sessions, and two awareness retrospection questionnaires, one completed immediately after the second treatment session and the other immediately after the third treatment session. The following is the 7-point scale that was used to operationalize awareness on the awareness retrospection questionnaires (p. 98):

-3 = I did not detect it at all (and thus was not interested in it at all).

-2 = I did detect it but was hardly interested in it.

-1 = I did detect it but was not so interested in it.

 0 = I did detect it but cannot say whether I was interested in it or not.

+1 = I did detect it and was a little interested in it.

+2 = I did detect it and was interested in it.

+3 = I did detect it and was very interested in it.

Takahashi found that learners noticed the targeted pragmalinguistic features to differing extents, suggesting the influence of individual differences. She also noted that, although the learners' awareness was not correlated with proficiency, it was correlated with their degree of intrinsic motivation.

The questions asked on a questionnaire obviously depend on the research questions being addressed in the study. For example, in qualitative research that is relatively unstructured at the outset, it may be more appropriate to ask open-ended questions and allow the participants' responses to guide hypothesis formation. Once hypotheses are formulated, researchers can then ask closed-ended questions to focus on concepts and themes that have emerged as important. As shown in the example study in Box 7.2, questionnaires need not be solely closed- or open-ended, but can blend different question types depending on the purposes of the research and on what has previously been learned about the research phenomenon. For a more indepth discussion of these considerations, as well as a practical guide to the use of questionnaires in second language research, Dörnyei's (2003) text provides many helpful recommendations, as well as a list of published questionnaires that illustrate the impressive range of research that has been carried out using this approach.

7.4 TOPICS IN QUESTIONNAIRE STUDIES

A considerable range of areas in second language research has utilized questionnaires as a means of gathering data. Topics include language attitudes, needs analyses, L2 learning strategies, computer familiarity, language anxiety, motivation, willingness to communicate, and various issues related to corrective feedback, among many others. In the boxes are some examples of studies that have employed various types of questionnaires. In each box, the purpose of the study (i.e., the research question or questions) and any survey-based research methods employed are briefly described. A study on language learners' willingness to communicate appears in Box 7.4, and a study on grammar instruction and corrective feedback appears in Box 7.5.

Box 7.4: A Study Using a Questionnaire to Investigate Learners' Willingness to Communicate

MacIntyre, P. D., Baker, S. C., Clément, R., & Conrod, S. (2001). Willingness to communicate, social support, and language-learning orientations of immersion students. *Studies in Second Language Acquisition, 23*, 369-388.

In a study designed to investigate relationships among the willingness to communicate, social support, and language-learning orientations of French immersion students, the authors used a four-part questionnaire presented in English, the L1 of the participants (79 ninth graders).

The four-part questionnaire included one section on the learners' willingness to communicate in the classroom, one section on their willingness to communicate outside the classroom, one section on their orientations toward language learning (i.e., their reasons for learning French), and a yes-no section containing six questions regarding who offered the students support in their learning of French. Each of the sections on willingness to communicate (both inside and outside the classroom) contained 27 items that were grouped into four L2 skill areas: speaking, listening, reading, and writing. Some examples of these items, along with the Likert scale used to respond to them, are presented here (p. 385):

1 = Almost never willing, 2 = Sometimes willing, 3 = Willing half of the time, 4 = Usually willing, and 5 = Almost always willing

Speaking in class, in French

_____ 1. Speaking in a group about your summer vacation.
_____ 2. Speaking to your teacher about your homework assignment.

_____ 3. A stranger enters the room you are in, how willing would you be to have a conversation if he talked to you first?

_____ 4. You are confused about a task you must complete, how willing are you to ask for instructions/clarification?

_____ 5. Talking to a friend while waiting in line.

_____ 6. How willing would you be to be an actor in a play?

_____ 7. Describe the rules of your favorite game.

_____ 8. Play a game in French, for example Monopoly.

The researchers found that learners who showed orientations toward learning French for the purposes of travel, job considerations, friendship, knowledge, and academic achievement also tended to demonstrate a willingness to communicate both inside and outside the language classroom. The support of friends was also associated with learners' willingness to communicate outside the classroom.

Box 7.5: A Study Using Questionnaires to Investigate Perceptions of Grammar Instruction and Corrective Feedback

Schulz, R. A. (2001). Cultural differences in student and teacher perceptions concerning the role of grammar instruction and corrective feedback: USA-Colombia. *The Modern Language Journal, 85,* 244-258.

In a study designed to investigate student and teacher perceptions regarding the role of grammar instruction and corrective feedback in foreign language learning in the United States and Colombia, Schulz employed two questionnaires adapted from a study she had conducted in 1996. One questionnaire was designed for foreign language teachers and the other for foreign language students.

The Colombian data were collected from questionnaires completed by 122 foreign language instructors (of English, French, German, Russian, and Spanish) and 607 Colombian language learners (predominantly of English as a foreign language). The comparable data from the United States came from Schulz's (1996) study with 824 students and 92 teachers. The closed-ended items on the questionnaires were judged on a 5-point Likert scale: agree strongly, agree, undecided, disagree, and disagree strongly. Some example items appear here (pp. 257-258):

Example Items

　　1A. The formal study of grammar is essential to eventual mastery of a foreign language.

(Box 7.5 Continued)

Box 7.5 Continued

> 2A. I believe my foreign language improves most quickly if I study and practice the grammar of a language.
> 3A. The study of grammar helps in learning in a foreign language.
> 4A. I like the study of grammar.
> 13A. I prefer to be corrected by my fellow students in small group work rather than by my teacher in front of the entire class.

When Schulz compared the results that these instruments had produced in the two foreign language learning contexts, she found similar beliefs among students across cultures and similar beliefs among teachers across cultures, but not always similar beliefs among students and teachers. In basic terms, students in both the United States and Colombia felt that explicit grammar instruction and corrective feedback were important in L2 learning. On the other hand, whereas many teachers in both locales agreed that grammar instruction was helpful, they felt less strongly about this than the students did.

Reference

Schulz, R. A. (1996). Focus on form in the foreign language classroom: Students' and teachers' views on error correction and the role of grammar. *Foreign Language Annals, 29,* 343-364.

The studies presented in the boxes below illustrate examples of how questionnaires can be used to investigate such issues as computer anxiety and preferred feedback methods in EFL writing (Box 7.6), vocabulary learning strategies (Box 7.7), and L2 learner variables such as language proficiency test scores, beliefs about language learning, and reasons and strategies for learning English (Box 7.8, in which interviews, diaries, and discussion sessions were also used for triangulation).

Box 7.6: A Study Using a Questionnaire to Investigate Learners' Computer Anxiety and Preferred Written Feedback Methods

Matsumura, S., & Hann, G. (2004). Computer anxiety and students' preferred feedback methods in EFL writing. *The Modern Language Journal, 88,* 403-415.

In a study designed to examine the effects of computer anxiety on Japanese EFL learners' writing performance and choice of feedback methods, Matsumura and Hann utilized a questionnaire containing seven items to be answered on a 7-point scale ranging from strongly agree to strongly disagree. Some sample items from this questionnaire are presented here (p. 415):

1. I hesitate to use a computer for fear of making mistakes that I cannot correct.
2. I feel insecure about my ability to interpret a computer printout.
3. I have avoided computers because they are unfamiliar and somewhat intimidating to me.
4. I have difficulty understanding the technical aspects of computers.
5. The challenge of learning about computers is exciting.
6. I look forward to using a computer on my job.
7. Anyone can learn to use a computer if they are patient and motivated.

Of the 218 Japanese EFL students from four beginning-level and four intermediate-level university EFL classes who participated in the study, some were more experienced with computers than others. In addition to completing the questionnaire, they also carried out an essay-writing assignment for which they wrote two drafts. During the revision process, which lasted 2 weeks, they were given opportunities to receive feedback on their first drafts and were allowed to choose freely among three feedback options: online posting to a web-based class bulletin board, where they could get feedback from the teacher and classmates; online indirect feedback, in which they looked at other students' drafts along with the teacher's suggestions; and face-to-face feedback, in which they signed up to meet with the teacher in person. Some students chose to use all three of the feedback methods, whereas others used two (e.g., either online indirect plus face-to-face feedback or online posting plus online indirect feedback), and some students used none. Their writing improvement was measured based on scores for grammatical accuracy, vocabulary usage, originality, consistency, and the use of formal essay structure.

Performing a multiple regression analysis, the authors found that the students' feedback choices were related to their level of computer anxiety. For instance, highly computer-anxious students tended to avoid the computerized feedback methods. They also found, however, that giving the students a choice of feedback methods in fact helped them to improve their essays. Students appeared to improve more when the feedback method(s) matched their preferences and minimized anxiety.

Box 7.7: A Study Using a Questionnaire to Investigate Vocabulary Learning Strategies

Fan, M. Y. (2003). Frequency of use, perceived usefulness, and actual usefulness of second language vocabulary strategies: A study of Hong Kong learners. *The Modern Language Journal, 87,* 222-241.

In order to examine Hong Kong Chinese learners' vocabulary strategies in terms of frequency of use, perceived usefulness, and actual usefulness, Fan employed a vocabulary learning strategy questionnaire as well as a vocabulary test.

Data came from 1,067 prospective first-year students newly admitted to seven institutions of higher education in Hong Kong. The questionnaire originally contained 60 items, which were grouped into nine categories of vocabulary learning strategies, as well as nine questions regarding the participants' background information. Among the 60 strategy items, only 56 of them were ultimately analyzed due to a revision made in the categorization. The vocabulary test was presented in a word-definition matching format and contained a total of 720 items at five frequency levels. Some of the items from the questionnaire, which were judged on a 5-point Likert scale, are provided here (pp. 237-239):

1. In reading a sentence or a passage, when I come across a word I have recently learned, I recall the meaning of the word to help me understand the context.
2. When I meet a word I have recently learned in reading, I pay particular attention to its new usage and new meaning.
3. When I meet new words in reading, I guess their meaning and then look in the dictionary.
4. I look in the dictionary to find out the grammatical pattern of the word.
5. I use the dictionary to find out the context meaning of the new word.
6. To remember a word, I analyze it by breaking it into sound segments.

Through this research, Fan was able to construct a strategy profile of these participants, finding out, for example, which strategies the students reported using the most and least frequently and which strategies they perceived as the most and least useful. She noted, in fact, that there were discrepancies between frequency of use and perceived usefulness; for instance, learners reported using guessing strategies more often than dictionary strategies, but considered the latter to be more useful. Another interesting finding was the discovery that the learners who were less proficient in vocabulary tended to depend more on repetition and association strategies.

Box 7.8: A Study Using a Questionnaire to Examine L2 Learner Variables

Wen, Q., & Johnson, R. K. (1997). **L2 learner variables and English achievement: A study of tertiary-level English majors in China.** *Applied Linguistics, 18,* 27-48.

Wen and Johnson utilized a language learner factors questionnaire in order to examine L2 learner variables and their relationship to English achievement.

Data came from 242 Chinese EFL students, second-year English majors from five tertiary institutions who were completing a 2-year intensive English program required for a BA degree. The three-part language learner factors questionnaire elicited data on 16 variables, including personal information, the participants' scores on national standardized English and Chinese language proficiency/matriculation tests, the approximate amount of time they spent studying English outside the classroom, their reasons for learning English, their beliefs about language learning, and their language learning strategies. The students responded using a 5-point scale for all items except those related to personal information. Qualitative data were also collected through interviews, diaries, and discussion sessions. The following are some sample items from the language learner factors questionnaire, as well as sample ques-tions from the interviews:

Example items (on tolerating ambiguity or risk-taking strategies)

1. When I come across new words in reading, I guess their meaning from the context.
2. When I come across a new word in listening, I just skip over the word and continue listening.
3. When I cannot understand the meaning of a sentence in reading, I guess its meaning from the context.

Example interview questions (related to students' questionnaire responses)

1. Why did you choose this particular response?
2. What do you do when using this strategy?

The data were interpreted by means of a hypothetical causal model, which allowed the researchers to find that six learner variables had direct effects on English achievement: three prior traits (gender, L1 proficiency, and L2 proficiency) and three clusters of strategies (related to vocabulary learning, tolerance of ambiguity, and avoidance of the L1). The learners' belief variables also showed strong and consistent effects on strategy variables. In addition, the authors were able to use the qualitative data to illustrate strategy differences between more and less successful learners.

As mentioned earlier, one useful feature of closed-ended items in particular is the uniformity that they build into questionnaire responses, which allows for relatively easy quantification and greater reliability. However, questionnaires can also be customized, not only to obtain highly detailed and individualized information, but also with the purpose of truly involving participants in the process of data collection and analysis so as to make use of their insights. An example of a data elicitation procedure of this nature is a grid-based scheme, which a researcher can create following the analysis of a completed questionnaire and/or after carrying out an in-depth interview with a participant. The grid is designed both to reflect the participant's input, as well as to uncover further information, including the participant's perceptions about the patterns and relationships in the data collected to date. For example, drawing on work in the areas of mathematics and science teaching, Breen, Hird, Milton, Oliver, and Thwaite (2001) created grids to uncover information about teachers' principles and classroom practices. An example of one of their grids, plotting actions against potential reasons for those actions, appears in Figure 7.1.

Breen *et al.* describe the process of grid creation as follows:

> Prior to the second interview, the researcher drew up a grid for each individual teacher, transcribing the teacher's descriptions of practices and their reasons for them from the cards. The teacher's practices were listed on the vertical axis and their reasons listed on the horizontal axis. ... At this second interview the researcher worked with the teacher on the grid eliciting information as to whether the teacher saw a relationship between each action in turn, and all the reasons on the vertical axis. (pp. 478-479)

7.5 ADVANTAGES AND CAVEATS

7.5.1 Advantages

One of the primary advantages of using questionnaires is that they can, in many cases, elicit longitudinal information from learners because they are easily repeatable and directly comparable. Questionnaires can also elicit

	Reasons for Actions				
Actions	Quieter students should have a chance to speak/ use the language	Students should do things they like doing if they think it's useful for learning	Student's contribution is important for confidence and motivation	Need to simplify or break down the task to give a sense of progress	Build on what students already know
Begins the lesson by revising work from previous lesson	2	2	2	1	1
Accepts and encourages students' spontaneous suggestions	1	1	1	3	1
Encourages students to write down new items of language	2	3	3	1	3
Gets students to highlight words on the handout	2	3	3	1	3
Expects students to speak in English in the pair work	1	3	3	1	1
Gets some students to sound out individual words that are new	1	1	3	1	1

NOTE: For Kate, 1 indicates a strong relationship, 2 a weak relationship and 3 no relationship between an action and a reason. Kate's full grid had 15 reasons on the horizontal axis and 11 actions on the vertical axis.

Figure 7.1. Sample grid. From "Making Sense of Language Teaching: Teachers' Principles and Classroom Practices," by M. P. Breen, B. Hird, M. Milton, R. Oliver, & A. Thwaite, 2001, *Applied Linguistics, 22*(4), p. 479. Copyright © 2001 by Oxford University Press. Reprinted with the permission of Oxford University Press.

comparable information from a number of respondents for cross-sectional study. Moreover, questionnaires are economical and practical in terms of time in-vestment; they can be administered in many forms, including via e-mail, Internet, phone, or mail-in forms, as well as in person. Researchers can ask learners to fill them out all at the same time, perhaps in class, or they can distribute the questionnaires and ask learners to bring them back a few hours or a few days later. The latter method allows participants more time and may possibly lead to more data; it also allows researchers a greater degree of flexibility in the data-gathering process although not as many questionnaires will be returned. Furthermore, because answers are usually written, and questions are hopefully unequivocal, the data do not need to undergo the time-consuming processes of transcription. Depending on how they are structured, questionnaires can provide both quantifiable data and qualitative insights; thus, they are flexible enough to be used in a range of research types.

7.5.2 Caveats

As with any method for eliciting data, there are potential problems related to the analysis of questionnaire data. One concern is that responses may be inaccurate or incomplete because of the difficulty involved in describing learner-internal phenomena such as perceptions and attitudes, for example. This may especially be the case for questionnaires completed in an L2, where lower levels of language proficiency may constrain the responses. Both learners and native speakers might be able to provide salient details, but they may not always be able to paint a complete picture of the research phenomenon. This being so, questionnaires usually are not able to provide a complete picture of the complexities of individual contexts, and other data elicitation methods should be used as well. This is particularly important to remember when using open-ended written questionnaires, because participants may feel uncomfortable expressing themselves in writing and may choose to provide abbreviated, rather than elaborative, responses. Hence, whenever possible, questionnaires should be administered in learners' native languages, learners should be given ample time to specify their answers, and learners with limited literacy, for example, should be given the option of providing oral answers to the questionnaire, which can be recorded.

Another concern is that even though it is often assumed that researchers can control or eliminate bias in designing and using questionnaires, it is possible, as with any type of elicitation method, that the data elicited will be an artifact of the device. Thus, for example, if a study utilizes a discourse completion questionnaire, the researcher should take particular caution when interpreting the results, as the situations depicted are usually hypothetical. In this type of questionnaire, learners indicate only how they think they would respond; this may or may not correspond to how they actually would respond in real life. A nonexhaustive list of guidelines for maximizing the effectiveness of questionnaires is presented in the box (for more information, see J. D. Brown, 2001, and Dörnyei, 2003).

Recommendations for Questionnaire Design and Use

(Based on J. D. Brown, 2001, and Dörnyei, 2003)

- The format should be simple and uncluttered. Where applicable, shade every other line in order to ensure that participants do not mark their answers in the wrong area.
- Make sure that the questionnaire seems well-organized and varied, not haphazard or repetitious, in the questions that are asked. To this end, also include titles, page numbers, and numbered questions.
- Provide specific instructions at the beginning of each section.
- Create unambiguous, answerable questions, keeping each item to one complete thought.
- Include some differently worded statements that focus on essentially the same content. This will give the data greater stability since participants may be sometimes swayed by words' connotations. Avoid loaded terms.
- Try to make statements sound as though they would be said by real people.
- For Likert-style items, attempt to reduce response bias (i.e., the tendency to mark answers on only one side of the scale) by including questions the participants are likely to agree and disagree with.
- Ask several researchers with expertise in the area(s) of interest to review the instrument.
- Pilot the questionnaire among a representative sample of the research population.
- Include written thanks for the participants' responses.

There are also some issues specific to SLA research that second language researchers should take into consideration when constructing questions. For instance, it is important to avoid biasing responses through the wording of a question and, if possible, to avoid negative questions. This is because learners may not see the *not* in a negative question. As mentioned earlier, outcomes should be reviewed and piloted before undertaking the main bulk of data collection to ensure that the format is user-friendly and the questions are clear. When this is done carefully, questionnaires will often be one of the most efficient data collection methods that second language researchers have at their disposal.

7.6 CONCLUSION

Second language research relies on a variety of data elicitation methods to conduct survey-based research with second language learners. Whether closed-ended questionnaire items or free ranging interviews are used, and whether the data elicited is categorized as either qualitative or quantitative, a range of important topics can be addressed through survey-based research. It is important to remember that survey-based research incorporates a wide range of techniques eliciting different data.

CHAPTER 8

Classroom-Based Research

The term *classroom research*, despite its seeming transparency, has received various definitions over the years. Long (1980) described it as "research on second language learning and teaching, all or part of whose data are derived from the observation or measurement of the classroom performance of teachers and students" (p.3). A decade later, van Lier (1990) defined classroom research as research that "investigates what happens in second language classrooms" (p.174). This chapter defines classroom research as investigations carried out in second and foreign language classrooms, whether by the teachers of those classrooms or by external researchers, and we also occasionally refer to this as classroom-based research.

Many categorization schemes have been proposed for classroom research as well (e.g., Bailey, 1999; Chaudron, 1988, 2000; R. Ellis, 1990; Long, 1980; van Lier, 1988). One of the most straightforward of these is Bailey's (1999) three-way distinction between naturalistic classroom research, experimental classroom research, and action research. Although it should be kept in mind that these three types are not mutually exclusive, this categorization nonetheless represents a useful first step in understanding what constitutes classroom research.

8.1 NATURALISTIC CLASSROOM RESEARCH

In naturalistic classroom research, second language researchers seek chiefly to observe and describe learning and teaching as they occur in intact classes; the point is not to intervene in the learning process, but rather to gain detailed information on existing phenomena. To this end, researchers often make use of some form of observation method (as discussed in a later section), as well as other means of obtaining information on less easily observed classroom phenomena, such as the students' attitudes and thought processes (e.g., through data collection procedures such as stimulated recalls, questionnaires, and interviews, which are treated in more detail in Chaps. 5, 6 and 7).

8.1.1 Observations

Observations, briefly defined, are "methods of generating data which involve the researcher immersing [him- or herself] in a research setting, and systematically observing dimensions of that setting, interactions, relationships, actions, events, and so on, within it" (Mason, 1996, p. 60). Observations are one of the most commonly employed data collection procedures in classroom research, as they allow researchers to gather detailed data on the events, interactions, and patterns of language use within particular foreign and second language classroom contexts.

8.1.1.1 Observation Schemes. In deciding to use observation to investigate the L2 classroom, researchers can be aided by the many schemes that are available to help guide the observation process (e.g., P. J. Allen, Fröhlich, & Spada, 1984; Fanselow, 1977; Mitchell, Parkinson, & Johnstone, 1981; Moskowitz, 1967, 1970; Nunan, 1989; Sinclair & Coulthard, 1975; Spada & Fröhlich, 1995; Ullman & Geva, 1983, 1985). Some of the simpler observation schemes involve straightforward checklists and tallies of overt behaviors (see Figure 8.1 for an example from Nunan, 1989). Here, observers mark the frequencies of observed behaviors or events (e.g., teacher questions) at regular time intervals (e.g., every 5 minutes). Categories such as those in Nunan's (1989) scheme are considered relatively low inference, as they are "clearly enough stated in terms of behavioral characteristics … that observers in a real-time coding situation would reach high levels of agreement or reliability" (Chaudron,1988, pp. 19-20).

In contrast to schemes such as Nunan's, other schemes include high-inference categories. Here, observers are required to judge the meanings or functions of particular behaviors, as with Ullman and Geva's (1985) Target Language Observation Scheme (TALOS) scheme (see Mackey & Gass, 2005, and J. McDonough & S. McDonough, 1997, for an overview of this scheme, as well as other examples of low-inference, high-inference, and combination schemes). In addition to low- and high-inference observation schemes, classroom researchers often work with systems that have been developed for focusing on very specific aspects of classroom discourse, for example, corrective feedback (e.g., Lyster, 1998a, 1998b; Lyster & Ranta, 1997), discourse types (e.g., R. Ellis, Basturkmen, & Loewen, 2001), and instructional decisions (e.g., K. E. Johnson, 1992). An example of one such observation study, by R. Ellis, Basturkmen, and Loewen (2001), is described in Box 8.1.

	Tallies	Total
1. Teacher asks a display question (i.e. a question to which she knows the answer)	/ / /	3
2. Teacher asks a referential question (i.e. a question to which she does not know the answer)	/ / / /	4
3. Teacher explains a grammatical point		0
4. Teacher explains meaning of a vocabulary item		0
5. Teacher explains functional point		0
6. Teacher explains point relating to the content (theme/topic) of the lesson	/	1
7. Teacher gives instructions/directions	/ / / / /	6
8. Teacher praises	/	1
9. Teacher criticizes		0
10. Learner asks a question	/ / /	3
11. Learner answers question	/ / / /	4
12. Learner talks to another learner		0
13. Period of silence or confusion		0

Figure 8.1. Classroom observation tally sheet. From *Understanding language classrooms: A guide for teacher-initiated action* (p. 78), by D. Nunan, 1989, New York: Prentice-Hall. Copyright © 1989 by Prentice-Hall. Reprinted with the permission of Prentice-Hall. All rights reserved.

Box 8.1: A Study Using Observation to Examine Classroom Discourse

Ellis, R., Basturkmen, H., & Loewen, S. (2001). Preemptive focus on form in the ESL classroom. *TESOL Quarterly, 35,* 407-432.

In this study, the researchers observed two intact classes in a private English language school in New Zealand, focusing on one particular type of classroom discourse: focus-on-form episodes (FFEs). FFEs are instances in which either students or teachers take time out of communicative exchanges to

(Box 8.1 Continued)

Box 8.1 Continued

deal with issues of linguistic form (e.g., grammar points, problems with vocabulary, or questions about pronunciation). The researchers' observations involved attaching a microphone to the teacher in each class so that instances of teacher-student interaction could be recorded. After identifying two types of FFE (i.e., reactive FFEs, which arose as a result of real or perceived student errors, and preemptive FFEs, which involved drawing the students' attention to linguistic form even though no errors had been made) and finding that both types occurred fairly often and at roughly the same frequency, the researchers narrowed their focus to the latter type of FFE, which has been less rarely studied.

The authors then examined the discourse moves involved in both teacher-initiated and student-initiated preemptive FFEs. They found that uptake moves (i.e., acknowledgments of responses to questions, attempts to use the information provided, or attempts to produce the target items) were more common in student-initiated FFEs than in teacher-initiated FFEs, noting that "student-initiated focus on form is likely to involve actual gaps in the students' knowledge," whereas teacher-initiated FFEs may target items that the students already know (p. 428). Additionally, examining the linguistic foci of the preemptive FFEs, the researchers found that over 60% of the episodes targeted vocabulary. Their observations allowed them to gather detailed data about classroom discourse in a systematic way without manipulating features of the classroom context.

8.1.1.2 *Mechanical Means of Making Observations.* Researchers typically rely on several data collection procedures when making observations in a classroom context. These may include field notes (i.e., detailed notes—generally freehand—of the phenomena under investigation), observation schemes (as discussed earlier), and a mechanical means of recording the lesson, such as audio or video recording. The last method is particularly useful in complex classroom settings, as it enables the researcher to review the lesson, focusing once perhaps on the learners' behaviors and another time on the teacher's actions. However, conducting audio and video recordings in classroom settings is not entirely unproblematic.

When selecting a digital or analog recording device, the particular nature of the data collection should be considered. An advantage of digital recordings is their higher sound quality and stability (they do not degrade over time). In addition, digital files can be manipulated easily for analysis and presentation. A disadvantage is that most transcription machines are made for cassette tapes, and depending on software availability, digitally recorded data can be more difficult or expensive to transcribe.

Researchers also need to be concerned with the use of microphones. Internal microphones (e.g., built into tape recorders) are sufficient if participants can speak directly into the recorder. This set-up is potentially better for researchers dealing with small children (less equipment to fiddle with) or for researchers worried about technical malfunctions. However, external microphones (e.g., boom microphones or lapel microphones) are useful, and often necessary, for capturing small-group work, pair work, or whole-class interactions. Lapel microphones are particularly useful when a researcher wishes to distinguish the hearer's voice from other voices on a recording; boom microphones, on the other hand, are useful in capturing the speech of several participants. The nature of the research should influence the choice of microphone. For example, if a large class activity is being recorded, then the most sensitive microphone possible should be used. However, if the research involves recording separate, simultaneous group activities, the use of a very sensitive microphone might pick up talk from both the target group and adjacent groups, making it more difficult to transcribe and analyze the small-group discussions.

In addition to using audio recordings, researchers may wish to consider the use of video recordings as well. This is useful as a form of backup for the audiotape (i.e., to pick up more data and/or in case of equipment failure or human intervention, such as learners turning the equipment on and off). Videotaping is also worthwhile for investigating nonverbal forms of communication in the classroom. Researchers needing to capture the instructor's input, as well as student interactions, may consider using more than one video camera. (The disadvantage of this, of course, is that it might require more than one operator, which can double the intrusion into the classroom.) If only one camera is available, then it may be helpful to place it in a corner of the room so that not only the instructor, but also as many of the students as possible are captured on tape. In this way, more information can be gathered on the interactions between the instructor and the students and among the students themselves. As always, researchers must make sure that informed consent has been obtained from all individuals who will be videotaped and that arrangements have been made for those who have declined to participate (e.g., by seating them behind the camera and ensuring that their voices will not be picked up).

When recording younger children, researchers must also keep in mind that the equipment will be novel, interesting, and thus a target for exploration. One way to help ensure that the equipment remains intact is to ask for colleagues or adult volunteers to come to the class and keep an eye on it.

However, again, this may be disruptive and alter the nature of the class being observed. As an alternative, a researcher can start bring ing the equipment to the class a few weeks before the observation. In that way, the children may become accustomed to the presence of both the researcher and the equipment.

Guidelines for Mechanical Means of Making Observations

- Select a recording format that will facilitate the ultimate uses of the data (e.g., for transcription, analysis, presentation).
- Consider whose voices and actions need to be recorded, as well as how sensitively and distinguishably this needs to be done and in which situations.
- Determine what kinds of microphones and other equipment should be used for these purposes and where they should be placed in order to collect as much relevant data as possible.
- Supplement the primary recording method with a backup, but try to gauge what is necessary and sufficient for the job in order to avoid equipment malfunction or undue complexity.
- Consider the amount of intrusion in the classroom caused by equipment and equipment operators.
- Take anonymity concerns very seriously and act accordingly.
- Plan the physical arrangement beforehand, taking into account the suitability and adaptability of the environment.
- Consider human factors, such as the age of the participants and how the equipment may affect them; acclimate participants if necessary.
- In all of these areas, pilot testing can be immensely useful.

8.1.1.3 Observation Etiquette. In addition to addressing the technical aspects of observations, researchers must also keep in mind important guidelines on observation etiquette. This is crucial for the sake of maintaining smooth relations among the researcher, teacher, and students. As is discussed next, it is also crucial for ensuring the validity of the study.

Because researchers often rely ultimately on teachers for access to class-room data, observation etiquette is important from the perspective of main-taining good working relationships. To this end, it is important for researchers to obtain instructors' permission to observe classes well in advance of any scheduled observations. This also allows teachers to provide crucial input con-cerning when and how the observations should take place. For example, if the date a researcher has chosen for an observation is one in which another individual, say a supervisor, is scheduled to observe the class, the teacher can re-quest that a different day be selected. Similarly, the teacher may want to ask any observers to arrive before the students come to class and to sit in back of the class so as to minimize the risk of distraction. The teacher may also recommend that researchers begin coming to class several days before the scheduled observation in order to habituate the students to their presence.

Observers should also consider how to explain their presence in the class to the students. In some classes, students may be used to the occasional presence of a supervisor or instructor trainer, and little explanation will be needed. However, other classes may never have experienced an observer before. For such classes, depending on the research problems being studied, researchers could request that the teachers introduce them to the students (briefly explaining that they are there only to observe a second/foreign language classroom), allow them to participate in the instructional activities, and/or describe them as teachers' aids, assuming that this is an accurate description of the researcher's activities. J. M. Murphy (1992) further recommends that when observers are asked why they are in the classroom, they should keep their responses to a minimum; in addition, they should keep in mind that their role is not to judge, evaluate, criticize, or offer constructive advice, but to remain as nonjudgmental and unobtrusive as possible.

After scheduled observations have been completed, it is important, first of all, for researchers to thank the teachers, students, and administration for their cooperation. It can be easy to overlook such simple things, but in fostering good relationships between instructors and future researchers, the importance of expressing courtesy and appreciation cannot be overstated. This gratitude can take the additional form of acknowledging the teachers and students in any publications stemming from the research and of sending copies of the publications to the schools and instructors because they may not have access to the same journals and publications as the researcher.

In addition to expressing gratitude, it is also important to debrief instructors about the research findings or the content of the observation notes and/or schemes. In fact, this is often a requirement of university IRBs. Timing, however, is an important consideration here. For example, researchers might provide instructors with a copy of their notes after each lesson or arrange a time to meet in order to discuss the research. By keeping the observation process as transparent and interactive as possible, researchers can often establish a more trusting and cooperative relationship with instructors. Of course, in some cases, the instructors themselves may be the focus of the research, or continual debriefings may unduly influence the research. In these cases, it may be preferable to make such contact after the project has been completed.

Guidelines for Classroom Observation Etiquette

- Contact the classroom instructor ahead of time (in person, if possible).
- Determine a schedule for observations that is in keeping with the classroom rhythms and activities.
- Negotiate the observer's role in the classroom, including regular previsits, arrival time, introductions, and seating arrangements in order to create a situation that is as naturalistic as possible.
- Debrief the instructor (either during or after the observational period) on the findings of the study when necessary and appropriate.
- Clearly express appreciation to the instructor, students, and administration after the observation/data collection period.

In relation to the validity of a study, it is important to note that when an observer in a classroom is obtrusive (e.g., distracting the learners' attention away from the lesson), it becomes problematic to claim that the behaviors observed are characteristic or typical of the learners. In fact, even when observers do not act in a distracting manner, their mere presence may cause learners to alter their behavior in subtle ways, as discussed in Box 8.2. In classroom research, students may feel honored or pleased that they have been selected for observation, potentially resulting in (perhaps unnaturally) good or attentive behavior. Similarly, students assigned to a particular treatment group in experimental classroom research (discussed in the next section) may be pleased about being selected to use new equipment, again resulting in possibly uncharacteristic behavior. When the presence of an observer or the ostensibly special treatment involved in an experiment changes the behavior of participants due to their feelings of pleasure about being included in the study, this is referred to as the Hawthorne effect.

Box 8.2: An Experimental Classroom Study Showing a Possible
Hawthorne Effect

Allen, L. Q. (2000). Form-meaning connections and the French causative: An
experiment in processing instruction. *Studies in Second Language Acquisition,*
22, 69-84.

One example of second language research in which the Hawthorne effect
may have influenced the results is an experimental classroom study of high school
students studying French as a foreign language (FFL) by L. Q. Allen. In this study,
nine classes of FFL students were assigned to one of three groups (processing
instruction, traditional instruction, and no instruction), and the students' ability
to interpret and produce sentences containing the French causative were measured.
Finding that the scores on the second interpretation posttest (i.e., a posttest
measuring the students' ability to interpret French causatives, given 1 month
after the instruction) were higher for all three groups, Allen speculated, among
other things, that "the novelty of having the researcher as their teacher and the
stimulation of working on something different may have had a subtle influence on
the learners, thus causing a Hawthorne effect ... a phenomenon not uncommon in
educational research" (p. 80).

8.2 EXPERIMENTAL CLASSROOM RESEARCH[1]

In addition to (or in combination with) naturalistic classroom research, inves-
tigators may also employ more experimental methods for examining second or
foreign language classrooms. In this case, besides observing and describing,
researchers seek to intervene in the learning process. Experimental and quasi-
experimental classroom research, like experimental research carried out
in laboratory settings, typically involves randomization, treatment groups,
and control groups. In classroom research, students in intact classes are assigned to different groups; for example, one class may be assigned to be the
treatment group, in which case they may receive a certain form of instruction,
and another comparable class may be assigned to serve as the control group.
This is done in order to isolate the effects of the variable under investigation
(in this case, the type of instruction) on, for example, the students' test scores
or attitudes toward the learning process. In brief, the researcher intervenes in
the learning process and then measures the effects of the intervention. An example of this type of study is provided in Box 8.3.

---

[1]Most classroom research is in fact quasi-experimental rather than purely experimental.

Box 8.3: A Classroom Study Using (Quasi-)Experimental Methods

Williams, J., & Evans, J. (1998). What kind of focus on form and on which forms? In C. Doughty & J. Williams (Eds.), *Focus on form in classroom second language acquisition* (pp. 139-155). Cambridge, England: Cambridge University Press.

An example of experimental classroom research using intact classes is Williams and Evans's investigation into whether some linguistic forms are more amenable to certain kinds of focus-on-form instruction than others. They used three intact classes: a control group, a group that received an input flood of positive evidence, and a group that received explicit instruction and feedback. For the two experimental groups, the treatments were rotated for the different linguistic forms under investigation; that is, each class received different treatments for participial adjectives and passives. Importantly, the researchers ensured that the instructional materials were appropriate for, similar to, and integrated with the normal activities and focus of the course. Each treatment lasted approximately 2 weeks. The analysis, which combined quantitative and qualitative data, suggested that not all forms were equal in terms of the effectiveness of focus-on-form activities and that individual learners could vary greatly in terms of readiness and ability to learn.

Despite similarities, experimental research conducted in a classroom setting differs from laboratory studies in important ways. It can be more difficult in the classroom than in the laboratory for researchers to isolate the variables for study, a situation that opens up possibilities for intervening variables to influence the research findings (R. Ellis, 1994; Hulstijn, 1997). These variables include the amount and type of exposure the learners receive to the target language outside of the classroom (something that also varies considerably across foreign language and second language contexts), differences in the students' previous instructional experiences in both the L1 and L2, and of course, differences in the classroom and educational contexts. Teasing apart the many variables in classroom research is difficult, if not impossible, which is one reason that researchers have called for more tightly controlled laboratory studies. At the same time, one drawback of laboratory studies is that they lack ecological validity (Lightbown, 2000). As Hulstijn (1997) explains, "because such research deliberately abstracts away from real-life learning situations, it simultaneously limits the possibilities to extrapolate their findings legitimately to real-life learning" (p. 132).

In light of these complementary strengths and weaknesses, experimental studies conducted in both laboratory and classroom contexts are essential if we are to understand the complex phenomenon of second language learning. Nevertheless, it should be kept in mind that classroom-based studies come with their own set of challenges, including—but not limited to—dealing with teachers not adhering to researchers' guidelines in the delivery of instruction, as Box 8.4 illustrates.

Box 8.4: A Study Demonstrating the Challenges of Ecological Validity vs. Experimental Control

Spada, N., & Lightbown, P. M. (1993). Instruction and the development of questions in L2 classrooms. *Studies in Second Language Acquisition, 15,* **205-224.**

In a well-known series of studies involving many years of collaboration with classroom teachers, Lightbown, Spada, and their colleagues have investigated the ESL development of young Francophone learners in Canada, using both description and experimentation to research the roles of instruction and error correction. Spada and Lightbown set out to examine the impact of instruction on question formation in ESL. Following a 2-week period of explicitinstruction and corrective feedback, they found that learners improved and maintained their gains on a delayed posttest 5 weeks later. Illustrating the many complexities involved in second language classroom research, however, Spada and Lightbown reported that control group comparisons were not possible because their control group teacher had been found to use similar instruction and correction techniques to the experimental group teachers, despite the researchers' assumptions (based on several data points) that her focus would be on the communication of meaning within an overall communicative approach.

Similarly, classroom researchers may find that their research goals and plans are incompatible with those of the instructors with whom they need to work (resulting perhaps in the sort of situation described in Box 8.4). In addition, other parties (e.g., administrators) may hold the view that research prevents students from focusing on their studies, such as preparing for the TOEFL or other institutional tests. The researcher, as a guest to the institution, needs to take these concerns seriously and remain flexible. By being willing to compromise, by listening to the concerns of teachers and administrators, and by keeping the research process as transparent as possible, researchers can do much to keep these important relationships running smoothly. In addition, it is beneficial for researchers to keep interested parties abreast of the developments (and conclusions) of the research so that they feel that valuable teaching time, effort, and expense has not gone to waste.

In pointing out these concerns, it is not our intent to discourage novice or experienced researchers from engaging in experimental or quasi-experimental classroom research, but rather to emphasize that classroom research is a particularly complex and multifaceted endeavor that must be planned carefully. We must also stress the importance of flexibility throughout the process. Even the most carefully designed studies rarely go exactly according to plan in second language classrooms; unforeseen events and problems arise from many sources (Ortega, 2005; Schachter & Gass, 1996), and matters that might be trivial in a normal classroom context can require quick thinking and adaptation for the purposes of research—from there being an odd number of students in the classroom when an experiment calls for pair work, to some students having to leave early and not being able to complete the tasks. However, if researchers are aware of these possibilities in advance and can be patient, flexible, and ready to utilize alternate contingency plans, then experimental classroom research can be extremely valuable and rewarding.

8.3 ACTION RESEARCH

The third major type of classroom research is action research. Although this type of research has received varying definitions and labels (e.g., collaborative research, practitioner research, teacher-initiated research), "one common thread is that participants in a given social situation or classroom are themselves centrally involved in a systematic process of enquiry arising from their own practical concerns" (Burns, 2005, p. 241). That is, action research does not involve an external researcher observing and investigating the classroom primarily (although not exclusively) for the sake of theory development. Rather, action researchers are commonly teachers, investigating various aspects of their classrooms primarily (although not exclusively) to improve their teaching practice and the quality of education delivered to their students (Allwright & Bailey, 1991; Crookes, 1993; Wallace, 1998).

As with most other forms of research, action research usually stems from a question or problem. For example, practitioners may be concerned that their students are reluctant to speak in class and decide to gather data to gain more information about this problem. In the example here, this could first involve the teachers in audio- or videotaping their own classes in order to analyze the patterns of interaction. They may also decide to supplement this information with multiple other sources of data, such as discussions with colleagues, questionnaires, and/or diary entries tapping the students' perspectives. As discussed in chapter 6 on sociolinguistic and pragmatics-based second language research, the process of obtaining data from more than one source (also known as triangulation) benefits many types of research, including action research.

Based on the information obtained from these data, or sometimes before the data are collected, practitioners may form preliminary hypotheses. For example, if they find that lower proficiency students are reluctant to speak in whole-group exercises, they may then devise and implement some form of intervention or treatment to address that problem—such as using pair or small-group work, which the students might view as a less-threatening speaking environment, or employing activities that are more closely related to the students' interests and goals. Finally, the instructor might evaluate the effects of this practice in order to determine whether or not the students have benefited from it and also to ascertain the learners' own views about the changes in instructional practice. Obtaining this kind of information may involve another round of data gathering, in which the instructor could reuse one or more of the data collection procedures employed earlier. As can be seen, action research of this form is a cyclic process, and it is one that many teachers engage in as part of their everyday practice.

If the instructors' treatment, changes in practice, or actions are found to be effective, then they can contemplate what else might be done to further support the learning process, also considering whether to disseminate their results to other teachers facing similar situations. If the changes are not found to be effective, then they can start again, considering what other measures might be taken to improve the teaching/learning situation. Box 8.5 illustrates a typical example of action research: The teacher identified a question to investigate and then gathered and analyzed data from his class in order to determine how well the instruction worked.

Box 8.5: A Study Exemplifying Action Research

Liu, J. (1998). Peer reviews with the instructor: Seeking alternatives in ESL writing. In J. C. Richards (Ed.), *Teaching in action: Case studies from second language classrooms* (pp. 236-240). Alexandria, VA: TESOL.

As a teacher of ESL writing to international graduate students at a large midwestern university, Liu made use of both peer review activities and one-on-one teacher tutorials. He discovered, however, that even though the students enjoyed the former activity, they often felt uncertain as to whether their peers' comments were accurate—an uncertainty that led to a lack of enthusiasm toward the activity. As a solution to this problem, Liu devised a new type of session: a peer review with an instructor who participated as a peer. More specifically, the teacher joined the peer review group, participating in (but not controlling) the discussion, occasionally questioning the comments provided by other members of the group in order to stimulate discussion, and providing written comments. As Liu explains, "My role was not only to offer comments but also to evaluate the other peers' comments so that the student whose paper was being reviewed would feel comfortable and confident in making decisions" (p. 238). To measure the effects of this solution, the teacher administered questionnaires, surveys, and interviews periodically throughout the quarter. He found that the students valued the peer review sessions in which he participated and indicated that the presence of the teacher alleviated their concerns about the inaccuracy of some of their peers' feedback.

Action research, with its concern for situated local contexts, teachers' intuitions, and practical applications, is occasionally criticized for not strictly adhering to the guidelines of experimental studies (e.g., regarding the use of control groups, randomly assigned students). In addition, no agreed-on criteria exist for evaluating the quality of action research studies (Bailey, 1999; Burns, 2005). It is occasionally said, therefore, that the results of action research cannot be generalized and are of limited utility to the wider population of second language learners beyond the immediate context in which the studies were conducted. However, it should be kept in mind that, even though much action research is "difficult, messy, problematic, and, in some cases, inconclusive" (Nunan, 1993, p. 46), it can provide valuable insights not just in terms of practice (e.g., to teachers who find themselves facing similar problems and concerns in their own classrooms), but even in terms of theory (i.e., theories of how second languages are acquired). Ortega (2005) has pointed out the importance of considering who research is for and who it benefits. As van Lier (1994) has noted, if practice and theory are separated:

> SLA would either disappear into the thin air of absurdity, or else fall to the earth with the dull thud of pomposity. SLA is about language learning. All around the world, billions of people are learning language, millions are teaching language, and they do so with effort, intelligence and ingenuity. These activities are the true data of SLA. ... In short, SLA and language pedagogy are interdependent pursuits. (p. 341)

Perhaps in recognition of these points, in recent years, collaborative approaches to research have become increasingly common and valued, with language teachers and researchers working together in teams to investigate various aspects of second language learning.

8.4 CONCLUSION

Although there are challenges involved in conducting and interpreting classroom-based studies, this kind of research, regardless of the specific approach taken, allows researchers and teachers to reach a better understanding of the multitude of factors involved in instruction and learning in different contexts, thereby enhancing our insights into how languages are learned and taught.

In summary, then, this book has provided a sampling of the many elicitation techniques that are commonly used in different domains of SLA research. The techniques selected for inclusion are, by necessity, limited and should be taken as a point of departure for research, not as an exhaustive list. We anticipate that researchers will use the information in this text as a means to investigate their own research areas and will modify, refine, and expand on the techniques we have described to make them compatible with and to support their specific research questions.

References

Akiyama, Y. (2002). Japanese adult learners' development of the locality condition on English reflexives. *Studies in Second Language Acquisition, 24,* 27-54.

Allen, L. Q. (2000). Form-meaning connections and the French causative: An experiment in processing instruction. *Studies in Second Language Acquisition, 22,* 69-84.

Allen, P. J., Fröhlich, M., & Spada, N. (1984). The communicative orientation of second language teaching. In J. Handscombe, R. Orem, & B. Taylor (Eds.), *On TESOL '83: The question of control* (pp. 231-252). Washington, DC: TESOL.

Allwright, D., & Bailey, K. M. (1991). *Focus on the language classroom: An introduction to classroom research for language teachers.* Cambridge, England: Cambridge University Press.

Altarriba, J., Kroll, J. F., Scholl, A., & Rayner, K. (1996). The influence of lexical and conceptual constraints on reading mixed-language sentences: Evidence from eye-fixations and reading times. *Memory and Cognition, 24,* 477-492.

American Psychological Association. (2001). *Publication manual of the American Psychological Association* (5th ed.). Washington, DC: American Psychological Association.

Baddeley, A. D. (1986). *Working memory.* Oxford, England: Clarendon.

Baddeley, A. D., Gathercole, S. E., & Papagno, C. (1998). The phonological loop as a language learning device. *Psychological Review, 105,* 158-173.

Baddeley, A. D., & Hitch, G. (1974). Working memory. In G. A. Bower (Ed.), *Recent advances in learning and motivation* (Vol. 8, pp. 47-90). New York: Academic Press.

Bailey, K. M. (1983). Competitiveness and anxiety in adult second language learning: Looking *at* and *through* the diary studies. In H. Seliger & M. Long (Eds.), *Classroom oriented research in second language acquisition* (pp. 67-103). Rowley, MA: Newbury House.

Bailey, K. M. (1990). The use of diary studies in teacher education programs. In J. C. Richards & D. Nunan (Eds.), *Second language teacher education* (pp. 215-226). Cambridge, England: Cambridge University Press.

Bailey, K. M. (1999). *Looking back down the road: Twenty-five years of classroom research.* Retrieved August 1, 2005, from http://www.linguistics.utah.edu/pdfdocs/Baileypaper.pdf

Bailey, K. M., & Ochsner, R. (1983). A methodological review of the diary studies: Windmill tilting or social science? In K. M. Bailey, M. H. Long, & S. Peck (Eds.), *Second language acquisition studies* (pp. 188-198). Rowley, MA: Newbury House.

Barcroft, J., & VanPatten, B. (1997). Acoustic salience of grammatical forms: The effect of location, stress, and boundedness on Spanish L2 input processing. In W. Glass & A. Pérez-Leroux (Eds.), *Contemporary perspectives on the acquisition of Spanish: Vol. 2. Production, processing, and comprehension* (pp. 109-122). Sommerville, MA: Cascadilla Press.

Bard, E., Robertson, D., & Sorace, A. (1996). Magnitude estimation of linguistic acceptability. *Language, 72*, 32-68.

Bardovi-Harlig, K., & Dörnyei, Z. (1998). Do language learners recognize pragmatic violations? Pragmatic versus grammatical awareness in instructed L2 learning. *TESOL Quarterly, 32*, 233-262.

Bardovi-Harlig, K., & Hartford, B. (1993). Learning the rules of academic talk: A longitudinal study of pragmatic change. *Studies in Second Language Acquisition, 15*, 279-304.

Bates, E., & MacWhinney, B. (1982). Functionalist approach to grammar. In E. Warmer & L. Gleitman (Eds.), *Language acquisition: The state of the art* (pp. 173-218). New York: Cambridge University Press.

Beebe, L., & Cummings, M. (1995). Natural speech data versus written questionnaire data: How data collection method affects speech act performance. In S. Gass & J. Neu (Eds.), *Speech acts across cultures* (pp. 65-86). Berlin: Mouton de Gruyter.

Beebe, L., & Takahashi, T. (1989). Do you have a bag? Social status and patterned variation in second language acquisition. In S. Gass, C. Madden, D. Preston, & L. Selinker (Eds.), *Variation in second language acquisition: Discourse and pragmatics* (pp. 103-125). Clevedon, England: Multilingual Matters.

Beebe, L., Takahashi, T., & Uliss-Weltz, R. (1990). Pragmatic transfer in ESL refusals. In R. C. Scarcella, E. S. Andersen, & S. D. Krashen (Eds.), *Developing communicative competence in a second language* (pp. 55-73). New York: Newbury House.

Berman, R. A. (1993). Marking of verb transitivity by Hebrew-speaking children. *Journal of Child Language, 20*, 641-669.

Berman, R. A. (2000). Children's innovative verbs versus nouns: Structured elicitations and spontaneous coinages. In L. Menn & N. Bernstein Ratner (Eds.), *Methods of studying language production* (pp. 69-94). Mahwah, NJ: Lawrence Erlbaum Associates.

Billmyer, K., & Varghese, M. (2000). Investigating instrument-based pragmatic variability: Effects of enhancing discourse completion tests. *Applied Linguistics, 21*, 517-552.

Birdsong, D. (1989). *Metalinguistic performance and interlinguistic competence.* Berlin: Springer.

Bley-Vroman, R., & Chaudron, C. (1994). Elicited imitation as a measure of second-language competence. In E. Tarone, S. Gass, & A. Cohen (Eds.), *Research methodology in second-language acquisition* (pp. 245-261). Hillsdale, NJ: Lawrence Erlbaum Associates.

Bley-Vroman, R., & Joo, H. R. (2001). The acquisition and interpretation of English locative constructions by native speakers of Korean. *Studies in Second Language Acquisition, 23,* 207-219.

Bley-Vroman, R., Felix, S., & Ioup, G. (1988). The accessibility of Universal Grammar in adult language learning. *Second Language Research, 4,* 1-32.

Bock, K. (1990). Structure in language: Creating form in talk. *American Psychologist, 45,* 1221-1236.

Bock, K. (1995). Sentence production: From mind to mouth. In J. Miller & P. Eimas (Eds.), *Speech, language and communication* (pp. 181-216). San Diego: Academic Press.

Bock, K., & Griffin, Z. (2000). The persistence of structural priming: Transient activation or implicit learning? *Journal of Experimental Psychology: General, 129,* 177-192.

Branigan, H., Pickering, M., & Cleland, A. (2000). Syntactic co-ordination in dialogue. *Cognition, 75,* B13-B25.

Breen, M. P., Hird, B., Milton, M., Oliver, R., & Thwaite, A. (2001). Making sense of language teaching: Teachers' principles and classroom practices. *Applied Linguistics, 22*(4), 470-501.

Brown, G., & Yule, G. (1983). *Teaching the spoken language.* Cambridge, England: Cambridge University Press.

Brown, J. D. (2001). *Using surveys in language programs.* Cambridge, England: Cambridge University Press.

Burns, A. (2005). Action research. In E. Hinkel (Ed.), *Handbook of research in second language teaching and learning* (pp. 241-256). Mahwah, NJ: Lawrence Erlbaum Associates.

Bygate, M. (1999). Quality of language and purpose of task: Patterns of learners' language on two oral communication tasks. *Language Teaching Research, 3,* 185-214.

Carroll, J. B., & Sapon, S. M. (1959). *Modern language aptitude test* (MLAT). San Antonio, TX: Psychological Corporation.

Case, R., Kurland, M. D., & Goldberg, J. (1982). Operational efficiency and the growth of short-term memory span. *Journal of Experimental Child Psychology, 33,* 386-404.

Chaudron, C. (1988). *Second language classrooms: Research on teaching and learning.* Cambridge, England: Cambridge University Press.

Chaudron, C. (2000). Contrasting approaches to classroom research: Qualitative and quantitative analysis of language use and learning. *Second Language Studies, 19,* 1-56.

Chaudron, C. (2003). Data collection in SLA Research. In C. Doughty & M. Long (Eds.), *The handbook of second language acquisition* (pp. 762-828). Oxford, England: Blackwell.

Chaudron, C., & Russell, G. (1990). *The status of elicited imitation as a measure of second language competence.* Paper presented at the ninth World Congress of Applied Linguistics, Thessaloniki, Greece.

Chen, M. Y.-c. (2005). English prototyped small clauses in the interlanguage of Chinese/Taiwanese adult learners. *Second Language Research, 21,* 1-33.

Chomsky, N. (1997). *The minimalist program.* Cambridge, MA: MIT Press.

Cohen, A. (1998). *Strategies in learning and using a second language.* New York: Longman.

Cohen, J. D., MacWhinney, B., Flatt, M., & Provost, J. (1993). PsyScope: A new graphic interactive environment for designing psychology experiments. *Behavior Research Methods, Instruments, and Computers, 25,* 257-271.

Conway, A., Kane, M., Bunting, M., Hambrick, D. Z., Wilhelm, O., & Engle, R. (2005).Working memory span tasks: A methodological review and user's guide. *Psychonomic Bulletin & Review, 12,* 769-786.

Corder, S. P. (1981). *Error analysis and interlanguage.* Oxford, England: Oxford University Press.

Cowan, N., Towse, J., Hamilton, Z., Saults, J. S., Elliott, E. M., Lacey, J. F., Moreno, M. V., & Hitch, G. J. (2003). Children's working memory processes: A response-timing analysis. *Journal of Experimental Psychology: General, 132,* 113-132.

Cowan, R., & Hatasa, Y. (1994). Investigating the validity and reliability of native speaker and second-language learner judgments about sentences. In E. Tarone, S. Gass, & A. Cohen (Eds.), *Research Methodology in Second Language Acquisition* (pp. 287-302). Hillsdale, NJ: Lawrence Erlbaum Associates.

Crookes, G. (1993). Action research for second language teaching: Going beyond teacher research. *Applied Linguistics, 14,* 130-142.

Daneman, M., & Carpenter, P. A. (1980). Individual differences in working memory and reading. *Journal of Verbal Learning and Verbal Behaviour, 19,* 450-466.

Daneman, M., & Case, R. (1981). Syntactic form, semantic complexity and short-term memory: Influences on children's acquisition of new linguistic structures. *Developmental Psychology, 17,* 367-378.

De Jong, N. (2005). Can second language grammar be learned through listening? *Studies in Second Language Acquisition, 27,* 205-234.

Dell, G. S. (1986). A spreading activation theory of retrieval in sentence production. *Psychological Review, 93,* 283-321.

Dörnyei, Z. (2003). *Questionnaires in second language research: Constructing, administering, and processing.* Mahwah, NJ: Lawrence Erlbaum Associates.

Dörnyei, Z. (2005). *The psychology of the language learner: Individual differences in second language acquisition.* Mahwah, NJ: Lawrence Erlbaum Associates.

Duffield, N., Montrul, S., Bruhn de Garavito, J., & White, L. (1998). Determining L2 knowledge of Spanish clitics on-line and off-line. In A. Greenhill, M. Hughes, H. Littlefield, & H. Walsh (Eds.), *Proceedings of the 22nd annual Boston University Conference on Language Development* (pp. 177-188). Somerville, MA: Cascadilla Press.

Egi, T. (2004). Verbal reports, noticing, and SLA research. *Language Awareness, 13,* 243-264.

Ehrman, M., & Oxford, R. (1995). Cognition plus: Correlates of language learning success. *Modern Language Journal, 79,* 67-89.

Ellis, N. (1996). Sequencing in SLA: Phonological memory, chunking, and points of order. *Studies in Second Language Acquisition, 18,* 91-126.

Ellis, N. (2002). Frequency effects in language processing: A review with implications for theories of implicit and explicit language acquisition. *Studies in Second Language Acquisition, 24,* 143-188.

Ellis, N. (2005). At the interface: Dynamic interactions of explicit and implicit language knowledge. *Studies in Second Language Acquisition, 27,* 305-352.

Ellis N., & Schmidt, R. (1997). Morphology and longer distance dependencies: Laboratory research illuminating the A in SLA. *Studies in Second Language Acquisition, 19,* 145-171.

Ellis, N., & Sinclair, S. (1996). Working memory in the acquisition of syntax: Putting language in good order. *Quarterly Journal of Experimental Psychology, 49A,* 234-250.

Ellis, R. (1990). *Instructed second language acquisition.* Oxford, MA: Blackwell.

Ellis, R. (1994). *The study of second language acquisition.* Oxford, England: Oxford University Press.

Ellis, R. (2003). *Task-based language learning and teaching.* Oxford, England: Oxford University Press.

Ellis, R. (Ed.). (2005). *Planning and task performance in a second language.* Amsterdam: John Benjamins.

Ellis, R., Basturkmen, H., & Loewen, S. (2001). Preemptive focus on form in the ESL classroom. *TESOL Quarterly, 35,* 407-432.

Ellis, R., Tanaka, Y., & Yamazaki, A. (1994). Classroom interaction, comprehension, and the acquisition of L2 word meanings. *Language Learning, 44,* 449-491.

Fan, M. Y. (2003). Frequency of use, perceived usefulness, and actual usefulness of second language vocabulary strategies: A study of Hong Kong learners. *The Modern Language Journal, 87,* 222-241.

Fanselow, J. F. (1977). Beyond Rashomon—conceptualizing and describing the teaching act. *TESOL Quarterly, 11*, 17-39.

Felser, C. (2005). Experimental psycholinguistic approaches to second language acquisition. *Second Language Research, 21*, 95-97.

Foster, P., & Skehan, P. (1996). The influence of planning and task type on second language performance. *Studies in Second Language Acquisition, 18*, 299-323.

Fotos, S., & Ellis, R. (1991). Communicating about grammar: A task-based approach. *TESOL Quarterly, 25*, 605-628.

Frenck-Mestre, C. (2005). Eye-movement recording as a tool for studying syntactic processing in a second language: A review of methodologies and experimental findings. *Second Language Research, 21*, 175-198.

Gass, S. (1980). An investigation of syntactic transfer in adult L2 learners. In R. Scarcella & S. Krashen (Eds.), *Research in second language acquisition* (pp. 132-141). Rowley, MA: Newbury House.

Gass, S. (1994). The reliability of second-language grammaticality judgments. In E. Tarone, S. Gass, & A. Cohen (Eds.), *Research methodology in second language acquisition* (pp. 303-322). Hillsdale, NJ: Lawrence Erlbaum Associates.

Gass, S. (2001). Sentence matching: A reexamination. *Second Language Research, 17*, 421-441.

Gass, S. (2003). Input and interaction. In C. Doughty & M. Long (Eds.), *Handbook of second language acquisition* (pp. 224-255). Oxford, England: Blackwell.

Gass, S., & Alvarez-Torres, M. J. (2005). Attention when?: An investigation of the ordering effect of input and interaction. *Studies in Second Language Acquisition, 27*, 1-31.

Gass, S., & Mackey, A. (2000). *Stimulated recall methodology and second language research*. Mahwah, NJ: Lawrence Erlbaum Associates.

Gass, S., Mackey, A., Alvarez-Torres, M., & Fernandez-García, M. (1999). The effects of task repetition on linguistic output. *Language Learning, 49*, 549-581.

Gass, S., Mackey, A., & Ross-Feldman, L. (2005). Task-based interactions in classroom and laboratory settings. *Language Learning, 55*, 575-611.

Gass, S., & Selinker, L. (2001). *Second language acquisition: An introductory course*. Mahwah, NJ: Lawrence Erlbaum Associates.

Gass, S., Svetics, I., & Lemelin, S. (2003). Differential effects of attention. *Language Learning, 53*, 495-543.

Gass, S., & Varonis, E. (1994). Input, interaction, and second language production. *Studies in Second Language Acquisition, 16*, 283-302.

Gathercole, S., & Baddeley, A. D. (1989). Evaluation of the role of phonological STM in the development of vocabulary in children: A longitudinal study. *Journal of Memory and Language, 28*, 1-14.

Gathercole, S., & Baddeley, A. D. (1993). *Working memory and language*. Hove,

England: Lawrence Erlbaum Associates.

Gathercole, S., & Martin, A. (1996). Interactive processes in phonological memory. In S. Gathercole (Ed.), *Models of short-term memory* (pp. 73-100). Hove, England: Psychology Press.

Geva, E., & Ryan, E. (1993). Linguistic and cognitive correlates of academic skills in first and second languages. *Language Learning, 43,* 5-42.

Glew, M. (1998). *The acquisition of reflexive pronouns among adult learners of English.* Unpublished doctoral dissertation, Michigan State University, East Lansing.

Goldschmidt, M. (1996). From the addressee's perspective: Imposition in favor-asking. In S. Gass & J. Neu (Eds.), *Speech acts across cultures* (pp. 241-256). Berlin: Mouton de Gruyter.

Graham, S. J. (2004). Giving up on modern foreign languages? Students' perceptions of learning French. *The Modern Language Journal, 88,* 171-191.

Gries, S., & Wulff, S. (2005). Do foreign language learners also have constructions? Evidence from priming, sorting, and corpora. *Annual Review of Cognitive Linguistics, 3,* 182-200.

Grigorenko, E. L., Sternberg, R. J., & Ehrman, M. E. (2000). A theory-based approach to the measurement of foreign language learning ability: The CANAL-F theory and test. *The Modern Language Journal, 84,* 390-405.

Harrington, M. (1987). Processing transfer: Language-specific strategies as a source of interlanguage variation. *Applied Psycholinguistics, 8,* 351-378.

Harrington, M., & Sawyer, M. (1992). L2 working memory capacity and L2 reading skill. *Studies in Second Language Acquisition, 14,* 25-38.

Hawkins, R., & Chan, C. (1997). The partial availability of Universal Grammar in second language acquisition: The "failed functional features hypothesis." *Second Language Research, 13,* 187-226.

Hendrick, C. (1990). Replications, strict replications, and conceptual replications: Are they important? *Journal of Social Behavior and Personality, 5,* 41-49.

Hermans, D., Bongaerts, T., De Bot, K., & Schreuder, R. (1998). Producing words in a foreign language: Can speakers prevent interference from their first language? *Bilingualism: Language & Cognition, 1,* 213-230.

Hulstijn, J. H. (1997). Second language acquisition research in the laboratory: Possibilities and limitations. *Studies in Second Language Acquisition, 19,* 131-143.

Inagaki, S. (2001). Motion verbs with goal PPs in the L2 acquisition of English and Japanese. *Studies in Second Language Acquisition, 23,* 153-170.

Ionin, T., & Wexler, K. (2002). Why is "is" easier than "-s"?: Acquisition of tense/aspect agreement morphology by child second language learners of English. *Second Language Research, 18,* 95-136.

Iwashita, N. (2003). Negative feedback and positive evidence in task-based interaction: Differential effects on L2 development. *Studies in Second Language Acquisition, 25*, 1-36.

Jasso-Aguilar, R. (1999). Sources, methods and triangulation in needs analysis: A critical perspective in a case study of Waikiki hotel maids. *English for Specific Purposes, 18*, 27-46.

Johnson, J. S., & Newport, E. L. (1989). Critical period effects in second language learning: The influence of maturational state on the acquisition of ESL. *Cognitive Psychology, 21*, 60-99.

Johnson, J. S., & Newport, E. L. (1991). Critical period effects on universal properties of language: The status of subjacency in the acquisition of a second language. *Cognition, 39*, 215-258.

Johnson, K. E. (1992). Learning to teach: Instructional actions and decisions of preservice ESL teachers. *TESOL Quarterly, 26*, 507-535.

Juffs, A. (2001). Discussion: Verb classes, event structure, and second language learners' knowledge of semantics-syntax correspondences. *Studies in Second Language Acquisition, 23*, 305-313.

Juffs, A., & Harrington, M. (1995). Parsing effects in second language sentence processing: Subject and object asymmetries in *wh*-extraction. *Studies in Second Language Acquisition, 17*, 483-516.

Just, M. A., & Carpenter, P. A. (1992). A capacity theory of comprehension: Individual differences in working memory. *Psychological Review, 99*, 122-149.

Kanagy, R. (1999). Interactional routines as a mechanism for L2 acquisition and socialization in an immersion context. *Journal of Pragmatics, 31*, 1467-1492.

Kasper, G., & Rose, K. R. (2002). *Pragmatic development in a second language.* Oxford, England: Blackwell.

Keenan, E., & Comrie, B. (1977). Noun phrase accessibility and universal grammar. *Linguistic Inquiry, 8*, 63-99.

Kinoshita, S., & Lupker, S. (Eds.). (2003). *Masked priming: The state of the art.* Hove, England: Psychology Press.

Kormos, J. (2000). The timing of self-repairs in second language speech production. *Studies in Second Language Acquisition, 22*, 145-167.

Krathwohl, D. R. (1998). *Methods of educational and social science research* (2nd ed.). New York: Longman.

Kumpf, L. (1984). Temporal systems and universality in interlanguage: A case study. In F. R. Eckman, L. W. Bell, & D. Nelson (Eds.), *Universals of second language acquisition* (pp. 132-150). Rowley, MA: Newbury House.

La Heij, W., de Bruyn, E., Elens, E., Hartsuiker, R., & Helaha, D. (1990). Orthographic facilitation and categorical interference in a word translation variant of the Stroop task. *Canadian Journal of Psychology, 44*, 76-83.

Labov, W. (1972). *Sociolinguistic patterns.* Philadelphia: University of Pennsylvania Press.

Lakshmanan, U., & Teranishi, K. (1994). Preferences versus grammaticality judgments: Some methodological issues concerning the governing category parameter in second language acquisition. In E. Tarone, S. Gass, & A. Cohen (Eds.), *Research methodology in second language acquisition* (pp. 185-206). Hillsdale, NJ: Lawrence Erlbaum Associates.

Lambert, W., Giles, H., & Picard, O. (1975). Language attitudes in a French-American community. *International Journal of the Sociology of Language, 4*, 127-152.

Lardiere, D. (1998a). Dissociating syntax from morphology in a divergent L2 end-state grammar. *Second Language Research, 14*, 359-375.

Lardiere, D. (1998b). Case and tense in the "fossilized" steady state. *Second Language Research, 14*, 1-26.

Lenngren, L. (Ed.). (1993). *Chastotnyi slovari sovremennogo russkogo yazyka* [Frequency dictionary of modern Russian language]. Uppsala: Acta Universitatis Upsaliensis.

Leow, R. (1998). Toward operationalizing the process of attention in SLA: Evidence for Tomlin and Villa's (1994) fine-grained analysis of attention. *Applied Psycholinguistics, 19*, 133-159.

Leow, R., & Morgan-Short, K. (2004). To think aloud or not to think aloud: The issue of reactivity in SLA research methodology. *Studies in Second Language Acquisition, 26*, 35-57.

Levelt, W. J. M. (1983). Monitoring and self-repair in speech. *Cognition, 33*, 41-103.

Levelt, W. J. M. (1989). *Speaking: From intention to articulation.* Cambridge, MA: MIT Press.

Levelt, W. J. M. (1993). Language use in normal speakers and its disorders. In G. Blanken, J. Dittmann, H. Grimm, J. C. Marchall, & C. W. Wallesch (Eds.), *Linguistic disorders and pathologies* (pp. 1-15). Berlin: deGruyter.

Li, P., & Yip, M. (1998). Context effects and the processing of spoken homophones. *Reading and Writing: An Interdisciplinary Journal, 10*, 223-243.

Lightbown, P. (2000). Anniversary article. Classroom SLA research and second language teaching. *Applied Linguistics, 21*, 431-462.

Liu, J. (1998). Peer reviews with the instructor: Seeking alternatives in ESL writing. In J. C. Richards (Ed.), *Teaching in action: Case studies from second language classrooms* (pp. 236-240). Alexandria, VA: TESOL.

Long, M. (1980). Inside the "black box": Methodological issues in research on language teaching and learning. *Language Learning, 30*, 1-42.

Long, M. (1996). The role of the linguistic environment in second language acquisition. In W. C. Ritchie & T. K. Bhatia (Eds.), *Handbook of second language acquisition* (pp. 413-468). San Diego, CA: Academic Press.

Loschky, L. (1994). Comprehensible input and second language acquisition: What is the relationship? *Studies in Second Language Acquisition, 16*, 303-323.

Loschky, L., & Bley-Vroman, R. (1993). Grammar and task-based methodology. In G. Crookes & S. Gass (Eds.), *Tasks and language learning: Integrating theory and practice* (pp. 123-167). Clevedon, England: Multilingual Matters.

Lyster, R. (1998a). Negotiation of form, recasts, and explicit correction in relation to error types and learner repair in immersion classrooms. *Language Learning, 48*, 183-218.

Lyster, R. (1998b). Recasts, repetition, and ambiguity in L2 classroom discourse. *Studies in Second Language Acquisition, 20*, 51-81.

Lyster, R., & Ranta, L. (1997). Corrective feedback and learner uptake: Negotiation of form in communicative classrooms. *Studies in Second Language Acquisition, 19*, 37-66.

Macaro, E. (2001). *Learning strategies in foreign and second language classrooms.* London: Continuum.

MacIntyre, P. D., Baker, S. C., Clément, R., & Conrod, S. (2001). Willingness to communicate, social support, and language-learning orientations of immersion students. *Studies in Second Language Acquisition, 23*, 369-388.

Mackey, A. (1999). Input, interaction, and second language development: An empirical study of question formation in ESL. *Studies in Second Language Acquisition, 21*, 557-587.

Mackey, A. (2002). Beyond production: Learners' perceptions about interaction processes. *International Journal of Educational Research, 37*, 379-394.

Mackey, A., & Gass, S. (2005). *Second language research: Methodology and design.* Mahwah, NJ: Lawrence Erlbaum Associates.

Mackey, A., Gass, S., & McDonough, K. (2000). How do learners perceive interactional feedback? *Studies in Second Language Acquistion, 22*, 471-497.

Mackey, A., Philp, J., Egi, T., Fujii, A., & Tatsumi, T. (2002). Individual differences in working memory, noticing of interactional feedback and L2 development. In P. Robinson (Ed.), *Individual differences and instructed language learning* (pp. 181-209). Philadelphia: John Benjamins.

MacWhinney, B. (1987). The competition model. In B. MacWhinney (Ed.), *Mechanisms of language acquisition* (pp. 249-308). Hillsdale, NJ: Lawrence Erlbaum Associates.

MacWhinney, B., & Pléh, C. (1997). Double agreement: Role identification in Hungarian. *Language and Cognitive Processing, 12*, 67-102.

Marian, V., & Spivey, M. (2003). Competing activation in bilingual language processing: Within- and between-language competition. *Bilingualism: Language and*

Cognition, 6, 97-115.

Marinis, T. (2003). Psycholinguistic techniques in second language acquisition research. *Second Language Research, 19,* 144-161.

Mason, J. (1996). *Qualitative researching.* London: Sage.

Matsumura, S., & Hann, G. (2004). Computer anxiety and students' preferred feedback methods in EFL writing. *Modern Language Journal, 88,* 403-415.

McDonough, J., & McDonough, S. (1997). *Research methods for English language teachers.* London: Arnold.

McDonough, K. (2006). Interaction and syntactic priming: English L2 speakers' production of dative constructions. *Studies in Second Language Acquisition, 28,* 179-207.

McLaughlin, B. (1990). Restructuring. *Applied Linguistics, 11,* 113-128.

Meara, P. (1978). Learners' word associations in French. *Interlanguage Studies Bulletin, 3,* 192-211.

Merzenich, A. (1989). *Relativity in research and the acquisition of reflexive binding.* Unpublished manuscript, University of Hawaii.

Miller, N. A., & Kroll, J. F. (2002). Stroop effects in bilingual translation. *Memory & Cognition, 30,* 614-628.

Milroy, L., & Gordon, M. (2003). *Sociolinguistics: Method and interpretation.* Oxford, England: Blackwell.

Mimica, I., Sullivan, M., & Smith, S. (1994). An on-line study of sentence interpretation in native Croatian speakers. *Applied Psycholinguistics, 15,* 237-261.

Mitchell, R., Parkinson, B., & Johnstone, R. (1981). *The foreign language classroom: An observational study.* Stirling, UK: University of Stirling Monographs.

Miyake, A., & Friedman, N. (1998). Individual differences in second language proficiency: Working memory as language aptitude. In A. Healy & L. Bourne (Eds.), *Foreign language learning: Psycholinguistic studies on training and retention* (pp. 339-364). Mahwah, NJ: Lawrence Erlbaum Associates.

Montrul, S. (2001). Agentive verbs of manner of motion in Spanish and English. *Studies in Second Language Acquisition, 23,* 171-206.

Montrul, S. (2004). Subject and object expression in Spanish heritage speakers: A case of morphosyntactic convergence. *Bilingualism: Language & Cognition, 7,* 125-142.

Montrul, S., & Slabakova, R. (2003). Competence similarities between native and near-native speakers: An investigation of the preterite-imperfect contrast in Spanish. *Studies in Second Language Acquisition, 25,* 351-398.

Morrison, L. (1996). Talking about words: A study of French as a second language learners' lexical inferencing procedures. *Canadian Modern Language Review, 53,* 41-75.

Moskowitz, G. (1967). The Flint system: An observational tool for the foreign language classroom. In A. Simon & E. G. Boyer (Eds.), *Mirrors for behavior: An anthology of classroom observation instruments* (pp. 1-15). Philadelphia: Center for the Study of Teaching, Temple University.

Moskowitz, G. (1970). *The foreign language instructor interacts.* Minneapolis: Association for Productive Teaching.

Munnich, E., Flynn, S., & Martohardjono, G. (1994). Elicited imitation and grammaticality judgment tasks: What they measure and how they relate to each other. In E. Tarone, S. Gass, & A. Cohen (Eds.), *Research methodology in second-language acquisition* (pp. 227-243). Hillsdale, NJ: Lawrence Erlbaum Associates.

Murphy, J. M. (1992). An etiquette for the nonsupervisory observation of L2 classrooms. *Foreign Language Annals, 25,* 215-225.

Murphy, V. (1997). The effect of modality on a grammaticality judgment task. *Second Language Research,* 13, 34-65.

Newton, J., & Kennedy, G. (1996). Effects of communication tasks on the grammatical relations marked by second language learners. *System, 24,* 309-322.

Nunan, D. (1989). *Understanding language classrooms: A guide for teacher-initiated action.* New York: Prentice-Hall.

Nunan, D. (1993). Action research in language education. In J. Edge & K. Richards (Eds.), *Teachers develop, teachers research: Papers on classroom research and teacher development* (pp. 39-50). Oxford, England: Heinemann International.

Ortega, L. (1999). Planning and focus on form in L2 oral performance. *Studies in Second Language Acquisition, 21,* 109-148.

Ortega, L. (2005). For what and for whom is our research? The ethical as transformative lens in instructed SLA. *Modern Language Journal, 89,* 427-443.

Ortega, L., & Iberri-Shea, G. (2005). Longitudinal research in second language acquisition: Recent trends and future directions. *Annual Review of Applied Linguistics, 25,* 26-45.

Oxford, R. L. (1990). *Language learning strategies: What every teacher should know.* New York: Newbury House Publishers.

Papadopoulou, D., & Clahsen, H. (2003). Parsing strategies in L1 and L2 sentence processing: A study of relative clause attachment in Greek. *Studies in Second Language Acquisition, 25,* 501-528.

Papagno, C., Valentine, T., & Baddeley, A. (1991). Phonological short-term memory and foreign-language vocabulary learning. *Journal of Memory and Language, 30,* 331-347.

Papagno, C., & Vallar, G. (1992). Phonological short-term memory and the learning of novel words: The effect of phonological similarity and item length. *Quarterly Journal of Experimental Psychology, 44A,* 47-67.

Pawley, A., & Syder, F. H. (2000). The one-clause-at-a-time hypothesis. In H. Riggenbach (Ed.), *Perspectives on fluency* (pp. 163-199). Ann Arbor, MI:

University of Michigan Press.

Philp, J. (2003). Constraints on noticing the gap: Nonnative speakers' noticing of recasts in NS-NNS interaction. *Studies in Second Language Acquisition, 25*, 99-126.

Pica, T., Kanagy, R., & Falodun, J. (1993). Choosing and using communication tasks for second language instruction. In G. Crookes & S. Gass (Eds.), *Tasks and language learning: Integrating theory and practice* (pp.9-34). Clevedon, England: Multilingual Matters.

Pickering, L. (2001). The role of tone choice in improving ITA communication in the classroom. *TESOL Quarterly, 35*, 233-255.

Pienemann, M., & Johnston, M. (1987). Factors influencing the development of language proficiency. In D. Nunan (Ed.), *Applying second language research* (pp. 45-141). Adelaide, Australia: National Curriculum Resource Centre.

Pimsleur, P. (1966). *The Pimsleur language aptitude battery.* New York: Harcourt Brace Jovanovich.

Polio, C., & Gass, S. (1997). Replication and reporting: A commentary. *Studies in Second Language Acquisition, 19*, 499-508.

Robinson, P. (2005). Aptitude and second language acquisition. *Annual Review of Applied Linguistics, 25*, 46-73.

Rosa, E., & O'Neill, M. D. (1999). Explicitness, intake, and the issue of awareness: Another piece to the puzzle. *Studies in Second Language Acquisition, 21*, 511-556.

Sasaki, Y. (1997). Material and presentation condition effects on sentence interpretation task performance: Methodological examinations of the competition experiment. *Second Language Research, 13*, 66-91.

Sawyer, M., & Ranta, L. (2001). Aptitude, individual differences, and instructional design. In P. Robinson (Ed.), *Cognition and second language instruction* (pp. 319-353). Cambridge, England: Cambridge University Press.

Schachter, J., & Gass, S. (Eds.). (1996). *Second language classroom research: Issues and opportunities.* Hillsdale, NJ: Lawrence Erlbaum Associates.

Schiffrin, D. (1996). Narrative as self portrait: The sociolinguistic construction of identity. *Language in Society, 25*, 167-203.

Schmidt, R., & Frota, S. N. (1986). Developing basic conversational ability in a second language: A case study of an adult learner of Portuguese. In R. Day (Ed.), *Talking to learn: Conversation in second language acquisition* (pp. 237-326). Rowley, MA: Newbury House.

Schulz, R. A. (1996). Focus on form in the foreign language classroom: Students' and teachers' views on error correction and the role of grammar. *Foreign Language Annals, 29*, 343-364.

Schulz, R. A. (2001). Cultural differences in student and teacher perceptions concerning the role of grammar instruction and corrective feedback: USA-Colombia. *Modern Language Journal, 85,* 244-258.

Schumann, J., & Schumann, F. (1977). Diary of a language learner: An introspective study of second language learning. In H. Brown, C. Yorio, & R. Crymes (Eds.), *On TESOL 77* (pp. 241-249). Washington, DC: TESOL.

Schütze, C. (1996). *The empirical base of linguistics: Grammaticality judgments and linguistic methodology.* Chicago: University of Chicago Press.

Service, E. (1992). Phonology, working memory, and foreign-language learning. *Quarterly Journal of Experimental Psychology, 45A,* 21-50.

Service, E., & Craik, F. I. M. (1993). Differences between young and older adults in learning a foreign vocabulary. *Journal of Memory and Language, 32,* 608-623.

Service, E., & Kohonen, V. (1995). Is the relation between phonological memory and foreign language learning accounted for by vocabulary acquisition? *Applied Psycholinguistics, 16,* 155-172.

Silverberg, S., & Samuel, A. G. (2004). The effect of age of second language acquisition on the representation and processing of second language words. *Journal of Memory and Language, 51,* 381-398.

Sinclair, J., & Coulthard, M. (1975). *Toward an analysis of discourse: The English used by teachers and pupils.* Oxford, England: Oxford University Press.

Skehan, P. (2002). Theorizing and updating aptitude. In P. Skehan (Ed.), *Individual differences and instructed language learning* (pp. 69-94). Amsterdam: John Benjamins.

Skehan, P., & Foster, P. (1999). The influence of task structure and processing conditions on narrative retellings. *Language Learning, 48,* 93-120.

Slimani-Rolls, A. (2005). Rethinking task-based language learning: What we can learn from the learners. *Language Teaching Research, 9,* 195-218.

Smith, B. R., & Leinonen, E. (1992). *Clinical pragmatics: Unraveling the complexities of communicative failure.* London: Chapman & Hall.

Sorace, A. (1993). Incomplete vs. divergent representations of unaccusativity in non-native grammars of Italian. *Second Language Research, 9,* 22-47.

Spada, N., & Fröhlich, M. (1995). *The Communicative Orientation of Language Teaching Observation Scheme (COLT): Coding Conventions and Applications.* The National Centre for English Language Teaching and Research (NCELTR). Sydney, Australia: Macquarie University.

Spada, N., & Lightbown, P. M. (1993). Instruction and the development of questions in L2 classrooms. *Studies in Second Language Acquisition, 15,* 205-224.

Stemberger, P. (1985). An interactive interaction model of language production. In A. W. Ellis (Ed.), *Progress in the psychology of language* (Vol. 1, pp. 143-186). Hillsdale, NJ: Lawrence Erlbaum Associates.

Sternberg, R. J. (2002). The theory of successful intelligence and its implications for language aptitude testing. In P. Robinson (Ed.), *Individual differences and instructed language learning* (pp. 13-44). Amsterdam: John Benjamins.

Stroop, J. R. (1935). Studies of interference in serial verbal reactions. *Journal of Experimental Psychology, 18,* 643-662.

Swain, M. (1995). The output hypothesis: Just speaking and writing aren't enough. *Canadian Modern Language Review, 50,* 158-164.

Swain, M., & Lapkin, S. (2000). Task-based second language learning: The uses of the first language. *Language Teaching Research, 4,* 251-274.

Swain, M., & Lapkin, S. (2002). Talking it through: Two French immersion learners' response to reformulation. *International Journal of Educational Research, 37,* 285-304.

Takahashi, S. (2005). Pragmalinguistic awareness: Is it related to motivation and proficiency? *Applied Linguistics, 26,* 90-120.

Tarone, E., & Liu, G. Q. (1995). Situational context, variation, and SLA theory. In G. Cook & B. Seidlhofer (Eds.), *Principle and practice in applied linguistics: Studies in honour of H. G. Widdowson* (pp. 107-124). Oxford, England: Oxford University Press.

Tarone, E., & Parrish, B. (1988). Task-related variation in interlanguage: The case of articles. *Language Learning, 38,* 21-44.

Trahey, M., & White, L. (1993). Positive evidence and preemption in the second language classroom. *Studies in Second Language Acquisition, 15,* 181-204.

Turnbull, W. (2001). An appraisal of pragmatic elicitation techniques for the social psychological study of talk: The case of request refusals. *Pragmatics, 11,* 31-61.

Ullman, R., & Geva, E. (1983). *Classroom observation in the L2 setting: A dimension of program evaluation.* Toronto: Modern Language Centre, Institute for Studies in Education.

Ullman, R., & Geva, E. (1985). Expanding our evaluation perspective: What can classroom observation tell us about core French programs? *Canadian Modern Language Review, 42,* 307-323.

Valdman, A. (1993). Replication study. *Studies in Second Language Acquisition, 15,* 505.

van der Veer, R., van Ijzendoorn, M., & Valsiner, J. (1994). General introduction. In R. van der Veer, M. van Ijzendoorn, & J. Valsiner (Eds.), *Reconstructing the mind: Replicability in research on human development* (pp. 1-10). Norwood, NJ: Ablex.

van Lier, L. (1988). *The classroom and the language learner: Ethnography and second language classroom research.* London: Longman.

van Lier, L. (1990). Classroom research in second language acquisition. *Annual Review of Applied Linguistics, 10,* 73-186.

van Lier, L. (1994). Forks and hope: Pursuing understanding in different ways. *Applied Linguistics, 15*, 328-346.

Von Stutterheim, C., & Nüse, R. (2003). Processes of conceptualization in language production: Language-specific perspectives and event construal. *Linguistics, 41*, 851-881.

Wallace, M. J. (1998). *Action research for language teachers.* Cambridge, England: Cambridge University Press.

Waters, G. S., & Caplan, D. (1996). The capacity theory of sentences comprehension: Critique of Just and Carpenter (1992). *Psychological Review, 103*, 761-772.

Wen, Q., & Johnson, R. K. (1997). L2 learner variables and English achievement: A study of tertiary-level English majors in China. *Applied Linguistics, 18*, 27-48.

White, L. (2003). *Second language acquisition and Universal Grammar.* Cambridge, England: Cambridge University Press.

White, L., & Genesee, F. (1996). How native is near-native? The issue of ultimate attain-ment in adult second language acquisition. *Second Language Research, 12*, 233-265.

White, L., & Juffs, A. (1998). Constraints on *Wh*-movement in two different contexts of non-native language acquisition: Competence and processing. In S. Flynn, G. Martohardjono, & W. O'Neill (Eds.), *The generative study of second language acquisition* (pp. 111-130). Mahwah, NJ: Lawrence Erlbaum Associates.

Wilks, C., & Meara, P. (2002). Untangling word webs: Graph theory and the notion of density in second language word association networks. *Second Language Research, 18*, 303-324.

Williams, J. (1999). Memory, attention, and inductive learning. *Studies in Second Language Acquisition, 21*, 1-48.

Williams, J., & Evans, J. (1998). What kind of focus and on which forms? In C. Doughty & J. Williams (Eds.), *Focus on form in classroom second language acquisition* (pp. 85-113). Cambridge, England: Cambridge University Press.

Williams, J., & Lovatt, P. (2003). Phonological memory and rule learning. *Language Learning, 53*, 67-121.

Yule, G., & Hoffman, P. (1993). Enlisting the help of U.S. undergraduates in evaluating international teaching assistants. *TESOL Quarterly, 27*, 323-327.

Zeno, S., Ivens, S., Millard, R., & Duvvuri, R. (1995). *The educator's word frequency guide.* Brewster, NY: Touchstone Applied Science Associates.

Zyzik, E. (2006). Transitivity alternations and sequence learning: Insights from L2 Spanish production data. *Studies in Second Language Acquisition, 28*, 449-485.

Glossary

Acceptability judgment: A judgment about the acceptability of a particular utterance (generally a sentence).

Action research: As applied to language classrooms, carried out by practitioners to understand, in the case of second language learning/teaching, the dynamics of how second languages are learned and taught.

Attitudes research: Investigations of learners' attitudes, beliefs, opinions, interests, and values.

Biodata questionnaire: Administered to collect basic information about a participant. The information gathered depends on the goal of a study. In general, age, amount, and type of prior L2 study, gender, first language of participant, and proficiency in L2s are collected and reported.

Classroom research: Research conducted in classroom settings, often involving variables related to instruction.

Closed role-play: Similar to discourse completion tasks, but in oral mode. Individuals are usually provided with a description of a situation and/or a character and asked to state what they would say in that particular situation. (See also *open role-plays.*)

Closed-ended question: Requires a specific answer from a respondent. Typically involve uniformity of measurement and therefore greater reliability in terms of data. They also lead to answers that can be easily quantified and analyzed (See also *open-ended question*).

Coding: Organizing data into a manageable, easily understandable, and analyzable base of information, and searching for and marking patterns in the data.

Coding system: A means of organizing data prior to analysis. Coding systems usually involve coding sheets, charts, techniques, schemes, and so on. Researchers develop their coding scheme based on their specific research questions.

Competition model: An approach that attempts to understand how people use information to understand the relationship among words.

Cognitive Ability for Novelty in Acquisition of Language as Applied to Foreign Language Test (CANAL-FT): L2 aptitude test that emphasizes measuring how people cope with novelty and ambiguity in language learning.

Consciousness-raising task: An activity intended to facilitate learners' cognitive processes in terms of awareness of a language area or linguistic structure.

Consensus task: A task in which pairs or groups of learners must come to an agreement on a certain issue.

Construct validity: The degree to which the research adequately captures the construct of interest.

Counting span task: Task used to measure working memory.

Cross-modal priming: Used to investigate antecedent reactivation. The task usually involves two parts: listening to a sentence and responding to a word that appears on a computer screen.

Data: Information (oral or written) available for analysis.

Data collection: The process of accumulating information pertaining to a particular research question, problem, or area.

Data elicitation: A subset of data collection, data elicitation refers to the process of directly eliciting information from individuals, for example, through an interview or a task.

Delayed posttest: In a pretest-posttest design, delayed posttests are tests given after the first posttest (e.g., 1 month or 1 year later) to measure the long-term retention of a skill or knowledge.

Diary research: Individuals' perspective on their own language learning or teaching experience, in the form of entries to a personal journal. Analyses usually focus on patterns and salient events.

Dictogloss task: A type of consensus task in which learners work together to reconstruct a text that has been read to them.

Discourse completion test (DCT): A test used to gather contextualized data. Generally, a situation is provided and then the respondents are asked what they would say in that particular situation. There is often a follow-up response (e.g., "I'm sorry that you can't come") so that the individual knows the type of response that is expected (e.g., a refusal).

Dyad: Two participants working together.

Elicited imitation: A procedure for collecting data where a participant is presented with a sentence, clause, or word and is asked to repeat (imitate) it.

Elicited narrative: Narratives gathered through specific prompts (e.g., "What did you do yesterday?" or "Tell me about a typical day for you.").

Ethics review board: See *Institutional Review Board.*

Experimental research: Research in which there is manipulation of (at least) one independent variable to determine the effect(s) on one (or more) dependent variables. Groups are generally determined on the basis of random assignment.

Eye movement study: A technique that uses special eye-tracking equipment to track participants' eye movement as they are performing a task.

Eye tracking sensor: See *Eye movement study.*

Field notes: Researchers' observations, often in the form of freehand notes, in relation to the phenomena under investigation

Gating paradigm: Used to determine the amount of phonetic/acoustic information needed to identify a word. Participants hear fragments of a word until the whole word appears. Following introduction of new information, participants are asked to identify the word.

Generalizability: The extent to which the results of a study can be extended to a greater population.

Grammaticality judgment: See *acceptability judgment.*

Hawthorne effect: Occurs when learners perform better due to positive feelings at being included in a study.

High-inference observation scheme: Observers are required to judge the meaning or function of particular behaviors that involve judgments.

Human subjects committee: See *Institutional Review Board.*

Immediate recall: An introspective data collection technique used to elicit data immediately after the completion of the event to be recalled.

Institutional Review Board: A committee established to review research involving human subjects to ensure it is in compliance with ethical guidelines laid down by government and funding agencies. (This term is often used interchangeably with *Human Subjects Committee* and *Ethics Review Board.*)

Interaction research: Usually examines the relationship between communication and acquisition and the mechanisms (e.g., noticing, attention) that mediate the learning process.

Interlanguage: The language system of a non-native speaker. It often differs from the L1 and the L2.

Interview: Comparable to a questionnaire, but usually in oral mode, interviews are often associated with survey-based research. Information is usually gathered by means of open-ended questions and answers. Interviews can be based around a stimulus, for example, a completed questionnaire or a videotape of a lesson.

Introspective methods: A set of data elicitation techniques that encourages learners to communicate about their internal processing and/or perspectives about language learning experiences.

Jigsaw task: See *Two-way task.*

Language aptitude: Facility for learning, argued to be a predictor of subsequent language learning achievement.

Learning strategy: Actions, steps, or techniques used by learners, often consciously, in their efforts to acquire the L2.

Lexical decision task: A type of task that requires participants to respond to a prompt, indicating whether or not the prompt constitutes a word.

Listening span test: A test designed to measure verbal working memory.

Longitudinal data: Data collected over a prolonged period of time.

Low-inference observation scheme: Observation scheme that usually allows observers to code material in objective real time.

Magnitude estimation: A procedure whereby judges are asked to rank a stimulus by stating how much better or worse the stimulus is from the previous one.

Map task: A type of a jigsaw task, in which learners are given a map of a section of a place.

Matched guise: A technique used to determine language biases. Individuals (or sometimes the same individual) are matched and produce speech in two languages or dialects. Respondents rate the individual speech samples according to their feelings about the person who is speaking (e.g., intelligent, likeable).

Moving window: A technique, generally carried out on a computer, whereby words are presented visually or aurally one by one. This technique may be used to measure reaction times (i.e., how long it takes a participant to press a button to have the next word presented) and thus, indirectly, ease of comprehension.

Modern Language Aptitude Test (MLAT): Language aptitude test developed by Carroll and Sapon in 1959.

Modern Language Aptitude Test-Elementary (MLAT-E): Language aptitude test developed for younger children (age 8-11).

Naturalistic data: Language data that is captured in a natural (nonexperimental) setting.

Naturalistic classroom research: Research in which the researcher does not seek to intervene in the learning process, but rather to observe and describe classroom learning and teaching as it occurs in intact classes.

Negotiation: An interactional process during which interlocutors modify their interaction, for example, by providing feedback, requesting clarification, checking comprehension, and making adjustments to linguistic form, conversational structure, and/or the content of their utterances in order to achieve mutual comprehension.

Observations: Researchers systematically observe different aspects of a setting in which they are immersed, including, for example, the interactions, relationships, actions, and events in which learners engage. The aim is to provide careful descriptions of learners' activities without unduly influencing the events in which the learners are engaged.

Observer's paradox: The goal of most observation is to collect naturalistic data; however, the act of observing will impact what is being observed.

Offline techniques: An experiment whereby the response is external to the stimulus, that is, whereby the response is given after a stimulus is presented as opposed to during the presentation of a stimulus. See also *online task*.

Online recall: See *Think-aloud*.

Online task: An experiment that has its response or probe internal to the stimulus; there is a response to an ongoing stimulus.

One-way task: A task in which one learner holds all the information, and information flows in one direction, from the holder.

Open role-play: Individuals are provided with a description of a situation and/or a character and each individual is asked to play out the part of one of the characters. In open role-plays, limits are not provided as to the length of the exchange. (See also *closed role-play*.)

Open-ended question: Open-ended questions allow respondents to answer in any manner they see fit, leading them to express their own thoughts and ideas in their own manner, and thus potentially resulting in less predictable but more insightful data (See also *closed-ended question*.)

Operationalize: To provide a precise, concrete definition of a variable in such a way that it can be measured.

Operation span task: Task used to measure working memory.

Parameters: Within Universal Grammar, the set of alternatives that is available to individual languages.

Picture description: A task that involves describing a picture or picture sequence to an interlocutor who draws the picture or who orders a sequence of pictures. At times, one interlocutor has all of the information and at other times, interlocutors might work together to complete the task.

Picture sequencing task: See *Picture description*.

Pilot study: A small-scale trial of the proposed procedures, materials, and methods. It may also include a trial of the coding sheets and analytic categories.

Pimsleur Language Aptitude Battery: Language aptitude test developed by Pimsleur in 1966.

Posttest: A test to determine knowledge after treatment and any immediate test.

Preference task: A task in which participants are asked to judge sentences in relation to one another.

Pretest: A test to determine knowledge before treatment.

Priming: A task in which two stimuli appear one after the other. The first is the *prime* for the second. Participants respond in some way to the second stimulus (the *target*).

Principles: Within Universal Grammar, these are invariant and constrain the acquisition of all languages.

Prompted production: Language production captured following a prompt.

Prompted response: Responses to a particular prompt.

Prompted story telling: This technique involves telling a story based on viewing (or listening) to a prior event (video clip, picture).

Pushed output: Output that "stretches" learners' linguistic repertoires as they communicate with their interlocutors.

Questionnaire: A (usually written) survey often used in a large-scale study to gather information. Can utilize open-ended questions and/or questions followed by a selection from a set of predetermined answers.

Reaction time: The time between a stimulus and a learner's response. Reaction time experiments are usually computer-based and can also be used to investigate processing.

Reactivity: Whether the act of doing something (e.g., thinking aloud) impacts what is being done (e.g., recalling thoughts or solving a task).

Reading span task: Task used to measure working memory.

Recast: A rephrasing of an incorrect utterance while maintaining a significant overlap in meaning.

Replication: Conducting a research study again, in a way that is either identical to the original procedure or with small changes (e.g. different participants), to test the original findings.

Second language: Used in this book as a cover term to include foreign language as well as second language learning and all language learning beyond first language learning (e.g., second, third).

Self-repair: A self-correction by a speaker.

Sentence combining: A technique used to elicit data on compound and complex sentences. Two sentences are presented and participants are asked to combine them to make one sentence.

Sentence matching: A procedure (generally computer-based) whereby participants are asked whether or not two sentences (usually appearing consecutively) are identical. This procedure is often used to determine grammaticality.

Self-paced reading/listening task: A variation on the *moving window* technique. In a self-paced task, the participant controls the speed with which the stimulus is presented.

Spot the difference: A task in which learners are asked to find a predetermined number of differences in pictures. Each learner has visual access to only one picture.

Stimulated recall: An introspective technique for gathering data that can yield insights into a learner's thought processes during language learning experiences.

Learners are asked to introspect while viewing or hearing a stimulus to prompt their recollections.

Story completion task: A task in which learners are given different parts of a story (written or pictorial) with instructions to make a complete story.

Strategic Inventory for Language Learning (SILL): Commonly used instrument for assessing language strategy use.

Stroop test: A task used to investigate inhibition. It is often used with colors. A word naming a color is printed in the same or a different color than the meaning of the word. The task is to name the color.

Think-aloud: A type of verbal reporting in which individuals are asked what is going through their mind as they are solving a problem or performing a task.

Transcription machines: Designed to facilitate transcription of oral data, these machines are often controlled by a foot pedal so that both hands are free for typing. As well as rewinding by a set number of seconds, the controls can be used to adjust the rate of the speech, to make it easier to distinguish individual voices.

Triangulation: Data collected using multiple research techniques and multiple sources in order to explore the issues from all feasible perspectives. Using the technique of triangulation can aid in credibility, transferability, and dependability in qualitative research.

Truth-value judgment: These judgments generally involve contextualized information, and individuals are asked if a particular follow-up sentence is true or not based on prior contextualization.

Two-way task: A task that requires two (or more) individuals, each of whom holds different information, to exchange that information in order to complete the task.

Universal Grammar: The system of principles and parameters that all human languages share and is proposed to be innate.

Verbal reporting: A type of introspection that consists of gathering information by asking individuals to say what is going through their minds as they are solving a problem or doing a task.

Veridicality: Whether something accurately depicts its target, for example, how representative a learner's reports about their thought processes are in relation to their actual thought processes

Word association task: A technique that asks participants to produce the first word that comes to mind following a prompt.

Working memory: Memory that not only involves storage capacity, but also processing capacity.

Author Index

Note: Page numbers followed by *f* indicate a figure

Subject Index

Note: Page numbers in **bold** refer to the Glossary